THE STONE MASON

STONE

THE

MASON

A History of Building Britain

ANDREW ZIMINSKI

JOHN MURRAY

First published in Great Britain in 2020 by John Murray (Publishers)
An Hachette UK company

2

Copyright © Andrew Ziminski 2020

Illustrations by Clare Venables

Extract on p.101 from *Aldhelm: The Poetic Works* by Michael Lapidge and James L. Rosier,
reproduced by permission of Boydell & Brewer

A CIP catalogue record for this title is available from the British Library

Hardback ISBN 978-1-473-66393-0
Trade Paperback ISBN 978-1-473-66392-3
eBook ISBN 978-1-473-66395-4

Typeset in Bembo MT Pro 12.5/17 pt by
Palimpsest Book Production Limited, Falkirk, Stirlingshire

Printed and bound in Great Britain by Clays Ltd, Elcograf S.p.A.

John Murray policy is to use papers that are natural,
renewable and recyclable products and made from wood grown in
sustainable forests. The logging and manufacturing processes are expected
to conform to the environmental regulations of the country of origin.

John Murray (Publishers)
Carmelite House
50 Victoria Embankment
London EC4Y 0DZ

www.johnmurraypress.co.uk

CONTENTS

PART FOUR: Concrete

Tradition is not the worship of ashes, but the preservation of fire.

Gustav Mahler

INTRODUCTION

Under its rusting corrugated roof, the tenement still managed to speak of a life well used. With windows gone and its lath and plaster covering kicked out, the exposed oak frame, silvery grey with age, was now nearly all that remained of its walls. The family of brewers who had worked and lived there since the late-1500s put it up in the 1620s as an extension to a long-gone medieval house. Although buttressed and propped at one end by a great external stone chimney, it was hard to see how on earth it was still standing.

I had become more aware of the slow dilapidation of the brewer's house as my mates and I passed it by each evening on our journey home from school. Narrow cobbled steps dropped through the town that clung to the ramparts of the long-demolished medieval castle. Crossing Reigate's busy high street into Cage Yard we legged it past the haunted town lock-up, where its former inmates still waited behind unhinged doors in the rubbish-strewn interior. And over it loomed the mournful hulk of the brewer's house.

Redemption finally arrived with a sign nailed high up on its gable end. The structure was to be dismantled and then moved to a museum where it would be rebuilt and preserved. Mrs Ward, our history teacher, told us that fragments of wall paintings – St George slaying the dragon over one of its two fireplaces, accompanied by a coloured floral design executed in black line – could still be found within. Volunteers were urgently needed if the 350-year-old structure was to be saved. My real education was about to begin in earnest.

I had stopped enjoying school years before. By my teens, it had become nothing more than a disastrous sequence of reports that complained 'Andrew must stop daydreaming and try harder'. For me, the standard history curriculum was too focused around flat pages of facts, events and royal personalities. It was the material aspects of the past, the tangible remnants that were left behind, that thrilled me. And there was no room for that at my school. I was once caught copying out illustrations from the *Collins Field Guide to Archaeology in Britain* during a mathematics lesson – my punishment: confiscation and three of the best from the headmaster's slipper. I still remember that page 158 was covered with simple line drawings of tumuli – burial mounds just like the ones I had already explored on the commons, downs and sandy heathlands that enclosed the town. I pictured them still filled with treasures, weapons, personal ornaments and pottery. These bell barrows were the burial places of prehistoric kings and earls, and I liked to imagine the lives that these objects had been part of.

I spent my weekends searching for treasures and it was on the heath that, aged twelve, I had made my greatest find. When the broad end of the flint axe-head connected with the heart of my hand, I felt the electric jolt of discovery and the desire to learn more coursed through me. An archaeologist at the Holmesdale Museum confirmed that it had been made four thousand years before, during the Bronze Age, and was probably an object of status rather than work. She told me how it had absorbed some of the background minerals so that, over time, they had turned its surface from the usual marbled blue-white to toffee-gold. She explained that the first sharp edge had been put on a flint for use as a tool over three million years ago and that the shaping of stones is our species' most ancient skill. The raw materials had probably come from the chalky heights of the North Downs and soon I was spending as much time there as I could, looking for nodes of this inner marbled colour, which I used to teach myself how to make my own copies of the museum's Neolithic tools.

Soon, instead of hanging around the castle grounds after school, I was to be found high on the rickety scaffolding that enclosed the brewer's house, hardhat-less in parka and monkey boots. The last remaining residents of the house shared their outrage at our presence; the jackdaws dive-bombed as the wrecking crew staved in the broad, stone chimney that had been the birds' family seat for many generations, sending tufts of their old nests out about amongst the dust and rubble. As the frame started to come down, I felt increasingly drawn into the puzzle of how this medieval building was still standing. I wanted to know everything about this old place and the other buildings I had started to notice. Who built them? How long did it take to put their frames up? Where did the oak come from? Where had they sourced the stone? How was all this heavy stuff brought here on what I had been taught were the terrible roads only used by armies and royalty?

My father would know some of the answers. After the war he had been taught to cut Scottish granite into wedge shapes – voussoirs the size of ancient TV sets – that he and his team of Highlanders, Irishmen and Polish refugees fixed into position to form horseshoe-shaped arches that were the outflows for hydroelectric power stations. His big hands still carried the scars. I remembered a day where he had been telling us about how gelignite must be handled in the tunnelling process. Blasted stone, he said, was no good for building with as the explosion would microfracture the stone and so it needed to be extracted by hand. He hadn't forgotten the whereabouts of the quarry – by then overgrown – and he took me there. As we explored, he explained how the place worked. This trip inspired an interest that has never left me.

When the brewer's house was razed to the ground, I knew that one day it would be rebuilt in the museum, and so I volunteered on-and-off as my funds allowed in its slow rebuild at the Weald and Downland Museum, near Chichester in Sussex. It was hard work and, with no pay, I lived on baked beans and hand-outs – but it was worth it.

Mick 'the Mason', who took me under his wing, told me of a working life that sounded like a Thomas Hardy plotline. A road mender and local builder, Mike could turn his hand to pretty much any job and understood intuitively how the old builders built with local materials. On my first day, while I made us mugs of tea, he asked if I had noticed that tea tasted different in other parts of the country and explained that it was simply a case of the land's personality having a bearing on everything. And as the taste of tea varied all around the country so too did the building materials that give a place its unique character. This variation of materials could be seen all around the museum's saved buildings, proof that folk once built with what was locally to hand, whether it was the oak that thrived in the clay of the Sussex Weald or water reed for thatched roofs in the Norfolk Broads. The stones of the Weald were not as renowned as other parts of the country, such as Dorset for example, with its famous limestones from the Isles of Portland and Purbeck. Looking around at the different walls of red brick, green sandstone, flint and chalk block, I could see that nature had still managed to give a good account of herself in her gift of building materials, the understanding of which is the foundation of architecture.

Mick showed me how to slake quicklime and mix it with sand to make the mortar that would bond the stones together. He explained how to use the right tools for each job. He lent me his broad-bladed all-steel chisel – a bolster, the head rounded like a button mushroom – for use with his mallet. I felt how the ash handle gave it some 'bounce', its curved beat – the part that makes contact with the also-curved chisel head – allowing me, as my position changed, to keep the same surface contact with its end-grain beech wood. It felt as if I had been passed the baton of a medieval tradition in a direct line from generation to generation of stonemasons. Later, on a visit to the quarry to pick up a freshly sawn load, I saw a mason's workshop for the first time – noisy and dusty, but tense with concentration.

My back yard soon filled up with grotesque figures and

green men, with chisels laid out in order of use alongside the other oddly named tools – the frig bob, cocks comb and French drag. I daydreamed about how my working life might progress as in medieval times, through the stages of apprentice, journeyman and then master. Over time I have become confident, but even today, three decades after I started, before I make the first cut into a new stone I still pause for a moment, my mallet hovering over the chisel, filled with the same trepidation I felt on my first day.

Towards the end of my training at South Dorset Technical College, we were set an assignment to fix freshly cut blocks into the ancient walls of Christchurch priory's great church that lifted from the edge of the natural harbour. It was an epiphany: this was the kind of stonemason I wanted to be – a fixer mason.

The fixer mason takes on, in many respects, the most challenging aspect of the craft. Fixers need strength, subtlety and an engineer's mindset as they have to lift and fix newly carved blocks sometimes weighing thousands of pounds into a pre-cut pocket with only a cigarette paper's width to spare. That day also taught me how the walls of old buildings tell the tale of their architectural evolution – of bodging, cut-corners and technical brilliance in equal measure. The strange mason's marks and superstitious graffiti carved into the walls of the priory's northern transept gave it all a very human touch. These were all themes that were to become familiar in the years to come.

Over the past three decades I have worked on many of Britain's greatest buildings and monuments – from the Roman ruins at Bath to Salisbury Cathedral's spire to St Paul's – and they have given me an unusual perspective on the warp and weft of English history, nature and geology. From the first stone megaliths put up by Neolithic farmers, to Roman temples, the Anglo-Saxon and Norman churches, as well as the engine houses, mills and aqueducts of the Industrial Revolution, each has given me a different view of our past to the one I learnt at school.

Thirty years ago, strolling down the longest church nave in the country, awed, cowed and a little dishevelled – my clothes rough under a covering of white dust that also sat thick on my boots – I felt like I finally belonged. I had chosen the itinerant path of the journeyman, one I happily still follow today.

In this book, I have tried to plot a roughly chronological journey through the building of Britain from the Neolithic to the present day, and across the year, exploring how our ancestors constructed the world we live in today. I am a stonemason not a historian and have concentrated on the buildings I have worked on and know best, so this is very much a partial and personal history, told from the inside out. I hope you enjoy it.

Orkney Islands

Simple
Geological Map
of
BRITAIN

SANDSTONE
&
GRANITE

Iona

SLATE

Edinburgh

CARBONIFEROUS
LIMESTONE

Durham

MAGNESIAN LIMESTONE

CLAY

York

Lincoln

N

SLATE

SANDSTONE

Coalbrookdale

OOLITIC LIMESTONE

Norwich

Ely

Sutton
Hoo

FLINT
&
CLAY

Preseli Hills

Carreg Cennen

Gloucester

Oxford

London

Bath

Stonehenge

Salisbury

CHALK
& FLINT

Reigate

Canterbury

SLATE,
GRANITE &
SANDSTONE

Exeter

Mên-an-Tol

Eddystone

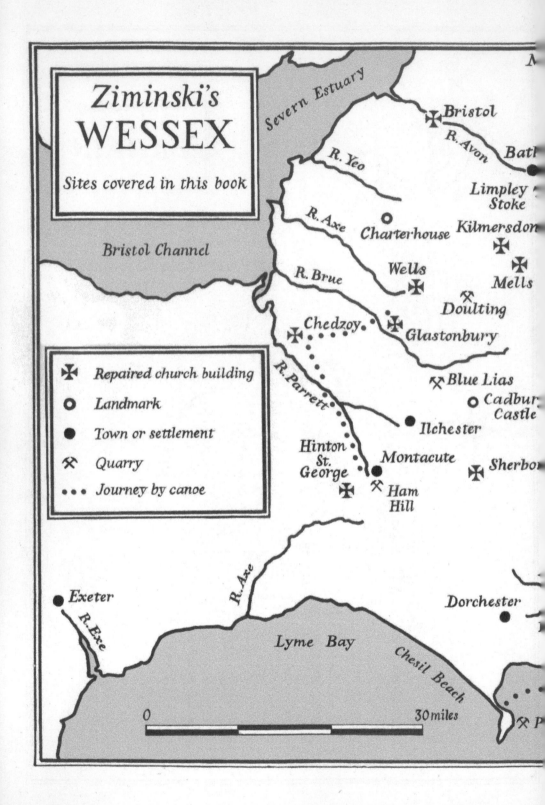

Ziminski's
WESSEX

Sites covered in this book

Bristol Channel

Severn Estuary

R. Yeo

R. Avon

Bristol

Bath

Limpley Stoke

R. Axe

Charterhouse

Kilmersdon

Wells

Mells

R. Brue

Doulting

Chedzoy

Glastonbury

R. Parrett

Blue Lias

Cadbury Castle

Ilchester

Hinton St. George

Montacute

Sherborne

Ham Hill

✠ Repaired church building

○ Landmark

● Town or settlement

⚒ Quarry

••• Journey by canoe

R. Axe

Exeter

R. Exe

Lyme Bay

Chesil Beach

Dorchester

0   30 miles

PART ONE
SARSEN

1

SAMHAIN

The stone-lined chamber was austere. Rough uprights, levered from the bedrock, supported an enormous slab, which formed a ceiling of sorts. A grassy mound may have covered all like a blanket, but as I shivered on the compacted chalk floor in my ineffectual sleeping bag, it was clear that this long barrow was far from the cosy hobbit hole I had imagined.

My torch lit a dim path across walls where tiny beads of condensation sparkled in competition with the eyes of cave spiders. As the cold night rolled on, so grew its disquieting atmosphere, but I was not visited by any of the apparitions that were supposed to lurk in its darker corners.

In the very early morning I awoke from a dream that my hipbone had fused through the camping mat on which I lay, my marrow spreading as rootstock through the compacted chalk. The connection between marrow and the chalk seemed appropriate, as this was once a mausoleum of sorts, built perhaps for a founding clan of farmers who had cleared the primeval woodland for pasture nearly six thousand years ago.

One of the largest and most impressive Neolithic, or new Stone Age, graves in Britain, the West Kennet Long Barrow was built around 3650 BCE and remained in use for at least the next thousand years. From my bed I could see across the narrow-roofed passageway to a twin chamber and down to a wall of massive stones forming the tomb's entrance. Another pair of chambers flanked the passage behind me, and behind them, deeper still in the long mound, the passage terminated in a central womb-like polygonal chamber, seven-and-a-half-feet high, which was occupied by Andy, my confederate and workmate since college days.

A mixture of work, convenience and professional curiosity had drawn us here. The custodians of the tomb had asked us to take a look and see if its collapsing walls could be repaired. I was fascinated to see how our stone-working forebears had managed to put together a structure that had been doing its job for so long. We had been told that there was evidence of the honing and polishing of prehistoric flint or some other stone tool inside. These marks were hard to find during the day so we decided to stay over in the hope that the morning's low-raking sunlight would help identify them.

I lay there a little longer, putting off the chill that unzipping the sleeping bag was sure to bring. Dawn probed its way along the corridor that connected the outside world to this realm of the dead. A finger of light touched the shoulder of a blocking slab at a point more highly polished than the rest. The sandstone here is so tough that it would have been regularly used to grind down and hone edges on local flint hand tools such as blades and axes. This procedure allowed for the increase in mechanical strength needed when cutting down a tree or in carpentry work, as friction would be reduced during the impact and make the cutting of the tool more efficient. Soon, other tool-rubbing spots caught my eye. One, smooth as glass and the width of a shoe, would have been made by the last tools to have been produced here. If this slab was laid on its back, it could have been used as a bench to sharpen some of my own chisels. I realised that I was surrounded by the remnants of a Neolithic tool manufactory, where already old stone slabs were recycled and incorporated into the later chambers. Suddenly those long-dead Neolithic people did not seem so remote. I imagined them clearing the woodland that gave us the landscape we know today, the timber they supplied propping up the tomb during its construction, cut with axes that had been sharpened on these stones.

The whippet – our other companion on this visit – led the way out of the tomb and she was soon over and through the gap in the row of megaliths. I followed her through the facade of colossal stones, stiff with damp and cold, into a new day. On an adjacent hill, anonymous under a coxcomb of knife-tattooed beech trees, lies another long barrow just as large, excavated only by badgers.

The straw chaff left by the combine harvester blowing around the whippet's legs reminded me that today was All Saints' Day, the festival used by local farmers to mark the end of harvest time. Considering our location, it seemed appropriate that All Saints had replaced the pre-Christian festival of the dead, where 1 November was the festival of Samhain which marked the beginning of winter and the first day of the Celtic calendar.

We walked around the barrow's grass bank. The whippet sniffed at the rabbit burrows, which pockmarked its scrubby base. Large anthills that looked as if they had built up over thousands of generations covered the rest of the mound, which tapered down three hundred feet to open fields. In the distance a hundred gulls rose and fell around the business end of a single red Massey Ferguson tractor. The soil folded neatly over the bedrock chalk suggested that the plough had been at work for some days already.

These hills form the roof of the south country: a watershed that creates a trio of rivers that rise in the surrounding valleys and drain away to separate seaward cardinal points. The first Homo sapiens came this way 11,000 years ago, tracking and stalking migratory herds of red deer and horse at the end of the last Ice Age. Soon a network of paths evolved that allowed humans and animals to travel safely above the swamps and forest. Perhaps the oldest of these followed the Ridgeway a few fields away. Gradually, a couple of centuries before West Kennet Long Barrow was built, hunters left their seasonal camps and hunting grounds to embark on early attempts at farming – trial-and-error ventures of deforestation, growing crops and managing livestock, watched over by pastoral dogs, quite different from the thin shadow loping by my side. Within a few generations, these first farmers became successful enough to have time to spare, creating the first sacred monuments.

Windmill Hill near Avebury is not only windmill-less but more of a low rise in the land than a hill, and is a landscape redolent with prehistory. Here large seasonal get-togethers would have drawn visitors from far and wide to this trading place and bustling market. These gatherings proved so profitable that time was spent in the slack parts of the farming year digging a series of concentric ditches and embankments connected with open causeways to create a vast enclosure that spread out below the brow of the hill. These causewayed enclosures had no defensive purpose as the earth, when dug from the ditch, was piled up in a bank on the outside. And over the next thirty generations, this form evolved into the first of the henge monuments. Even though Windmill Hill is the largest of the many causewayed enclosures, a visit today does not reveal much. The earthworks of Britain's first farming communities are long ploughed-out, but kicking around its molehills will throw up an occasional thumbnail-sized sherd of 'grooved ware'. I prefer the old name that early archaeologists used for tribes indigenous to this part of Wessex who developed megalithic civilisation and the first pottery: the Windmill Hill people.

These 'grooved ware' sherds come from pots with a flat base used for casseroling, dating as far back as the early third millennium BCE, and are one of the earliest pottery types found in Britain. Decorated with imprints that imitate wicker basketry, the style remained in fashion for more than a thousand years. Some regional variants had a curved base that allowed the pot to withstand the heat of the fire and its contents to be evenly cooked. Analysis has found residues of the meals that were cooked in them. In Neolithic times, spring-born piglets were slaughtered after about nine months of fattening for the feast, when the clans gathered at midwinter. This would have been the last opportunity to give thanks to the gods' controlling powers as winter (and famine) approached. I imagined them in procession as family groups to the nearby high places on a ritual visit to their ancestors up at West Kennet.

A mile away, the village of Avebury sat hazy under a pall of woodsmoke. The few sunbeams that broke through illuminated the old church tower of St James. The previous day, we had finished our job there, trying to save the rotten stone mullions and tracery that kept the west window's stained glass from collapse. Although built by medieval hands and listed Grade 1, the church tower seemed flashily new contrasted with the earthworks of the biggest stone circle in the world that encloses the rest of the village. We had come up to the barrow from Avebury after a few drinks to celebrate the end of the job. Spending the night there saved us the two-hour return drive to our yard in Somerset before we began the repair of the creaking walls of the seventeenth-century nonconformist chapel, on the other side of Avebury village, the following day.

St James's window was built from limestone, a material that we work with all the time. This particular limestone is soft enough to saw in any direction, yielding easily when cut with a chisel and perfect for architectural detailing. Sarsen, the stone we were using to repair the chapel's walls, is a different beast altogether. It can still be found in outcrops, protected as sites of special scientific interest, so some scavenging skills would be needed to source replacement material. Sarsen is diamond-hard and tougher even than granite, and because of a tendency to bend ploughshares, large lumps are often found on the margins of fields. Ploughboys must have been moving them out of the way since the time of the first farmers. We had been collecting this rare commodity for some time. While driving the previous day a small cairn of fieldstones hidden away around the base of a roadside hawthorn provoked a cry of 'Sarsen!' from Andy. 'There's many a fine sight for those who have eyes to see such things,' I observed after we had tossed the stones into the back of our old Toyota pickup.

Up until the end of the eighteenth century, most country buildings were built from the materials most readily to hand.

This can complicate a modern stonemason's daily task of maintaining the integrity of old buildings and churches because if stonework or the mortar that holds it in place has been worn away by time and weather, it needs to be repaired with replacement materials that are often no longer readily available on a like-for-like basis. Builders' merchants or DIY stores are not much help, so large roadside nodes of flint and sarsen are fair game. I could visualise a squared-up block within each medicine ball-shaped lump that could be put to good use in repairing damp, tired walls.

Warmed by the morning sun, Andy and I squeezed back through a gap in West Kennet Long Barrow's facade and clambered over the deep kerb that forms the thirty-two-foot base of a rudimentary isosceles triangle. The depth into the tomb is twice the length of the base and is perhaps the earliest use of geometry to set out a sacred space.

My eyes took a few moments to adjust to the gloom and focused on the infill of sarsen sat on low walls, skilfully built from thinly split forest marble. This flat limestone, each piece the size of a chopping board, had been brought over twenty-five miles of rough country from the edge of Somerset's distant Mendip Hills.

In some places the guts of the tomb had spilled out onto the chalk floor, perhaps vandalised. We could see that it would only be a quick job to put the fallen areas back together, so we decided to crack on. With no tools but our hands, we sorted the pieces, pulled out the muddy backing and 'knocked it up' with our boots like a winemaker treading grapes and spread the chalky mud – the oldest of building materials – as a backing mortar to stick together the otherwise dry-built walls.

It was satisfying to labour in the same way as the ancestors who built this place.

On my knees and with the wall stripped away, the sequence of their construction was apparent. Once the plan was set out, the Neolithic builders laid the upright sarsens down on their edges to create a revetment that would retain the chalk soil tamped down behind it as the tomb rose up. Large numbers of timber props would have provided temporary horizontal support to the walls. The course of huge slabs would have been dragged up the earthen ramp until they projected a small way above the walls at head height on either side.

The row of stones supported another row that projected forward, making a corbelling course – this was named from the way the upper beak of a raven (*corvus* in Latin, *corbeau* in French) overlaps the lower. Each course of stone on either side was gradually edged forward over the void until the slabs nearly met in the middle (the top of the arch) and then spanned with a flat capstone. The proto-arch, when repeated along the entrance gallery, created a simple vault that was an improvement on the load-bearing efficiency of the more usual timber post-and-lintel method. The disadvantage was that this wall-and-chalk packing needed to be thick enough to counteract the effects of gravity and prevent the sides of the vault collapsing inwards.

I remembered a lecture at stonemasonry college. Geoffrey Teychenne, our tutor, who had been taught by a pupil of Rodin, tried to sprinkle a good amount of culture into the heads of woodentops like me. He taught us about the Roman architect Marcus Vitruvius, who in *De Architectura* suggested that architecture should satisfy three characteristics: solidity, usefulness and beauty – principles that I thought also applied to this most ancient of places. That our Stone Age, stone-working forebears had put together a structure that had stayed up over thousands of years was proof enough of its solidity. The accommodation it offered was admittedly basic, but the rituals that modern visitors continue to practise here when the sun or moon mark certain points of the year reflect its ongoing usefulness. No one could describe this place as beautiful, but the gnarled entrance facade of massive boulders as well as the corridor and chambers that lead away from it were proportionally and aesthetically pleasing.

Building in stone was a method already well used by the early Neolithic cultures of Brittany and the Loire Valley. And the early fourth millennium BCE megalithic culture of western France in turn gave rise to its development in south-west England. These ideas could have arrived here via the Cotentin peninsula that lies opposite the natural harbour at Hengistbury Head in Dorset, only a couple of days' crossing in a small boat. From Hengistbury, where the Wiltshire Avon empties, it would have been natural to follow this riverine route to its headwaters that rise only a few miles from West Kennet. These French tombs were oriented on particular astronomical alignments important to early agriculturalists. This tradition continues at West Kennet twice yearly, at the time of the spring and autumn equinoxes, when the rising sun sends a ray of light dancing across the back face of the main chamber. This spectacle would have been witnessed by many generations of people who had made their way here to participate in the rituals that allowed them to venerate and even take away the body parts of their ancestors that they thought most important.

Professor Stuart Piggott's excavations here in the mid-1950s found the disarticulated remains of about fifty bodies. They had been carefully placed on the floor of the different chambers. Prior to this the corpses would have been left open to the elements and birds in an air burial, where the flesh would fall away to leave only the bones. Perhaps the body would have been left on an elevated platform nearby in the same way that some Zoroastrian still do today. According to their ancient belief, a body becomes tainted at death, when evil spirits, or *nasu*, attack the flesh and soul of the departed. These *nasu* also threaten the living. As fire and earth are sacred to the Zoroastrians, cremation and burial are deemed sacrilegious and air burial is considered the purest way of dealing with the dead. As carrion-eating birds strip the body of flesh, they act as intermediaries between earth and sky and liberate the deceased's soul.

Within the long barrow the skulls of a child, a middle-aged individual and an older woman had been placed carefully in a row. Anatomical reports noted 'suspicious collocations' of other bones that suggested 'the ghoulish picture of a visitor to the barrow picking up a partly decomposed arm, detaching the humerus and flinging the other bones into a dark corner'. The shoulder bones of one person were found in one chamber and their feet in another. 'Who knows the fate of his bones?' wrote Sir Thomas Browne in 1658. His disgruntled indignation goes on, 'To be Knavd out of our graves, to have our sculs made drinking bowls and our bones turned into pipes to delight and sport our enemies are tragical abominations.' Professor Piggott adopted a more reasoned approach. He thought that 'the concurrence of beliefs in classical antiquity seems to have linked both the head and the thigh bones as the seats of generation and fertility'.

People came here to honour their ancestors. Many of the

missing skulls and long leg bones would have been taken by the tribe back down the path to be buried in the ditch of Windmill Hill's causewayed enclosure, as a *pars pro toto*. This is where one body part was taken to represent the whole, a way of keeping the ancestors working for the community, ensuring the continuing fertility of the crops and livestock from the other side. If they had had a flag, I wondered, would it have resembled the Jolly Roger?

Over many generations, this mansion of the dead was progressively incorporated into the creation of a vast ritual landscape of huge mounds, henges, stone circles and avenues that focused on the River Kennet and its meadows. The tomb remained in use for a millennium, with occasional community projects to prise and haul the top slabs open. The interior was then deliberately filled to its ceiling like a skip with a mix of chalk blocks, shellfish from the River Severn, soil, beads and charcoal mixed with the bones of a few domesticated animals, a goat as well as wild horse, beaver and corncrake.

Once we had finished the long barrow's drystone walling, we gathered up our waste as well as the plastic tat and old tea lights left by others. We noticed the wax stains and burn marks left behind by candles on what the visitors thought was sacred. Then a siren drew us out of the tomb. Across the valley on Overton Hill, a fire engine, blue lights pulsing, climbed and overtook other vehicles on the busy A4 as it approached the crossroads with the great Ridgeway. Its noise intensified for a moment as the engine passed the now-destroyed Neolithic site known as the Sanctuary, a place that the archaeologist Aubrey Burl thought had at one time been a mortuary house for air burials.

For a moment, standing in front of the long barrow's concave facade, I fancied the sound of the siren dissipating across the surfaces of the slabs to leak away into the interior chambers. Had the succeeding generations of worshippers, who had used West Kennet for over a thousand years, drummed and chanted like this in ceremonies up on the Sanctuary, their beats carrying across the valley to the facade, constructed to amplify and focus the transmission to whatever of their ancestors remained within the barrow's chambers? It reminded me of another concave masonry listening device I had come across that was also east facing and long obsolete. Constructed in the 1920s the concrete sound-mirrors at RAF Denge in Dungeness, Kent, acted as an experimental listening station for slow-moving enemy aircraft and bomb-laden airships.

The red tractor was still ploughing the open fields, its threatening spike pacified by a bayoneted straw bale. It slowed as it passed us, and the farmer hopped down, his face expressionless. He knew all about our work at the chapel he went to. He nodded to our carrier bag of rubbish. 'Good work on tidying up after you,' he said. As a reward he told us the whereabouts of a secret valley, where some of the last sarsen outcrops remain hidden away among a preserved landscape of great antiquity.

It is only a short walk along the River Kennet to Piggledene where visitors are uncommon. Its usual name comes from the Saxon for 'valley of the hawks', suggesting it has always been private territory for birds. The busy high-pitched tremolo of the community of sparrows dissipates respectfully about the coombe. Skylarks stay there all year. A well-camouflaged sarsen train over twenty-five thousand strong remains hidden in the scrub. Distant slabs look like sheep, which could explain the alternative name – 'greywether' – used by the locals for a castrated ram. They were also known as 'sazzens', a shortening of 'Saracen' – the dialect term for anything considered foreign or unusual.

Up until the nineteenth century these quartzite slabs lay on the surface of the downs in such abundance that they streamed down all the local valleys like stone rivers. A traveller in the nineteenth century claimed that you could 'walk from Avebury to Lockeridge without ever touching the ground as there were so many sarsens to step on'. As this is the only hard stone that outcrops in any quantity on the chalk it is easy to understand the power this place would have held for the pioneering settlers of six thousand years ago. Piggledene would have been seen as a special, holy place that combined by chance with rivers and paths. There was nowhere better for the construction of shrines, mausoleums and sanctuaries in southern England. Once the first sarsen was prised from its resting place to be incorporated into a shrine or barrow, the days of the rest were numbered.

Today, they have been hunted almost to extinction. Starting as a quarry for the nearby prehistoric monuments, over time the extraction accelerated and once they had been skilfully cut by hand, the sarsens became kerbs and cobbles, gateposts and walling for barns and houses. William Stukeley, the eighteenth-century clergyman and antiquarian genius, lamented that in places only turnips remained. This was the start of the modern denudation of the chalkland. There are now gaps in the hedgerows from long-departed elms, the chain-sawn stumps of ash trees, and even the Kennet river has been over-abstracted;

once it would have been dammed by beavers, but now it remains dry for half the year.

It was still relatively early and the pickup that had been left on the byway leading to the chapel was not far away. The now-open downland held even more sarsens. Eventually we found the place the farmer had told us about. Encrustations of an ancient colony of orange, green, grey and brown lichen almost hid a series of clearly defined robust grooves. This was a *polissoir*, a different type of prehistoric polisher, where axes were sharpened 'edge on' at an angle of 90 degrees. Somehow this 5,000-year-old axe-grinding bench had managed to avoid incorporation into any other later monument.

We crossed the ancient Ridgeway that followed the top of the escarpment and took the rutted chalk course of the Saxon *hereweg* or military road down the slope toward the chapel, stopping by an old marl pit where we had left the pickup the night before. Enclosed by unkempt barbed-wire fencing and smothered with old man's beard, its mossy bottom was a tangled mess of old tyres, black plastic and dead nettles through which Jenny Wren was hemstitching her way to her little cave. It hid another material important for our work at the chapel, and we spent a profitable hour shovelling sticky batches of marl – a chalk/clay mix – into the back of the pickup.

It was a short, bumpy ride along Green Street to the quietest of Avebury's four prehistoric crossing points through the henge. As at Windmill Hill's causewayed enclosure, the ditch that enfolds the 28.5-acre site of the Avebury stone circle is on the inside of the rampart. The dense stand of beech trees that guards the entrance carried ribbons on their lower branches left by modern worshippers. The exposed matting of thick roots looked as if it preferred not to penetrate the earth, gripping the surface and slope of the bank instead. Tolkien thought of these beeches as his soulful walking trees, the Ents. From here, the other side of the circular embankment can be seen a quarter of a mile away, with St James's Church beyond. The church had been built a respectful distance from the monument as if the Saxon priest in charge had been 'afeared' of the place.

Avebury is a near-circular henge formed from a massive chalk-cut ditch – deep enough to toboggan down on snowy days – from where the spoil had been dumped to form an external bank enclosing the stone circle. From 2900–2600 BCE, when the henge was newly dug by people whose pickaxes were the antlers of reindeer and shovels the shoulder blades of oxen, it would have been waterlogged for much of the winter. Perhaps it was built to help prevent the spirits of the ancestors from escaping the circle to the open downland where the living people were farming. The large stone circle in turn encompasses the remains of two smaller stone circles. An avenue, delineated by pairs of great stones, wanders away from the henge and stone circle past Silbury Hill, the tallest prehistoric mound in Europe.

We parked the truck at the centre of the monument and started to unload our haul into the chapel's graveyard. The traffic on the busy Swindon–Devizes road that divides the village was heavy. Many people must pass the black-and-white timber-framed Red Lion, the brick-built Georgian houses and humbler cottages of chalk-cob and think Avebury is just a typical Wiltshire village. Some miss the diamond-shaped stones, the height of a large van, loitering by the monument's north and south entrances. Six thousand years ago the Neolithic people probably thought of this now-unremarkable spot, right at the centre of the stone circle, as the *axis mundi*, the centre of the world.

Part of a curious arrangement known as the Cove can be seen through a gap in the cottages. Two of the original three large upright slabs remain, as colossal as the neighbouring barn wall. They lean conspiratorially, making what would have been a square open-ended 'box' in the centre of one of a pair of now much-depleted stone circles. The other circle sat immediately to the south and also held a stone structure at its centre. The sequence of construction is unclear, but the largest Cove stone was erected in about 3000 BCE.

The gap in the once three-sided box faces north-east, ready to greet the rising sun on midsummer's day, which it has done about five thousand times. Another cove at the end of the Avenue to Beckhampton was possibly oriented to face the midwinter solstice, the most important day in the Neolithic calendar, and these two form Avebury's only possible solar alignments. Of all its many eerie parts, the spot around the Cove has the most sinister atmosphere, a place to be felt rather than analysed. The limbs of an adjacent alder sag under a platoon of preening starlings as a solitary big-eyed field pigeon stares knowingly down from what may have been the top of the first stone to have gone up. This type of standing stone, known as an 'orthostat', looks the most immovable of objects and has probably always been at this spot, until the forest around it was cleared and it became grass-covered in newly created pasture. At some unknown date before 3000 BCE, farmers used long, timber levers to wrench it from its setting. One end was gradually lifted until the stone could be propped up on a lashed-together lattice of timber baulks. The lifting of the stone continued until it hit the crucial seventy degrees of tilt. It would then have slid naturally into the huge clay-lubricated chalk mortice dug to accommodate half of its hundred-ton mass. Over the next few centuries the farmers from Windmill Hill continued to develop the area around the Cove before they dug the great circular arena of ditch and embankment. In creating the inner stone circles, the on-site stone supply would perhaps have been exhausted, and more sarsens must have been sourced from the adjacent heights and coombes.

Just before the middle of the second millennium BCE, during a time of great religious change and revival, the scale of this megalithism increased greatly. More stones were sourced and moved to create Avebury's great circle of undressed uprights, the largest in existence. An abundance of stone circle types are found throughout the British Isles from this time. They may have assisted in the creation of a backdrop to enhance the theatrical rituals that Burl thinks were carried out in order 'to appease the malevolent powers of nature'. Each of the hundred or so known stones of Avebury's outer circle closely followed the henge's strange plan, maintaining an average of eleven feet between each other and the same constant, cautious distance from the inner lip of the ditch. The surviving uprights are planted among molehills of black humus packed with pieces of Willow Pattern plate and burnt glass. The lichen-coated outer face of each stone is thought to be smoother than the inner, the effect of weathering over millions of years as they lay on the turf line.

This place is a great natural temple, the character of which changes in each quadrant. In the north-west, the stones are more geometric than their far larger equivalents in the south-west. This was a design common to other late-Neolithic stone circles that face the winter solstice sunset. The remaining Avenue of re-erected standing stones demonstrates an unrivalled mastery of form. Some say they were selected for their pleasing male and female shapes, as broad and squat contrast with their tall and thin partners. They do seem to have a relationship with the one opposite, as if enjoying 'a long way set' folk dance, in a way that draws the disparate parts of the ritual landscape together into a great dramatic sculpture. Following subtle topographical changes, they curve and kink their way towards their separate termini at Beckhampton's Cove to the west, and to the south-east at the Sanctuary, which may have acted as a turnstile through which Neolithic pilgrims from the Ridgeway would pass after a respectful nod to the bodies exposed for air burial on wooden platforms.

We stood for a moment in the small graveyard of the Dissenters chapel, and studied the self-effacing facade of flint, brick and sarsen that was enlivened only by a seemingly frivolous date stone that indicates that it was put up five years after the Five Mile Act of 1665. After the Civil War Dissenters were banned from preaching a sermon within five miles of any town corporation or their old parishes. Avebury sat at the centre of a hub of good roads that brought the faithful from the surrounding towns of Swindon, Calne, Marlborough and Devizes. The preachers thought this position at the centre of a pagan temple was a divine sign and, clearing this area by the crossroads, they built their own place of worship.

They weren't the first to interfere with Avebury. On the eve of the Black Death in the early fourteenth century, its stones were buried as they were thought to be the embodiment of evil. For the villagers, this happily created more tillage, and some of the toppled stones were incorporated into hedge boundaries and the walls of cottages. In the seventeenth century, the destruction escalated. For those of a puritanical or speculative bent, the magnetic attraction of the five hundred or more megaliths in the wider complex proved too much. In what has come to be known as 'the shame', Avebury became a quarry; uprights were toppled and then broken up to produce pieces of a usable size to build the Dissenters chapel. William Stukeley summed up the scale of the slaughter when he wrote:

> This stupendous fabric, which for some thousands of years, had brav'd the continual assaults of weather, and by the nature of it, when left to itself, like the pyramids would have lasted as long as the globe, hath fallen a sacrifice to the wretched ignorance and avarice of a little village unluckily plac'd within it.

The campaign was continued in the same manner by the preacher Thomas 'Stone-Killer' Robinson, who boasted that he had killed forty stones and was only defeated by the scale of the project. A woodcut of him hangs in the National Portrait Gallery; the banner draped about his person declares him *Alburae Depopulator* – 'the Avebury devastator'.

Our job was to mend the chapel's collapsing walls that had been built with sarsens from this most destructive phase, and we were caught by the view from the small workspace we had set up in its back garden. Framed by the turf grandstand of the henge's embankment, a huge pair of impassive diamond-shaped megaliths formed one of the original entrances. A flock of sheep grazed among the concrete markers of the lost stones of the southern circle. Here, once, stood the mightiest of all stones, a 21-foot-high obelisk that was destroyed and replaced by a maypole. A broken stump was all that remained of another enigmatic holed sarsen, once the size of the tractor tyre-sized Mên-an-Tol in Cornwall, a stone with a hole, where children who passed through were sure to be cured of their scrofula, while women would be ensured the pregnancy they longed for.

Preservation of Avebury's heritage is a continuing problem. On cold days the walls of the chapel, recently covered by an impermeable hard cement render, would sweat, the windows thick with condensation. Long strands of mycelium had accepted the invitation to feed under the damp pew bases where the kingdom of rot ruled. Its grip was so total that the organist fell through the floor during a service. The gallery creaked so much that I felt it was sure to collapse as soon as a visiting choir clapped in evangelising unison.

We had the first half-hundredweight fieldstone lifted onto the waist-high workbench, ready to be squared off. It was destined to replace missing stones, in an area where the chapel's walls had collapsed. As sarsen is such a hard material, and unlike many of the local limestones it cannot be cut with a handsaw, I needed to use a hammer, punch (a chisel with a point) and claw tool (a toothed chisel) for the removal of superfluous material. I cut a marginal draft as a lip around the circumference of the stone, which would guide the working of the flat plane into the pumpkin-shaped top.

Making a flat surface using traditional tools and techniques is still one of the first activities an apprentice learns today. Even Michelangelo and Bernini would not have achieved a flat surface immediately. Practice makes perfect, especially when training the most important tool of all – the eye, which once sharpened never blunts.

Normally, with a job like this I would cut the surface with a mallet and chisel; but this needed the sturdier approach of steel hammer and punch. These were used to flatten the lumpy area between the marginal drafts and remove the waste. Afterwards the flattened area looked something like a furrowed field. The next stage was to use the claw tool to take off the ridges; then finally a wide chisel would remove the marks of the claw tool and make a good surface, which is checked with a straight edge. This was such hard work that at the end of the day, for the first time on a job, I noticed wear on the steel tools and the back of my hands were blue with iron dust. Sir Christopher Wren noticed that sarsens 'doe pitch all one way like arrows shot', an evocative description of the small explosions each blow created, which released a subtle sulphurous tang from within the stone.

With the face perfectly flat, and the waste removed roughly from the sides, it was ready for fixing into the wall. Each stone differed in colour across varying hues of toffee and burnt toast. At the front of the chapel next to the pile of marl and chalk waited the galvanised bath tub that was the only container strong enough to deal with the most volatile of building ma-terials: quicklime. This quicklime was limestone cooked at 1000 degrees at the kilns at Cheddar near its famous Gorge. With the bath half-filled with water, we added the marl and chalk and some coarse aggregate. The bags that held the fist-sized grey-white lumps of rock looked harmless enough, but were covered in warnings to keep them dry. I knew they needed handling with respect. Having togged ourselves up in goggles, masks and sou'westers, we lit the fuse by carefully emptying the bags into the water. We quickly stepped back and picked up our rakes and waited, as builders have done for over four thousand years, since a Minoan or Egyptian alchemist first discovered the peculiar reaction that we were about to experience. After a pregnant pause and a few innocuous-looking vapours, the bubbles came. Quite suddenly all hell broke loose and the tub erupted into a spitting volcano-like cauldron, its contents hot enough to strip flesh from bone – a use to which quicklime had been extensively applied in the plague pits of London. Going at it in unison with rakes, as the chapel's builders would have done, we took it in turns to mix it up, the steam so intense that visibility disappeared. Then, as quickly as it had started, it suddenly slaked and the ferocity ebbed away.

We shovelled the hot putty out and used it immediately to fix the new work into the wall. Satisfyingly, it was a perfect match for that used by the original country builders, and once it had set the walls would be able to breathe. It was an irony that the hardest of stone needed to be bedded with the softest of mortars to ensure the building survived for another few hundred years.

Leaning on the truck's tailgate, tired after the day's exertions, I rolled a cigarette and contemplated Silbury Hill with West Kennet Long Barrow behind it on the hillside above. I decided to take the whippet on a final leg, following the footpath and watercourse, braided by the first floods of winter, that led from Avebury towards the prehistoric mountain's sight line.

Silbury Hill's shaved top can be seen peeping over adjacent hills from many directions. It is the hub on which the older trackways focused. The imperial Roman surveyors two thousand years ago made good use of the hill's already ancient heights and abruptly changed the direction of their new military road from London to skirt around its fat curving rump and on to the next high point, in the direction of Bath.

Silbury's watercourse drained into a vast moat, also filled by the many springs that rose near the hill when the bedrock was saturated. Radioactive-looking water vapours lifted around the excavation quarry that supplied the material for the mound. The higher water table during the early Bronze Age when it was constructed in stages would have ensured the hill remained an island all year round. I hoped that the night's full moon might encourage King Sil – who, legend said, rested armour-clad beneath – to rise and take his golden horse to drink from the nearby Swallowhead Spring.

The whippet and I followed in the footsteps of generations of visitors and pilgrims on sarsen stepping-stones the size of car bonnets. The Kennet, a source of the Thames, chattered from a couple of holes the size of a badger sett. I looked between Silbury Hill and the long barrow and understood that this was the sort of sacred place the ancient Greeks would have called an *omphalos*, or 'navel', a metaphor for the centre of the world.

This was the point where it all started and finished. After twelve hundred years of co-opting the population into constructing these enormous projects, which started at West Kennet around 3750 BCE, they came to an end with the completion of Silbury Hill around 2400 BCE. Once complete, Silbury would have been scoured and chalk-white, the biggest single human endeavour undertaken in prehistoric Europe, with as many as 18 million working-hours expended in its construction. Its completion signified a time of momentous and catastrophic change for the

Windmill Hill people. Great blocking stones were levered into position to seal the entrance portal of the long barrow and give some suggestion of the scale and nature of events that were taking place. Over time these blocking stones fell. In one of the sockets into which the butt-end of a stone once fitted, archaeologists found a small, carefully placed piece of pot; a calling card left by the new blood that was soon camped out on the downs. This type of differently shaped pot was evidence that a new population of migrants was beginning to arrive, individuals who had been migrating in small groups across Europe for several generations. For them the construction of massive stone monuments for ritual use and to commemorate the dead was an alien concept. They preferred burial in a more modest way, on their own in a pit or under a round earthen mound. It may even have been they who blocked up the long barrow.

These were the first Celtic peoples to arrive in Britain. The package of personal possessions buried with them tells the tale of a revolution in religion, technology and language. They were buried with flint tools and daggers, more refined in their making and design; leaf-shaped arrowheads of the earlier inhabitants were replaced with barbed and tanged versions. Often they were buried with the new type of pot, one that would have been well used while they lived – a beaker, shaped with a flat bottom, filled with enough beer or mead to see them through to the other side, which gave their culture its name – Beaker folk.

Most significantly, they had objects made from the first metals to be refined; personal adornments in gold or weapons in copper. Their arrival coincided with the short transitional period between the Neolithic and the Bronze Age. This Chalcolithic or 'Copper Age' was a time when copper ingots and objects were cast without being toughened by the simple addition of tin to make bronze.

Recent DNA research has shown that it was then that the blue-eyed and fair-skinned people of the Beaker culture from the steppes of the Ukraine and Russia started to arrive in Britain. From around 2450 BCE, and over the next few generations, the dark-skinned Windmill Hill people and other native communities were replaced almost entirely, possibly through the diseases that the new arrivals brought with them to which the locals had no immunity.

These changes took place only a couple of generations after the building around Avebury reached its peak and its power drained away towards the south, down the Avon's riverine way to Stonehenge. Stonehenge evolved, perhaps, in competition over several phases at roughly the same time as these henge and stone circles, but its extraordinarily sophisticated design was to completely eclipse Avebury's unworked stones.

Had the Beaker people caused this shift? The dates are too close to call but an entirely new way of thinking about the business of construction, surveying, design, geometry and engineering had appeared without any European precedent, drawn it seemed out of the thin air of Salisbury Plain's coombes and downs. Stonehenge was the highpoint of European cultural prehistory, the only circle where the stones are shaped and jointed one to another. Was this the work of the insular Windmill Hill farmers or that of the new migrants, or even a mix of the two? We don't know. But we do know that eventually the area around Stonehenge became a draw for Beaker folk from across Europe. And it would be the place where, once our work at the chapel was complete, I was heading next.

2
WINTER SOLSTICE

A couple of days before the year's shortest day, I was working three hundred feet above a remarkable sacred landscape.

Looking out, I could see the transition from the shallow chalk hills of the alkali plain to the acid sands of the New Forest. Rivers with differing geological signatures came and went like curved streaks of mercury. A few miles north, among distant pollarded willows, I could just make out the stretch where people once tied up their coracles and rafts as they journeyed to Stonehenge. To the south, the water's pulse quickened as it was drawn irresistibly into Christchurch Harbour, a day further downstream.

Beams of midwinter sun dazzled and diffracted their way carelessly about the forest of metal poles that supported our work platform. The scaffolding hugged the grove of pinnacles at the base of the greatest and most intact of medieval spires, Salisbury Cathedral, which rose up another 104 feet into the clouds. We were working on an elevation populated with carved dog's-head grotesques that snarled at the city's roofscape below. My workmates were on the lee side of the tower, sensibly keeping out of the icy wind, cutting out the decayed stone to a depth that would allow the retention of the maximum amount of ancient carving. This was dentistry, but on a cathedral-sized scale.

Above, at the spire's top, just below the red glow of the aircraft-warning light, where the cups of the anemometer turned ceaselessly, a lead box had been built into the capstone. Could it still contain a piece of silk, a relic of the Virgin Mary, to whom Salisbury Cathedral was dedicated? Way below, a channelled grid of streams fed the water meadows that defined the city of Salisbury. In the medieval canals and watercourses, long fingers of pondweed waved on gelid waters with winter quickness.

As we worked, a hoppy odour rose from the nearby Gibbs Mew brewery, and the conversation kept coming back to Bishop's Tipple, their much missed masterpiece 6.5 per cent ale. (I had known worse. On an early freelance job inspecting the spire of the church of St James in Trowbridge, this torment had been doubled when the aroma of the Ushers brewery merged with the aromatic delights of the adjacent Bowyers sausage and pork-pie factory.)

The job at the cathedral was to replace some stone panels near the top of the tower, just below the corner pinnacles that abut the spire. The panels, traceried sections of silage-green Chilmark stone cut in the cathedral's workshop, could only be hefted into position with a team effort. One mate rapidly dragged on the chains of the block-and-tackle hoist, another was ready to trowel the wet mortar down at the right time so that its moisture wasn't sucked out too quickly as we slid our new work, a perfect fit for the gaps that had been cut to accommodate it, into position.

On the other side of the scaffolding's handrail, a lone resident peregrine gyred round, picking off a straggling pigeon. Even higher up, a clattering family of jackdaws nested among the pinnacles, where the octagonal base of the spire met the square tower. Their ill-humoured saturation bombing had been directed against us all winter; and large quantities of ancient stinking twigs and the odd corncob husk rained down as we worked. Later in the season, a fallen jackdaw chick, wedged behind a crocket, was to resist all our attempts at rescue while it returned our attention with a gaze of baleful, human-like calculation.

Inside the spire, ancient rickety worm-eaten ladders were still tied into the original timber scaffolding, as disorientating as an Escher drawing. When the clerk of works was absent, I took to their forbidden splintered steps. My claustrophobia, anxiety and excitement mounted with the ascent into the narrowing inner space of the spire, lit thinly by a dim festoon of 40-watt bulbs. Far below was a windlass built into the timber framework in the mid-fourteenth century, and used until recently to lift material and scaffolding up from the crossing of the nave. Looking down to it from the top through the cobwebs was not an option for the faint-hearted. My climb terminated at a heavily cobwebbed weather door, where I felt the top of the spire sway subtly.

It was curiosity that had lured me upwards to see if the ancient sites that were reputed to be skewed together in a curious alignment were visible. As the little door graunched open, it wasn't just the sudden inward gust of wind that took my breath away. A couple of miles to the north lifted the upturned saucer of the vast Iron Age earthwork of Old Sarum, within which, set like an intaglio, lay the low-ruined outline of this cathedral's predecessor. I imagined the alignment continuing on its south-east–north-west axis to where it terminated at Stonehenge. There, Druids and partygoers would soon be gathering for their hazy cosmic jive, one of the two days per year when Stonehenge perhaps rediscovers some echo of its original purpose.

I made my way safely back down the spire and returned to the job of filling the gaps around the newly fixed Gothic panel with a soft lime mortar, to hold it in place and keep the weather at bay for a few hundred more years. Looking west over the parapet at eye level, I could see two of the five river systems that were drawn to this nodal point. Were they the route by which the thousands of tons of medieval stone below me had been brought? It would have been easier than hauling it by horse and cart.

Some years later, while unpicking the collapsing vault of a nineteenth-century farm bridge that crossed the River Nadder, I found more supporting evidence for my hunch. The bridge had been built to improve access to the quarry at Chicksgrove that, along with those at the nearby village of Chilmark, was the cathedral's main source of stone. The clear chalk river had reached its lowest summer level, and the bridge's footings were exposed. To my great interest, they rested on a far earlier causeway of flagstones. Could this be part of a small wharf where the newly quarried stone was loaded onto rafts and punted the few miles downstream to the Nadder's confluence with the River Avon?

All wild things, such as migrating birds, follow the route of least effort and humans are no exception. Rivers and watercourses were well used by ancient peoples. When I visited the quarry that had supplied the white limestone that once clad the exterior of the Pyramid of Cheops at Giza I learnt that those huge blocks had been floated to the site from a few miles up the Nile. Why would their contemporaries, just starting to move the first stones to Stonehenge, not have used the same method to get them to Salisbury Plain? This feels much more likely than the image we have of hundreds of fur-clad savages struggling to drag a bus-sized block up escarpments, through dense forest, and across marshes and rivers.

I decided to take some time out from cathedral life to survey what I thought had been the likeliest route for transporting the raw materials for the megaliths: from the familiar stone fields between Avebury and Marlborough on sledges, across the downs, to the River Avon which fortuitously headed straight to our destination.

Although the trip was only twenty or so miles in distance, it would mean time-travelling back forty-five centuries or more on a journey that few would have made since. If the timings worked out, I would arrive at Stonehenge in time to make the most of the access that English Heritage granted to the inner part of the monument for the midwinter solstice sunrise. (Access has not always been so generous. One pre-solstice dawn my dad and I set out along a public footpath through fields of wheat to be turned back by bored police officers. The old soldier was infuriated that his right to roam on public footpaths should be barred.)

I had other motives for coming. An item in the *Wiltshire Archaeological and Natural History Magazine* about a new solstice eve alignment discovered by a local farmer had intrigued me. But the main reason was to use the access to see the many faded tell-tale marks and workings that survive on the megaliths' surfaces, clues as to what methods were used to work them. These would help guide my hand better when I experimented with prehistoric stone-working techniques on the sarsen that awaited its fate back at my workshop. I had discovered it near Avebury languishing under silage wrappers and galvanised cattle feeders next to a barn we were working on. The rectangular slab, nine feet by four and a knobbly foot and a half thick would be the perfect subject. The farmer was quite content with the fifty quid I gave him for it, telling me that his grandfather thought 'they sazzens' grew out of the ground like mushrooms.

A few days later I lifted *Laughing Water*, my canoe, from the roof of the pickup and balanced it upside down at its midpoint onto my shoulders. It was a long carry with my head enveloped by darkness and the faint aroma of cedarwood.

With canoe hidden away next to the river that twisted through the woodland, and Ordnance Survey map unfolded, I plotted a route across the open downland towards the stone fields beyond Piggledene. My destination was a quiet coombe long since denuded of its sarsens. After a few hours I had crossed the broad expanse of bare open downland and was standing in front of what looked like a stone skeleton crouched alone on a low mound. Two standing and two fallen slabs supported a horizontal capstone, or table, that formed the single chamber of the Devil's Den. Was this monument built as a ceremonial marker? Local tradition says that water poured into hollows on the capstone's top disappears overnight, drunk by a demon who appears from the shadowy interior. Examining the monument up close, I saw nothing stranger than a handful of golden hawk-moth cocoons that hung like heifers' teats from the capstone's underside.

The restoration of the Devil's Den in the 1920s was based on the eighteenth-century sketches of William Stukeley. His books, *Stonehenge: A Temple Restor'd to the British Druids*, *Abury: A Temple of the British Druids* and *Itinerarium Curiosum,* are in many instances the only remaining records of monuments long demolished or ploughed out. Stukeley thought the Den was a dolmen or *kist-vaen*, a name derived from the Welsh language for a storage chest (*cist*) and (*maen*) stone. Originally it was thought that the Den had been covered with a turf mound for interments in a passage like that at the West Kennet Long Barrow which had since weathered away leaving only the 'skeleton' intact. Excavations have since shown that its interior had always been exposed.

To me the Devil's Den felt out of place, an aggressive and jarring intrusion in the calm Wessex downland where no other *kist-vaens* are to be seen. Their natural habitat, where they reflect a moorland geology, is along Britain's western fringe. There they stand proud against the skyscape.

The original lifting of the Devil's Den's capstone would have been one that required organisation, strength and the taking of risks. In common with most other dolmens it would have been levered from the bedrock where it was 'earth fastened' and lifted further by one of two methods. The first involved raising one end of the capstone a few inches, where a log could be pushed under at ninety degrees to the longest edge. This was repeated at the other end where the structure would then have resembled Fred Flintstone's car. Both logs would have had a pair of notches cut close to each end to allow the placement of another pair of logs, again at the sides, and this process would have been repeated until a lattice was formed of the right height. The stone uprights were then levered and manipulated into place, dropping into a pre-dug socket on each corner. There must have been a few heart-stopping moments when the lattice's top sections were removed.

My preferred method, however, echoes that used to create the corbelled roof structure at the West Kennet Long Barrow and involved the piling up of a temporary mound over previously erected stone pillars that act as uprights. Once compacted the capstone could then be mounted onto a sledge and dragged up the mound slope along log sleepers that would reduce friction as it was dragged. When removed from the sledge, it was a short haul onto the uprights where its weight would hold the structure in place. The mound could then be dug out to expose the dolmen with the soil redistributed to the ditch.

Turning my back to the Den and its secrets, I pictured the area where the coombe fanned out into the river as a vast place of assemblage. Here corralled oxen would have been yoked together in the early morning before the big pull. The heights around here, as at Piggledene, would once have been thick with sarsen and a likely starting point for the journey south for the eighty or so main components of Stonehenge. Neolithic Britain did not have the wheel. At Salisbury Cathedral, we had found that dragging large elements on rollers – such as scaffolding poles on a flat, planked surface – was much easier than lifting or carrying, but pulling a dead weight in this way would not be possible on rough terrain, because the logs ceased rolling when they hit a root or rock. I had some ideas about how the stones were dragged and looked forward to experimenting with log, rope, lever and sledge at the workshop.

After negotiating a way through the water meadows, and across the ford point of the Kennet river, it would have been a relatively gentle three-mile uphill pull by livestock and the assembled clans to the heights that overlooked the Vale of Pewsey, through which the Avon drained away due south. Then it was a gentle gradient down to the river, which in the late Neolithic era flowed broader and deeper than today, and the woodland where the canoe waited.

In a research paper that reconstructed the palaeohydrology of the River Kennet, English Heritage suggested that the water table was between two and five metres higher in the late-Neolithic period 4400 years ago. I imagine that it was the same for the Avon. The land here often rediscovers its former self during winter floods. The width of the now canalised Winterbourne can double and its original braided course returns as it spreads across medieval water meadows. It was along this stretch of the river that the stone could have been lashed to the centre point of a timber raft.

A typical stone of the outer circle is fifteen feet high by five feet broad by three feet thick, and can weigh anything from twenty to thirty tons. This should be impossible to float on a smallish English river, but a little Neolithic know-how and an intuitive understanding of buoyancy may have made it happen. This size of sarsen would displace about ten tons of water, which means it has an upward pressure of ten tons trying to force it up, so when submerged it effectively becomes

40 per cent lighter. All objects are subject to 'specific gravity'. The SG of water is one and any other material less than that will float. Wood's SG is about half that of water, but sarsen has an SG of about two and a half. This means that it is relatively straightforward to calculate the amount of wood required to keep a sarsen afloat when lashed to a raft. These principles were well understood at the time, as the smaller bluestones that were the first to go up and form the inner ring would have made much of their journey from Wales across open water. Each stone would require thirty cubic metres of wood to allow it to float – the equivalent of six one-yard-thick trunks of about twenty feet long. When lashed together in a lattice this craft could then be punted or pulled downstream, perhaps in winter when the river was at its height, arriving in the monumental landscape after a journey of only a few days.

The next morning, I was up even before the birds and pushed off following what I imagined was the path of the last long-departed raft. Gaffer-taped black bin liners provided protection for my sleeping bag and spare clothes. It was an easy paddle, going with the flow along what in prehistory was a well-used communication artery. I silently trespassed through cultivated fields and the remnants of ancient water-meadow systems. The heavy flow had long washed away the entangled green places. Familiar church towers appeared with regular timing, indicating past projects and the position of villages that had formed along the river, away from the downland pastures.

Nodding to Fittleton's spire as it rose above garden walls of chalk, flint and brick, I could still remember every stone that we fixed back into position after the lightning bolt that tore it open like a peeled banana. When we first arrived, it looked suspiciously as if it had taken a hit from artillery on the nearby live-firing range. The strike was so powerful that the top of the spire had exploded, leaving a sizeable split down its side.

The fast flow of the water made it difficult to dodge around the numerous barbed-wired properties and fishing boundaries that stretched across the river – all festooned with weed, plastic bags and sanitary products. By lunchtime I tied the canoe up to the root of a willow and climbed the steep riverbank covered in nettles to lunch within the low, circular rampart of Durrington Walls. This was the biggest of Wiltshire's three super-henges that, along with Avebury and Marden, had been connected by the Avon's common thread to form the valley of the henges.

Recent excavations in the southern part of the Durrington enclosure discovered that below the grass lay the remains of the largest village known from the third millennium BCE. Inside the earthen ring, the users and perhaps builders of Stonehenge had lived in small, standardised houses, rectangular in plan and of the same design and proportions as those found on the Orkney Isles, several hundred miles away by sea.

Winter solstice was the most important day in the Neolithic ritual calendar. Stonehenge, which was carefully aligned to take in the view of the summer solstice sunrise and winter solstice sunset, was primarily a winter monument. Durrington's wooden world of the living and perhaps Stonehenge's builders connected, via the few miles of the Avon, to another processional avenue that led to Stonehenge's world of the dead. On the sun's journey through the day of the midwinter solstice, Woodhenge – just outside Durrington Walls – may perhaps have been the place to watch sunrise and Stonehenge to watch sunset.

Woodhenge's timber circle, with its similar axis and size, was possibly one of the prototypes for its more sophisticated stone cousin. Concentric rings of modern capped-off concrete drainpipe now mark the position of timbers, making a visit there just about as inauthentic a Neolithic experience as it is possible to have.

It was easy to picture the ancient festival-goers, full from the midwinter feast, staggering along the short Avenue for their downstream journey in their light coracle or currach boats. Perhaps they clutched the cremated remains of their relatives in their flared groove-ware pots, as Stonehenge in its early phase when the bluestones were erected was the largest cremation cemetery in Britain.

I pushed off again in the canoe through a lingering mist, the taser-like '*waou waou waou*' of a solitary swan passing low overhead. On the far side of the river, the dim figures of beaters, identified by their large revolutionary flags, stood waiting in the marsh to flush out snipe for waiting guns.

The river's character changed – looping in and out – and became less of a straightforward paddle. My spirits lifted as the tower of Amesbury's medieval abbey church came into view. From across the water meadows, the outrollings of its peal of bells greeted all-comers. I admired the tower's huge lancets, filled with the new oak louvres we had made and fixed into position the previous summer. We ignored the wishes of the churchwardens and left gaps in the mesh meant to block the openings and stop swifts nesting as their forebears would have done since the tower went up several hundred years before. I pictured the bells inside their chamber rocking in their frame just below the level of the windowsill, the sound lifting and dropping the jumble of tones down through its slanted boards, like the first fat raindrops of a spring shower.

The flooded water meadows suddenly broadened out where, among the crack willows, the site of the West Amesbury henge, better known as Bluestonehenge, lay hidden under the turf. Was this where the sarsens were disembarked before a cere-monial haul along the Avenue to their destination? I subsequently read that the twin banks of the linear earthwork were not thrown up until five hundred years after the sarsens had arrived, so some unknown quayside perhaps awaits discovery upstream.

The site of Bluestonehenge was clearly private land; there was not much to see, so I pressed on downstream to Wilsford and tied up at a footbridge where beech trees crowded down to the Avon's edge. The woodland either side of the footpath bristled with hi-tech surveillance equipment, giving the impres-sion that this was a place where important people lived. Now bare, the trees no longer shielded the Elizabethan walls of Lake House from prying eyes. Chequerboard panels of Chilmark stone and flint rose dramatically towards serrated gables. The demi-griffin of the Duke family, who lived in the house for over three hundred years, peered down from a shield above the front door to where one of the most mysterious objects taken from the Stonehenge landscape spent many years as a boot-scraper, slowly corroding away.

The large rusty medicine ball of an object, which today sits in a modern glass cabinet in Salisbury Museum, would be easy to pass by. But it is the oldest exhibit in the museum – older, in fact, than the establishment of the city of Salisbury, the artefacts from Stonehenge, anything in the British Isles or even on our planet. Almost as old as the solar system itself, this lump of iron, known as a chondrite, started its long journey in the asteroid belt between Mars and Jupiter. These 4.5-billion-year-old migrants are some of the most primitive rocks in the solar system and have been coming this way for millions of years. They are thought to have brought the conditions for life to Earth when it was newly formed, helping to establish water. Drawn into our gravitational pull, its great girth would have been much reduced by the blazing heat of entry into Earth's atmosphere about thirty millennia ago when – *pow!* – its teeth sank into the frozen wasteland of Salisbury Plain. The meteorite lay preserved in the ice-age tundra for many thousands of years. Who knows when it was first discovered? The chalk that still clung to it suggested it had been incorporated into some local monument or burial mound, which continued its fortuitous preservation, as its high iron content would have led to its corrosion and destruction. The chunk of corroded metal would have been a wondrous thing to the flint-using population who, at the time the sarsens were going up, were in the transition from flint to copper and so had an awareness of large metallic nodes. The young King Tutankhamun was entombed with a dagger made from meteorite iron at about the same time. The Egyptians knew it as a gift from the heavens, and so perhaps did the priests who looked after the temples that spread across the open chalk plateau.

I took to the footpath that led out of the valley and away from the tree cover that now obscured Lake House. Across open downland vast numbers of barrows gently punctured the turf in strung-out groups. It may have been from one of these that the Reverend Edward Duke dug out the meteorite.

Standing in the middle of Normanton Down round-barrow cemetery as dusk was drawing in, I was spooked by its solemn atmosphere. This was hardly surprising, as its inhabitants have watched over Stonehenge since the twenty-sixth century BCE. This is the greatest concentration of round barrows in Britain, the final stop for dynasties of chieftains and the grander Beaker people of the later Bronze Age: the archers, chieftains and wise women who had been buried with plenty of gold to see them on their way. Two-thirds of all gold found in Britain from the Bronze Age has come from here, a return of the tariffs-in-kind they could have levied on the minerals brought along the trade routes such as the ridgeways and River Avon, where they controlled supply. As with Avebury, archaeologists are still not sure if it was Beaker settlers who put up the arrangement that we can see today, but they certainly had a hand in the Stonehenge monument's final phase between 2300 and 1900 BCE, moving and re-erecting the blue stones a few more times.

In recent years the surrounding fields have shifted slowly from arable to managed pasture. Sheep have replaced springtime fields of yellow rapeseed and so the once isolated barrow groups have been drawn together to recreate that grassland habitat that had largely disappeared since the war. Wildlife has benefited hugely and both the stone curlew and the rare Adonis blue butterfly have returned. I stopped at each venerable turf lump, until I stood atop the famous Bush Barrow where the bones of the chieftain still lay below, stripped of his gold daggers, lozenge and mace in the eighteenth century. The busy traffic of the A303 sliced through the loneliness and what once would have been a place of black solitude. Dusk was drawing in to change the mood of the distant monument that seemed to

43

absorb and refract the last rays of sun before the days began to lengthen imperceptibly.

Turner caught Stonehenge best in his famous sulphurous watercolour. Its bare bones are thrown upwards, as a lightning strike briefly illuminates the scene in stark relief, the focus drawn to one particular stone that leans at an extreme angle. (Today, that stone, number fifty-six, has been righted.) I decided to bed down in a sheltered spot among the barrows on an under-
mattress of old grass straw so the following morning I would be ready to walk the short distance along the drovers' road before first light and enjoy unfettered access to the monument.

The night sky was tainted by the orange glow of Salisbury, but it did not diminish the impact of the Milky Way in the otherwise clear inky heavens.

The next morning, I awoke to blackness, somewhat disorientated and in need of a brew. There was no need to hang about and I was soon on the ancient byway which led to the stones. All was quiet on the rutted chalk track that glowed in the darkness. What I took to be a giant fungus, a puffball perhaps, much to my surprise sprang to life and scurried away. It was going to be that sort of morning. The second puffball I recognised as a great bustard, a turkey-sized migrant, more at home on the vast Russian steppe than on a scrappy verge near the A303. Long ago these birds were so common on the Salisbury Plain that the bird is depicted on the county of Wiltshire's coat of arms, but here was proof that the scheme of reintroduction had been successful.

The distant beat of drums began to intensify. In the darkness, a swirling accordion player, dressed like a Christmas tree, gave a taste of what was to come. Drawn past Stonehenge's dark uprights into the middle of the horseshoe I forgot the purpose of my visit, overawed at the place that was starting to fill up with other early risers. The sounds bounced back and forth from the stones and their dramatic resonance turned it from a taken-for-granted ruin into a vibrant and still great temple.

At the centre of things, in a white gown and straw boater, a Druid, Rollo Maughfling, chief of the Glastonbury Order, held court for the benefit of the crowds, TV cameras and global peace. Classical writers describe the Druids inhabiting groves, wells and holy places two thousand or so years after the final phase of Stonehenge's construction. None mention any relationship with the stone circles that neo-Druids and pagans are drawn to today. It seemed to me that although these groups didn't appear to get on that well, they did share a common need to add their own personal interpretation to the gathering, which culminates for them at the time of the solstices at ancient places like Avebury and Stonehenge.

Outside the stones in self-imposed exile stood King Arthur Pendragon, surrounded by his loyal warband of gentle Druids. In his tin crown, white robe and hefting a broadsword he cut a fine figure. His warband take a more militant stance than the other Druidic orders, seeing themselves as the protectors of the remains of the ancestors and the temple. Their exile was in protest against issues such as car-parking charges and the disrespectful display of the bones of the ancestors in the visitor centre. 'English Heretics', as they called the temple's custodians, certainly have a difficult job keeping everyone happy.

Passing around a pack of Marlboros, Arthur, Merlin and

their mates sheltered in a huddle by the towering Heel Stone. The Friar's Heel, as the Druids called it, stands sentinel in an important position just off the centre of the Avenue. If one were to stand next to the Heel Stone at about four o'clock that afternoon and cast an eye south along the line of axis through the centre of the henge, the sun would be seen to set over the Bush Barrow. Its occupant respected and understood the importance of this axis when he had been buried in it several centuries after it was laid out.

I was drawn back to the overwhelming reality of the stone grove. The elements of the temple when looked at in plan compress concentrically inwards, starting with the outer turf henge. Stonehenge is the site from which all other henges are named, but it is not actually a henge, since its low outer embankment has its ditch on the outside. The word 'henge' comes from the Saxon for hanging stone, a word they took from here. It relates to the lintels that span the space between two vertical supports of the outer ring of thirty uprights, of which seventeen still stand. They weigh about twenty-five tons each.

The concept of the upright and lintel is the simplest and most popular type of construction method. All structural openings have evolved from this idea, which was the first significant leap forward in architecture. The lintels reveal themselves to have been end-connected. One of the outer ring, exposed at one end, had a central vertical ridge running down it, while the vertical slot cut as a groove into its opposing end meant when complete it would have all been locked together by their now exposed tongue-and-groove joints. This was belt and braces engineering, and unnecessary as masonry structures only need to depend on the inertness of their sheer mass and the down-pull of gravity to stay up.

Could this technology, more appropriate for a wooden structure, mean that it had all been designed and engineered by a carpenter? The mason-carpenter was a common trade in the limestone-rich Holy Land of the Old Testament and was known in Greek as a *tecton* – or maker – from where the word architect comes. Perhaps timber components, including upright posts and horizontal trusses, were copied in stone, with the jointing techniques becoming architectural embellishments. The earliest type of roofed wooden Greek temple, such as that dedicated in about 590 BCE to the goddess Hera at Olympia, was constructed in the same way. Over time the original wooden columns were gradually replaced with stone equivalents. When the travel writer Pausanias visited the temple in the second century CE, an oak column was still in place.

Other common ground exists with classical Greek architecture. Each upright tapers towards the top and this refinement, known as *entasis*, was also used on classical columns to correct the optical illusion of concavity that the fallible human eye would create if a correction were not made to the upright. The lintels also suggest an understanding of perspective as the internal face leans outwards from the bottom to the top.

A cuckoo-clock opening in one of the outer lintels, crammed with the usual giveaway twigs, held a pair of jackdaws that stared down suspiciously. The overbearing otherworldliness of the temple's inner space manifests itself in small strokes. Storm-blown strands of wool cling to tiny twig-like lichens that populate the upper faces, each twitching horizontal tuft indicating the direction of the wind that hummed about the place in an unending vortex. I notice on the south-west side of Stone 52 some graffiti, but of a classier sort cut into the stone by someone who was handy with a chisel. The letters are 'I WREN' but the 'I' has a small slash across its midpoint, which may be an abbreviation for Christos or Christopher. Christopher Wren knew the properties of sarsen and could well have assisted his fellow Wiltshireman and Royal Society member John Aubrey as he surveyed the stones. Legend certainly has it that Wren's design of the diameter of the inner dome of St Paul's Cathedral is the same as that of the sarsen circle at the monument.

Within the ring stands a circle of single pillars, human size and of different character and colour to the sarsens. These, and those that make up a smaller inner horseshoe, are the famous bluestones that were brought from the Preseli Hills in south-west Wales. They weigh between two and five tons each. When wet, a bluish tinge can still be seen under the lichen that covers their surface. Some think that the bluestones could have been brought to Salisbury Plain by glacial movement, but they are all too similar a size not to have been transported by people. How they were brought a distance of more than a hundred and fifty miles across mountain, moor and estuary will never be known, but the water network must have played a part.

An arc of bluestones shadows the plan of the largest settings, which comprise the horseshoe arrangement that towers over everything else. These are the well-known trilithons, so named by William Stukeley, from the Greek for three stones. The horseshoe arrangement is open to the north-east and the apex of the curve faces the south-west. This axis gives Stonehenge its purpose: a temple aligned with the movements of the sun. The winter sunset would have been more important to the priests, builders and farmers than the summer sunrise as the day's turning point in the depths of winter promised the beginning of a new cycle and the eventual return of light and warmth.

Stone fifty-six is the tallest, squarest, smoothest – and most charismatic – standing stone here. It once formed one of the pair of legs of the largest trilithon, which was situated at the curved apex of the inner horseshoe. Its twin, fifty-five, lies on the ground in three well-trampled sections. Its base resembles a not-so-massive club foot, which would have been woefully inadequate at keeping it upright. Several inches had been taken away from its outer face to create its near-perfect flat plane, giving it the profile of a hockey stick. It pins down a recumbent altar stone, which also straddles the solstitial axis. This is the business end of things – the great trilithon acting in the same way as the most important part of a cathedral where the host is elevated, illuminated by the sunlight as it floods in from the windows of the lady chapel, symbolically oriented towards sunrise and Jerusalem. And it was surrounded. The excited crowd that covered fifty-five, despoiling its surface, quickly responded to intimidating appeals from its face-tattooed, self-imposed custodian to respect and clear its exposed back.

Fifty-six was eased back into its socket to match its original upright position in 1901 under the supervision of the Society for the Protection of Ancient Buildings (SPAB) who engaged the architect Detmar Blow to oversee the work. Excavations by the stone's side revealed a sloping pit from which a large object – perhaps a natural, locally grown sarsen – may have rested before it was dragged out. I can't help thinking that another object, far older even than the sun, could have been buried on the line of the solstice. Could it have been Detmar Blow, rather than Duke, who discovered the Lake House meteorite? Blow, after all, was also the architect in charge of repairs to the house after it was gutted by fire.

I watched for the south-easterly glow of dawn to see if the outer face of the largest trilithon was oriented to indicate sunrise at midwinter, as suggested by a local farmer and archaeologist Tim Daw. This axis is 80 degrees of difference to the converse midsummer sunrise/midwinter sunset, an angle coincidentally celebrated in the corner angles of the chieftain's mysterious gold lozenge found in the Bush Barrow. With my nose frozen to the south-western corner of fifty-six, I cast my eye south-east along its flat face towards the pre-dawn horizon that was developing an orange cast. This didn't feel like a particularly weird thing to be doing among the ravers, the purple-clad stone huggers and the spliff monkeys I was surrounded by. My pulse quickened as the first rays of the rising sun caused the flecks of silica on the polished face to shimmer under the lichens. I looked around at the crowd, most of whom had their backs to this remarkable point of observation. Would this effect be repeated by eyeing across its face from the opposite direction as the sun set on the eve of the midsummer solstice? I planned to return in six months' time.

I was distracted by a solitary preening jackdaw, faintly lit by the midwinter's first light, that roosted on a projection, like a half-cut pumpkin, from between the giant upright's square shoulders. At its foot, the solstice crowd cleared away towards the car park to reveal the long-fallen lintel that had spanned the pair of uprights where a cup had been scooped out at either end. This had acted in the same way as the carpentry-type mortice joint, to accommodate the rounded tenon that once fit in the hollow. After four and a half thousand years of enduring the agents of weather, vandalism and time, it was amazing that some of its megalithic parts should remain held fast without the need for any modern intervention. Skilled selection of the most durable of materials and the brilliance of its construction ensures it still retains the power to tell much of the tale of its architecture and making.

There are many theories – some very outlandish – about Stonehenge's construction. At the gate of my workshop, I put aside the notion that it was antigravity devices or the levitational powers of Merlin the magician that had moved the stones. I had heard one solstice raver argue it was aliens with plasma cutters who did the work, as sarsen was impervious to human tools, either modern or primitive. It was time to translate what had been learned at Stonehenge into something practical.

I hoped, over a week of experimental work, to knock into shape and erect a monolith in the yard using only Neolithic methods. Getting to know the glassy, iron-like surface of the silcrete, I bore in mind the words of a long-retired sarsen-cutter that 'this was the hardest stone known to man' and as I started to pound away I soon realised how difficult a task this was to be.

I turned to the beautiful sarsen that lay on the yard floor. I tested its suitability in a way that the Neolithic mason-carpenters would have understood. Flaws and shakes within could lead to premature fracturing during the cutting process so, in the same way that Michelangelo selected marble for the *Pietà*, I crouched down and struck it all over with the end of a steel chisel. Listening closely, it rang true and sounded bright, its unflawed self ready for work.

My workshop sits under a corrugated tin roof and is fronted with a wall of north-facing, skip-recycled sash windows. Built into a deep garden wall, in the middle of winter, with the log burner going at full tilt, it is the place to be. Summer work is done outside, canopied by a crown of sycamores, surrounded by old bits of church and other buildings brought back to copy if they were too far gone to be repaired in situ. Finials, pinnacles, volutes, balustrade-bottles and old weatherworn crosses lurk in corners or bookend lever-arch files. Plaster and cracked clay models that should have been thrown out years ago remain for someone else to deal with.

I don't know the bigger answer as to *why* Stonehenge exists, but evidence, observation and the application of craft knowledge was to help me find out the *how*. Essential to the making of Stonehenge was the cutting down of the forest that would be needed to transport, lift, support and provide scaffolding for the builders. To achieve this, they had to make and maintain their own cutting tools: I remembered the stone polishing benches of West Kennet Long Barrow. A piece of flint was to them like a Swiss army knife is to us. One I found, a biface, sits on my workbench. It would have been used by early hunter-gatherers, a precursor of the tools found in the ploughed fields around Stonehenge. Its toffee colouring and texture belie its still razor-sharp edge. The two symmetrical faces of the chert teardrop meet at a point, in a form that originated in Africa over a million years ago and continued in use for over four hundred thousand years by different species of human. This is perhaps the most revolutionary tool in human history, marking an important step in our evolution: its manufacture implying the ability to project a three-dimensional mental image of the tool in a raw material.

The knapper would have made it in only a few minutes, roughing out the tool from the node with a sarsen hammer. This would remove large flat chips from the surface before finishing with a soft hammer of antler tine to create a multi-tool that could be used as a knife, axe or saw to work wood or process a carcass. I like to keep mine close, as a reminder that this is a product of one of the oldest professions in the world. It feels like a natural extension of my hand.

In the cursus field to the north-west of Stonehenge, archaeologists have identified a workshop area where all the second-part finishing, surface-dressing and joint-cutting was done. Here, among the large quantities of sarsen and bluestone offcuts, are not only broken and discarded tools but also clues about the methods of working.

Some of the uprights exhibited flaking scars like those left on worked flints. Some admittedly were the result of vandalism – a local enterprising Victorian rented out hammers to souvenir hunters. Some others were much larger and indicated an early stage of the dressing process where protrusions and nodes were simply lumped off. I thought back to the distinctive ridges of stone 59, lit by the low raking light of that solstice morning: it showed that they used the same method of removing waste with a large tool before finishing with something smaller.

Parts of the monument were finished more carefully than others. Apart from 55 and 56 only the inner faces of the horse-shoe were finely dressed; when approaching from the Avenue this would have been the side to view the midwinter sunset.

This work was undertaken with hammer stones – spherical nodes of sarsen and flint known as mauls that ranged in size from a football to an orange. Many mauls have been found in the stone dressing areas and packed around the bases of uprights.

Over the years I have found a few maul-shaped sarsens while walking the fields of Wessex and put them aside for experimental use. Sarsen or the hardest stones were used for the masonry work; anything else would have been ineffective, as only a diamond can cut a diamond. Thin plank templates would have helped in the prefabrication of each element and guided the shapes the cutters and dressers needed to achieve. Stone 59-A, where the face had been left curiously unfinished to reveal a pair of deep furrows that ran longitudinally from top to bottom, seemed a good specimen to replicate. This involved little more than using the maul to pound away in a straight line on the surface of the slab. It produced so much dust that it meant that the workers must have had a short life. Sarsens are essentially silica sand bound together by silica cement: the inhalation of large amounts of this dust leads to silicosis, a particularly horrible lung disease with a bleak outlook. I quickly donned a facemask. After a few minutes of beating away on the surface with a large two-handed maul of about ten pounds my clothes were impregnated and boots covered in its white flour. My eyes were gluing up with the insoluble dust and my breathing was restricted by the sweat accumulating in the mask. Removing enough imperfections to create a small, roughed-out flat surface area a foot square took all day, whereas the same area dressed with a hammer and punch, the way I did at the Avebury Dissenters chapel, only took an hour or so.

The next phase, to take off the wave-like surface ridges, was done with a smaller maul (of about five pounds) and by working at an angle of ninety degrees to the deeper-cut channel. By now I was getting into the rhythm of things and the area got a little easier and quicker. The flour-like dust made me wonder if they might have used ancient milling techniques to grind down the face of the stone. Perhaps children were involved in the pushing and pulling of hand stones on the surface, as if on a quernstone grinding wheat into flour.

At the day's end, sat with a beer in my sweaty, blistered hand and feeling quite broken, I recalled the farmer's odd comment that the 'sazzens grew out of the ground like mushrooms' and how much easier the fieldstone, destined for the Avebury chapel, had been to cut. I suddenly realised I had been working at a disadvantage. In the late-Neolithic period, sarsens would originally have been buried beneath the wild wood that then filled the coombes and valleys, with only the occasional outcrop to indicate their presence. Once first extracted the surface crust would be full of the quarry sap that would make it softer and therefore easier to work. Over time, as the quarry sap evaporated, the surface developed a dense rind. The 'grooved ware' folk would have known all about this and so perhaps had a slightly easier time of it than I had on my great slab, the surface of which could be said to have been curing for at least hundreds of years.

It was time to dig the pit into which the menhir would be tipped. This was earth-bound carpentry. A couple of hours pick-axing with a red deer antler (retrieved from the council tip, of all places) and shovelling with an ox scapula from the local butcher's excavated a yard-deep hole in the middle of our nice lawn. The Stonehenge uprights vary in length so the sockets that held them like a tooth would have been dug to varying depths to reflect this, and so keep the top of the lintels exactly level. The sloping site would have compounded this difficulty. How on earth did they manage to work out the levels?

With a shallow ramp formed from the pit spoil I hammered in a row of stakes with the tops level with the ramp's lip, the edge of which I hoped would be strong enough to act as a pivot to help the monolith tip once it had been hauled length-ways along the ramp. With a short trackway of logs laid as sleepers along the ramp, like that theorised at the Devil's Den dolmen, and the stone levered and lashed onto a pair of friction-reducing logs turned up at the front like a sledge, the time to haul had come.

To our surprise the stone, which was about a ton in weight, was easily pulled in bursts by a tug-of-war team half-a-dozen strong, while two others picked up the last sleeper to replace the first as it moved along the track. The blue nylon rope, lashed to either side, tightened and creaked until the bottom of the stone teetered on the edge of the pit. We paused for thought and someone had the bright idea of loading some concrete blocks onto its foot, to aid its tipping. As we piled them up tidily one at a time, it slowly began to tilt, see-sawing slightly in the wind. One last grunt focused everybody's might together and the foot, counterweighted and powered by gravity, pivoted into the hole with surprising quickness accompanied by a rousing cheer as it hit the soily bottom of its socket. All that was left was to pull it fully upright. We lashed together a wooden A-frame to form a pair of sheerlegs which would multiply the weight of our final pull, with a guy rope tethered from the apex of the frame to the menhir, and stage by stage hauled and levered it upright before we packed and rammed the hole securely with rubble. My menhir stood white and sparkling like a totem for future generations to mull over, though in reality it is nothing more than an oversized knick-knack, put up by a modern-day Obelix. Will future Ordnance Survey maps record this in Gothic letters as a standing stone?

Stonehenge was the last and the best of the sequence of megalithic structures that spread across Britain. The true mystery, apart from how it appeared without precedent or evolutionary development from elsewhere, is where, on the evening that the last sarsen lintel was dropped into position, did everyone go? How is it possible that such a renowned place could be a one-off and not influence monuments elsewhere? Other contemporary temples maintained their unhewn natural roughness. But once Stonehenge was complete, there would have been many dozens of workers, well versed in the practical side of masonry, the logistics of transportation and erection. They were also the first to understand many different principles of architecture – the allowance required for perspective distortion, and why it was important to cut the lintels wider on the upper surface than the lower. Why did nowhere else try to emulate it? Perhaps the inevitability of an early, dust-sponsored demise for the workers ensured Stonehenge's unique place in wider European culture at that time.

Later Beaker folk continued to tinker, digging a double ring of oblong pits, known as the Y and Z holes, outside the outermost sarsen circle, which may have been designed to take another setting of stones or timber posts. The unfilled holes seem to signify the end of meaningful activity. In the middle of the second millennium, as at Avebury, Stonehenge suddenly became a place to be avoided, a boundary place of bad spirits, execution and superstition. Around this time, during the later part of the Bronze Age, land use and settlement changed. On the Ordnance Survey map these changes and improvements in efficiency can be seen in the many Celtic fields marked on open downland. Taming the landscape and filling grain stores became more important than the creation of gigantic monuments.

By the eighth century BCE the tribes of the south and east were trading and communicating with Europe far more frequently, and the first Iron Age objects such as weapons, closely related to those on the continent, start to appear. The use of iron does not become widespread until after 500 BCE when tribes and kingdoms were developing on the more strategic hilltops. There their gigantic fosses heave up in waves forty feet high to flat crowns where palisades would have protected the thatched roundhouses, agricultural buildings and seed-corn storage pits of the occupants. Today after a hot summer, the low dimpled depressions of these pits can still be made out from the air.

There is a particularly dense concentration of hill forts on the route home from Stonehenge, an old folkway which hugs the River Wylye north-west out of Salisbury. Corvids are especially attracted to these high places, as if at the expense of all other creatures, apart from the distant swarms of starlings that lift in the wind or sit along telegraph wires looking like musical notation. Crows frog-march about the empty harrowed fields that crowd the adjacent turf heights of Cley Hill, Battlesbury and Scratchbury. These defensible land sculptures advertised the status and power of the incumbent tribe to those who tramped the local ridgeways and valley tracks.

Over this period, religion changed. Offerings were now made to the groves, rocks, wells and springs. The old road along the Wylye valley must have been well trodden by pilgrims en route to what would have been one of the most famous holy places in the British Isles a day's walk distant: the hot springs in what is now the city of Bath, which the Celts knew as the waters of the goddess Sulis.

The hill forts of Scratchbury and Battlesbury are close together, separated only by a shallow dry valley, from which the aptly named Middle Hill rises to a solitary bowl barrow sitting on its low summit. The whippet and I go there all the time. Every step forward from the dirt track takes me through medieval agricultural terraces. The hill fort's adjacent ramparts rise to eye level. Siegfried Sassoon thought that they 'seemed more hill than history'. This dramatic panorama is the haunt of ravens. To the north, Salisbury Plain's green wall was once an ocean, formed from nothing more than the skeletons of coccolithophores: single-celled algae dying in their trillions every day in the ocean. Over millions of years their calcium bodies have grown into the formation of a sedimentary rock: chalk.

The nucleus of hill forts and their relationship with the Roman roads that pass close by make this a great place for the lens of history to focus. Once, while kicking over the molehills that pepper the sward, I found an object that in a small way captured the transition from the *prehistoric* to the *historic*. I picked up what I thought was a shotgun cartridge top. Scraping away the mud, the faint impression of a head developed and on the obverse was what looked like a charging bull, but stylised and very Picasso. A visit to the library confirmed that this was a coin, a 'potin', a mixture of copper, lead and tin, metals sourced from the nearby Mendip Hills and other parts of the West Country. Dating from the end of the second century BCE this could be one of the first coins made in Britain. The head with a haughty nose was that of Apollo struck in imitation of those being produced across the sea in Roman-occupied Gaul. This was some of the first evidence that fresh winds were blowing north from the Mediterranean. Roman influence had definitely started to take hold in southern England, if the tribes were modelling their coinage on imperial equivalents.

Sitting atop Middle Hill's barrow, I always feel that for all the renown of Stonehenge, and Avebury's earlier and mightier monuments to the north, I wouldn't swap either of them for this conical chalk tump at the centre of Wessex, where magical birds haunt an island once washed by a vanished sea, now changed into stone.

PART TWO
LIMESTONE

3

QUINQUATRIA

The old road stretched away, arrow straight up and down over the Cotswold Hills towards our destination, the city of Bath or Aquae Sulis as it was known in Roman times. The back of the pickup was now loaded with bags of lime and humdrum-looking aggregates akin to those used by the Roman stonemasons who had built the temple wall we were set to repair. This was the last job to be done in the year's winter project of conserving aspects of the surviving structure and sculpture within the complex of baths and temples.

The undulating fields of the Cotswolds had a very different atmosphere from the chalklands of the Avon Vale we had left behind. This area, known as Bannerdown, comes from an Anglo-Saxon name that means Holy Hill. Bath lay in the valley only a few miles away, reached by a sudden drop down a steep escarpment to the river and what in the first century would have been an important junction with the road from the east that led from Londinium, the capital. Along one side, an endless drystone wall had provided agreeable company for some miles. I was surprised when it was interrupted by the sudden transition to a linear copse of beech trees. Something strange caught my eye in the brief interval between wall and tree and I pulled the truck onto the verge. By the wall's end, huddled in sulky togetherness, the strangely placed uprights and capstone of the Three Shire Stones marked the point where the counties of Somerset, Gloucestershire and Wiltshire come together. This was once a chambered tomb, moved by a local landowner in the eighteenth or nineteenth century.

I looked west towards the distant Welsh mountains from what was once the western frontier of the Roman Empire. It is marked by the Roman military road that follows the Jurassic limestone belt north-east from the Dorset coast, through the Cotswolds to Lincoln, where a spur goes on to terminate at the River Humber. It cuts through towns and cities that carry variations of the suffix 'cester'. These derivations – from the Latin 'castra' for military camp – can be tracked on the map from Exeter through Ilchester, Bathcaster (Bath), Cirencester and Leicester. The path of the Fosse Way, which never deviates more than six miles from a straight line, allowed the mobilisation of the legions and quick movement to protect the territories gained a year or two after they had landed in Kent in 43 CE. Across the Severn Valley a local tribe of Celts, the Silures, maintained a fierce guerrilla campaign against the Romans along the line of the frontier.

Returning to the pickup, I took in the newly harrowed fields spreading away in all directions. The cold snap was aiding the slow geological job of breaking down by frost action the small stones spread evenly throughout the soil. The limestone around here is known as cornbrash and is particularly suitable for growing cereals as the stones near the surface provide shelter for germinating seedlings. Over time the stones become so tiny they wash away into the rivers and valleys. When quarried, this aggregate is an important raw material for concrete and render, as valuable to the builders of today as those of the first century CE.

The materials we had collected would create a good, strong mortar copy of the Roman material. For it to look right and perform well for hundreds, perhaps thousands, of years required analysis of the original Roman mortar and some thought. Studying the sand type, size and proportions with a jeweller's hand lens was simple enough, but then breaking the lime component down with hydrochloric acid in a test tube to identify the amount added took a little more care. Like an unusual cooking ingredient that reflects a regional flavour, we had found our ingredients on the other side of the Cotswolds near Cirencester where they have been scoured out by the young River Thames.

The truck dropped down the deep escarpment, overlooked by twin Iron Age hill forts situated either side of the valley, protective of the strategic communication corridor around the crossing point of the Avon – a different river from the Avon I had earlier explored. This one flows towards Bristol. We passed through the outskirts of Bath, recognisable by the sombre but elegant terraces, set back behind solitary trees that accompanied the approach to the city. Their facades, smoke-blackened by three hundred years of coal fires and heavy industry, were given a vague, sodium-yellow cast by street lamps. The neoclassical frontage of one mansion block had been cleaned to a positively jaundiced finish. In the morning's darkness, it gave the impression of a single gleaming tooth in an otherwise empty mouth.

From Roman times until the mid-nineteenth century this was the main route into the city. The road forked and we approached the abbey and Roman Baths along Walcot Street, which led us to the position of the long-gone town wall near today's Waitrose supermarket. On the other side of the wall lay the most important 'castra' of the Roman Empire's western province and one of the holiest places in Europe at that time. Walcot is thought to mean 'the cottages of the Britons', and two thousand years ago the hostelries and workshops of Walcot Street would have jostled for the attentions of passers-by in a way that would be recognisable to shopkeepers and their customers today. Over the centuries since the expansions of the Georgian town, antiquarians and archaeologists have regularly encountered not only the foundations of their shops and inns near today's frontages, but Roman tombs and headstones, as well as fragments of more elaborate funeral sculpture and mausolea.

The Roman 'regulation of the Twelve Tables', the legislation which formed the foundation of Roman law, stated 'Thou shalt not bury or burn a dead man within a city'. This was also adhered to in Bath where its citizens were buried in groups in the linear cemetery established along Walcot Street. From the third century CE, when inhumation in sarcophagi became the norm, Bath-stone monuments of all sizes lined both sides of the street for some distance. Unusually, this was a place where it seemed the dead coexisted with the living and where their monuments would remind the living of the dead they once knew.

After we had unloaded our kit at the museum, I passed the display of stone sculpture we had conserved during the museum's refurbishment: here a theatrical mask of tragedy, perhaps from a monument to a Roman actor, there a life-sized wild boar, a symbol of Vespasian's twentieth legion that had been stationed here. Those happy to be portrayed on their tombstones clutching large purses contrasted with long-retired centurions on horseback crushing their opponents underfoot. The bust of a rather grand lady, her hair tied in a bun with tight corkscrew curls, would have once adorned a tomb so colossal that it would have blocked the pavement. She is commemorated in a style favoured by the wives and daughters of the Flavian emperors Vespasian, Titus and Domitian. Many visitors to the Roman Baths Museum have stroked her curls over the years, leaving heavy deposits of grease that we had drawn out with a gentle warm poultice.

I passed through a secret door into the network of underground Georgian vaults that were connected to the museum. They act as a store for an assemblage of random masonry, some of it moss-covered and unidentified, accompanied by yet more tombstones from Walcot Street, dedicatory altars, sculpture and sections of column. I looked up through a narrow iron grille fixed in the pavement above to the street scene of faux-Georgian shopfronts that rose a few storeys to the backdrop of the dawn-lit sky. This perspective is somewhat at odds with the heavy atmosphere, thick with sulphurous vapours released from the adjacent vent in the earth's crust, which gives this place life. From far above, the random, eerie notes of a piano being tuned trickled down from the chandeliered Pump Room.

We had completed the preparatory repair work to the wall and our attention now focused on the temple remains that we needed to build above it. On a pallet lay four slightly curved blocks, about eighteen inches deep, elaborately carved with flowing tendrils, flowers and human figures that looked as if they could have formed some part of a decorated frieze. Each section would have rested on a column to form a classical building monumental in scale. These were the remains of a *tholos*, a type of large circular temple that would have been more at home among the olive groves and cypresses of the eastern Mediterranean than this Romano-British outpost. I pictured the continental architect of the *tholos* wrapped against the elements in his thick *birrus britannicus* – a (mostly) rainproof, hooded woollen cloak – stopping at Stonehenge en route from the Roman harbour near Poole, inspecting its outer sarsen circle and reflecting on its scaled-up similarities to his design.

The fact that Bath had a Hellenic-influenced temple is significant. It suggests that the town the Romans knew as Aquae Sulis was no ordinary military or commercial settlement, but one of only a handful of sacred cities to be found in the empire north of the Alps. This was probably helped by the peaceful nature of the Dobunni, the local tribe around the Bath hills, who, when the legions of the Emperor Claudius landed on British shores in 43 CE, were content to be a client kingdom and to continue trading coal and lead with the Romans in France. This was not true for all local tribes. Just to the south, the Second Legion made a devastating example of the belligerent Durotriges. Archaeologists uncovered the arrow-head-punctured bones of its defenders, their wives and children, along with masses of British and Roman weapons, in the ditches of their hill fort at Cadbury Castle.

The Roman conquest followed the straightforward formula of all successful, colonising empires: huge state investment funded the invasion and then the construction of an infrastructure, such as the Fosse Way, consolidated their grip. Food supply was subsidised to further pacify the locals. Superficially, it seemed that an ancient culture had been destroyed. The hill forts were abandoned and its tribes incorporated into the empire as the province of Britannia. However, within the newly built towns that were developing around the sites of the most important hill forts, the locals interpreted Roman life in their own way. Outside the town walls and rich villa estates, life would have continued pretty much unchanged.

The subjugation seemed to be going well until the revolt by Boudica in 60 CE when Colchester and London were attacked, with consequences for Bath as the state became more involved in the running of the province. A military base developed around a ferry point on the River Avon. The fame of Bath's hot spring waters – the only ones in the British Isles – would have quickly spread as they provided the frontier troops with basic civilising comforts. But that was not the only factor that drew the Romans here. The rich farming estates and the mineral wealth won from the nearby hills by the usual Roman use of convict and slave labour gave the state a return on its investment that paid for the army and civil service. In time the most profitable mineral to be extracted was the local stone.

This stone was drawn from the mines and quarries that surround the city and beyond; the later workings still scar the hills. Four different quarries, Combe Down and Bathampton Down, Limpley Stoke and Westwood, all supplied oolitic limestone of similar consistency and strength. Oolites, aptly named from the ancient Greek word for egg, form the biggest ingredient in the Bathstone cake mix. Their individual spherical grains, which resemble fish roe, were deposited in layers of marine sediment during the Jurassic era 195–135 million years ago. As they rolled around the shallow seabed, they became lime-coated, forming the Bathonian series of rocks. These oolites give the stone its most important quality. Unlike coarse-grained or easily fractured stones such as sarsen or flint, Bath stone is a freestone that can be sawn or cut in any plane or direction. The stone leaves the mine a pale, dusty-yellow colour. Then, as oxidisation prevails, the surface changes to the slightly rusty, sometimes honey colouring due to the presence of a small amount of limonite, an iron-based compound that gives the city of Bath its distinctive appearance.

At the Sacred Spring, the Romans co-opted and formalised the dedication of requests to the Celtic goddess Sulis by coupling her with Minerva, her equivalent in the Roman pantheon. What would the hardy Roman sappers and surveyors sent to assess the realm of the goddess have made of it as they stepped through the dense mists that lifted from the hot bubbling pools, accompanied by the call of wildfowl through alder and willow stained orange by the minerals from the spring? Both Celt and Roman would have felt the need to make an offering to the goddess: perhaps by tossing a coin into the green, mineral-rich waters that emerge from a few miles' depth at a constant 115 degrees Fahrenheit.

The water that rises today fell on the Mendip Hills at about the time the West Kennet Long Barrow was put up. Immense pressure sends the waters heavenwards to where it is squeezed through the Pennyquick Fault, a place sacred since the retreat of the glaciers when hunter-gatherers deposited flint scrapers and arrowheads in the spring. Within a single generation, this new Romano-British civilisation had cleared the round huts and replaced them with buildings that reflected an alien culture from thousands of miles to the east. Local resources were soon marshalled to enclose the sacred flow. The fine, easily squared limestone was the perfect choice to wall the reservoir that is eye-shaped in plan. Lead sheets half-an-inch thick, sourced from the Mendip Hills a few miles to the south, kept it watertight. The first complex of baths and temples was constructed around this time and dedicated to both local and Roman deities and so provided a communal culture. This in turn brought more money, trade and craftspeople into the town.

In our cordoned-off workspace that overlooked the deserted Great Bath, the tang of an old egg boiling in an electric kettle hung in the air. We had carefully removed the centuries of grime from the *tholos* so its surfaces could be accurately read and sketched to record any shades of pigment that may have survived the centuries. Loose fragments of carved work, tips of acanthus leaf and tiny pieces of human anatomy were consolidated with liquid lime putty that was carefully injected with a veterinary syringe to fill tiny voids and cracks. Gaps between the vine tendrils were reconnected with a colour-matched blend of lime putty and Bath-stone dust.

The oil-drum-sided sections of the limestone column had been rebuilt to support the foot of a specially made metal frame. This would allow visitors to view the stones from below at their true angle of perspective. The topmost drum hid a deep inch-wide slot, drilled and flared out to a dovetail shape within the block by a Roman to accommodate a bit of kit indispensable to any mason, and which has remained unimproved since it was used to build the Athenian Acropolis: the Lewis pin, its name deriving from the Latin to levitate or lift.

Rope haulers, after knotting onto its D-shaped shank, would work in conjunction with pulleys fixed to scaffolding to lift the heaviest of loads. A pulley wheel, perhaps an offering to the goddess by one of the masons, was found within the spring.

I pulled our modern three-leg Lewis from its canvas bag and out of interest slid its legs into the slot and locked it into position and ancient and modern proved a comfortable fit.

During the original construction the blocks, once hefted into position, were connected with blacksmith-wrought metal staples. To finish the job, molten lead was poured into the sockets from a ladle to lock the staples in place. We were fixing the remains of the *tholos* in a new position, but it had originally shared a common axis with the similarly sized temple dedicated to the goddess Sulis-Minerva across a large courtyard. I wondered if this axis, which is a few degrees north of east and governed the entire layout of the temple complex, was aligned on purpose with sunrise on the festival sacred to the goddess Quinquatria, which commenced on the spring equinox on 19 March.

The flagstones of the sacred space, tinged with green algae, still lie some metres beneath the wide precinct that today fronts the abbey church. Although the once-colonnaded enclosure wall has been decapitated and the buildings are gone, a sense of the worship, sacrifice and ceremonies that took place around the great sacrificial altar remains. Next to it, a stone – used by an official diviner, a *haruspex,* for reading the entrails of a sacrificed animal, in the same way as people read tea leaves – has remained in position. Were the cat-sized rats that breeze along in the shadows after dark the descendants of those specially bred for that purpose?

Pilgrims of all classes and ages would have crossed the precinct. Some would have brought an altar with them. On a shelf in the museum store sits a small altar without an inscription, but, it seems, ready for purchase by a visiting communicant who could then commission its personalisation and dedication. One such was Peregrinus, a name that means pilgrim or wanderer, who travelling from the Rhineland sometime in the first or second century, had presented his inscribed altar to an area set aside for dedications to gods other than Sulis-Minerva.

Many would have pulled a few coins from their purses to seal a contract with the presiding goddess as they pleaded for a cure or prosperity, love or a child. Others inscribed curses onto small lead sheets instead; over a hundred and thirty of these *defixiones* have been found in the reservoir. Once folded, they were thrown into the portal believed to connect them directly with the underworld. This understanding continues. Once, in frustration, I scratched my own curse onto a piece of lead, folded it up and sent the message to the deity:

From Mr Z.
To the most holy goddess Sulis.
  I curse him who damaged my black van and stole my Barbour and best Nilfix Axe. Whether youth or man, crack smoker or otherwise. Goddess Sulis, inflict benefit withdrawal now, and further blackening of their teeth in the future, until he has returned these chattels to my black van.

The springs provoke a reaction from all kinds of visitors. While working on the edge of the cold plunge pool – the *frigidarium* – I found a number of laminated tokens with an image of Confucius stamped on them, pushed under a loose stone. I like to imagine one of a family of modern tourists furtively climbing over the handrail to get there as the others kept a lookout for a custodian.

By 80 CE, Aquae Sulis was booming and the development

of a bathing complex was well in hand. The new walls of the Great Bath were built into that of the sacred reservoir enclosing one side of the precinct. This gave the city its association with health and well-being that has endured on and off ever since. I wonder how many the waters killed instead of curing over the centuries. Even testing the temperature by dipping in one's fingers has its dangers, as its innocent turquoise waters harbour the *Naegleria fowleri*, colloquially known as the 'brain-eating amoeba', which tragically killed a young girl in 1978.

Layers of the city's history lift to the open sky from ancient lead-lined steps that rise out of the great rectangular bath. A heavy pall of steam perpetually swirls around low walls, pavements and piers that tell the story of long-forgotten collapse and subsequent Victorian reconstruction. The colonnade they built was a sympathetic job, which most visitors think is original. In turn this supports the famous terrace, lined with statues of Roman emperors and governors that overlook the waters. The governor we know most about is Agricola, because his historian son-in-law, Tacitus, vividly described his policy towards the barbarous Britons:

> His object was to accustom them to a life of peace and quiet by the provision of amenities. [Agricola], therefore, gave official assistance to the building of temples, public squares and good houses. He educated the sons of the chiefs in the liberal arts and expressed a preference for British ability as compared to the trained skills of the Gauls. The result was that instead of loathing the Latin language they became eager to speak it effectively. In the same way, our national dress came into favour and the toga was everywhere to be seen. And thus the population

was gradually led into the demoralising temptation of arcades, baths and sumptuous banquets. The unsuspecting Britons spoke of such novelties as 'civilisation', when in fact, they were only a feature of their enslavement.

Tacitus, *Agricola*, translated by H. Mattingly

(Penguin: 1948, 1973)

There are three kinds of sculpture found in Britain under the Romans: the work of the Celts that lacks the influence of a Roman figurative tradition, the entirely Roman and a blend of the two. On the wall near the *tholos* a small panel in flat relief was protected by an illuminated cabinet. The uplighting enhanced its otherworldly pallor. A trio of faintly abstract square-shouldered mother goddesses is cut into a flat piece of schist. The three frowning matrons, their tiny arms folded above simple pleated skirts, have eyes with a power to keep the viewer in check. These were known in ancient Celtic religion as the *Suleviae*, who looked after wells and springs and perhaps were related in sisterhood to Sulis-Minerva.

Most of the sculpture within the museum is standard off-the-peg stuff decidedly less skilful than that created by the Graeco-Roman sculptors of Rome. But Bath was on the margin of the empire so the work that was created there reflected the provincial world around it. The huge tombstone from Walcot Street of cavalryman Lucius Vitellius Tancinus provides a good example of the limited abilities of local sculptors. The tomb had fractured diagonally and needed careful handling as we prepared it for display. The upper part of the relief depicts a cavalryman, maybe Lucius, trampling from left to right over a poor unfortunate native. Underneath, the inscribed panel records him being 'a tribesman of Caurium in Spain, trooper of the Cavalry Regiment of Vettones, and a Roman citizen, aged 46 with 26 years' service'. Although the rider's body and horse's head are missing we can immediately appreciate that this is the work of a provincial hack. It has been executed in the same rough and irregular, freehand way that can be seen on most other monuments. The lettering of the inscription is skittish and cut without basic planning and setting out. The depiction and scale of Lucius's hanging legs, which nearly touch the ground, and the horse's fairground-carousel anatomy suggest not only a lack of skill but an unfamiliarity with some of the basic conventions of Graeco-Roman sculpture.

The failure of the imitation of these classical traditions was hardly surprising given that the introduction of Roman architecture and sculpture needed skills that the local Britons did not have. The Romans would have brought in architects, as well as skilled craftspeople and their tools, from northern and eastern Gaul where the limestone is very similar. Local youngsters would have been taken on as apprentices to fill the labour gap in the quarries and stone yards, much as we take on apprentices today. These apprentices would have quickly picked up the skills needed to square off blocks for the huge developments that were going on around them, the more capable going on to reproduce mouldings and architectural details. Others would have been schooled to knock out more profitable objects at speed, such as altar commissions for visitors to the temple.

In 1790, during the rebuilding of the Pump Room, more than seventy blocks of carved Bath stone were dragged out of the foundation mud. These were remnants of the principal shrine to the goddess Sulis. The temple survived for three hundred years until it was toppled, perhaps by Christians in an attempt to efface the pagan gods. We know of a possible witness to this iconoclasm; centurion Gaius Severius Emeritus inscribed on the altar he dedicated to Sulis–Minerva:

Locum religiosum per insolentiam erutum virtuti et n(umini) Aug(usti) repurga tum reddidit G(aius) Severius Emeritus reg(ionarius)

This holy spot, wrecked by insolent hands and cleansed afresh, Gaius Severius Emeritus, centurion in charge of the region, has restored to the Virtue and Divinity of the Emperor.

Good fortune evidently continued to linger at the shrine, as some of the carved stones were deliberately laid face down and used as paving, an act of preservation that would lead to their resurrection thirteen centuries later.

We were there to fix a newly discovered piece, which meant that the layout of the pediment now needed to be re-jigged. Opportunities to work on large-scale monuments from the classical world are rare, so once the scaffolding went up, it was exciting to find myself face to face with its central famous deity, choosing to avoid her still deathly stare, just in case.

Originally the temple facade consisted of four fluted columns rising to capitals, broad at the top, that mediated and channelled the thrust down from the great triangular pediment. This fronted an inner space, or *cella*, where the formal spirit dwelt. It would have been busiest during the five days of the festival of Quinquatria, dedicated exclusively to Minerva. From 19 March sacrifices would have been made and horns blown to purify the temple, and it seems that fortune-tellers and diviners were consulted on this day.

As the foundations of the Pump Room cut across the site of the temple, it wasn't possible to rebuild what was left in its original position. The discovery was forgotten until 1867 when further remains were found, and then in 1880 the rediscovery of the Great Bath prompted the building of a gallery to house the pieces and allowed them to be displayed on a wall.

I climbed onto the scaffolding to inspect the sole remaining column and capital, decorated with acanthus leaves. Most classical decoration was based on details from nature and the use of acanthus has a strange origin. Around 500 BCE, the Greek sculptor Callimachus was inspired by seeing a votive basket placed over the grave of a young girl. A square tile had been placed on top of the basket, which contained a few toys. Callimachus noticed the pleasing form that acanthus leaves growing through the weaves of the basket gave and he imitated it on buildings around the city state of Corinth, establishing the Corinthian order. In common with other capitals throughout the classical world, this one was originally created in two parts, top and bottom, to make moving and hoisting the capital into position easier. When these pieces were discovered the Georgians took things further, gouging out the innards, then quartering them with a saw, a process they followed on the column. Thinking about this shameful work always makes me feel rather jumpy, but it proved a big help to us as it proved much easier to take down, move and rebuild.

This temple building – with its sculptured pediment – must have been astonishing to the British inhabitants of Bath. As we carefully removed the carved blocks and entablature, leaving the central section in situ, the methods and techniques employed could be better understood. The cornice is adorned with a repeat design of acanthus to the front and a random mixture of vine tendrils, bunches of fruit, flowers and stylised foliage to its underside.

The temple sculptures needed to have something Roman, something local, and something unique to draw the pilgrims in. All of these aims were achieved in the central dominating feature: an image of the goddess carved with great power and accomplishment. Following Roman tradition, the gods of the conquered were co-opted and continued to be venerated. Sulis was identified with Minerva, the Roman goddess who was also associated with healing and well-being. She was also the goddess of craft and identified with stonemasons. When we were looking for a name for our business, there was only one option.

In this design for some reason the sculptor has depicted the goddess as a gorgon, the mythical creature whose look turned men into stone and who was killed by the Greek hero Perseus. He gave her head to Athena (the Greek name for Minerva), who is represented by the small owl that peeks out below the central wreath. Her shield, the *aegis*, bore a *gorgoneion*: an apotropaic image showing the gorgon's head wreathed in snakes with a frontal stare that undoubtedly influenced the pediment's design. In a final twist, Medusa's gender was transformed into a figure with robustly male features. This captured the Celtic tradition of venerating male water gods while maintaining the reference to the Roman Minerva. His wild hairiness, flaming and anti-social, meets a serpent-entwined beard under a broad moustache. Prominent almond-shaped eyes glower down beneath beetling brows. A small dent on the bridge of a charismatic nose is the remnant of the central point from where a large compass once pivoted to set out the geometry that defines the pediment's proportions, its central circular shield fringed with a pair of oak-leaf wreaths. With elegantly executed hands, a pair of winged Victories – or Nikes, as the goddesses who personify victory are known – support the shield to each side, their toes springing from armillary globes, proof that the Romans saw the world spherically and not flat.

The Victories are classically depicted in flowing drapes, and the working of their deeply cut vertical folds attracted my attention. The mason has achieved this by deft use of either a starburst chisel for drilling or a long chisel called a quirk – twisting the tool left and right, cutting the letter X deeper and deeper over and over again with each blow of the hammer. It was a technique that allowed undercutting of a depth and angle impossible to drill. This carving of drapery remained unparalleled until the early Middle Ages.

Servants of Neptune, the water god, are squeezed tightly into both bottom corners, and these tritons – half fish, half men – blow into their shell horns as if heralding the Nikes that they in turn support. Much of the imagery suggests that this is a celebration of the invasion of 43 CE. Just below the apex a single star, the Sidus Iulium, or Caesar's comet, which appeared in 44 BCE, may represent the deified emperors Claudius or Vespasian who presided over the invasion, as signified by the oak wreath, tritons and figures of victory, all of which were well-recognised symbols of imperial iconography.

Whoever designed and created the gorgon pediment managed to interpret classical art using a Celtic, British vocabulary. We know the names of two masons or sculptors, Sulinus and Priscus – Celts perhaps drawn to set up shop as Bath developed a European reputation. Could the genius who created this masterpiece have been one of them, their names cut into altars dedicated to their goddess, no doubt with their own hands? The lettering on Priscus's fractured altar, on display in the museum, reads:

Priscus Touti filius lapidarius cives Carnutenus Suli deae votum solvit libens merito.

Priscus, son of Toutius, stonemason, a tribesman of the Carnutes, to the goddess Sulis willingly and deservedly fulfilled his vow.

I'm not sure that Priscus, who was from the Carnutes, the tribe who gave their name to Chartres in France, was our man. Only a fragment of his altar remains, but it provides enough evidence that although he was a *lapidarius*, a mason who specialised in relief carving, he wasn't the best to be found in the city. The quality of the well-spaced lettering, although calligraphic, was by a strangely jittery hand and more the work of a competent amateur. If, instead of genuine devotion, this were an advertisement for his skills, then an intervention from the goddess would definitely have been required. The other altar from a stoneworker in the museum is much more intriguing:

Sulevis Sulinus scultor Bruceti filius sacrum fecit libens merito.

To the Suleviae Sulinus, a sculptor, son of Brucetus, gladly and deservedly made this offering.

On this altar, although no more accomplished as a letter-cutter, the Matres Suleviae appear, perhaps as the mother goddesses of the hot springs. Sulinus and his father Brucetus are also mentioned on another altar found on a site at Cirencester in

1899. When revealed, the site was described as having 'so many other pieces of Roman stonework, some apparently new, in the sense of being unfinished or unused, as to suggest that the place in which they were found was the site of sculptor Sulinus's workshop or stoneyard'.

Several of the altars were of the local Cirencester oolite, but one was of Bath stone, which means that Sulinus must have travelled as a journeyman through the region, in the same way that we do from church to church. He may have taken his name from the Suleviae in honour of having worked on their great temple.

I imagine that Sulinus would have understood his way about my workshop, because such places haven't changed much over the last two thousand years. I can picture his aged father sat in the corner, keeping himself busy by endlessly sharpening chisels beneath the many dozens of wooden templates, like dress patterns, hanging from a roof beam and swinging gently in the wind. At waist height on the banker would have sat a stone, supported by a straw-filled cushion to protect its edges; on a table by Sulinus's side a mason's hammer and old apple-wood mallet, handle up. These were the main chisel-striking tools, already old but still supple enough to provide many more years of service, as long as the apprentice didn't use them with the wrong sort of chisel – flat-headed for a metal hammer, round for wood. Use of the wrong chisel will quickly destroy the conical head of a mallet. All would be laid out in dusty order so that the right chisel could be picked up without having to look down and not break the mental flow of working a straight line.

I am not a sculptor, but can put myself in his shoes or, judging by the deep wear patterns of his contemporaries on the floor slabs of the baths, his hob-nailed clogs. I also enjoy using a stone-cutting axe – bladed on one side, toothed on the other – to square up basic square forms. The tool marks left on the stones that surround us show that it was used as much as a hammer and chisel.

Sulinus's business as a sculptor would have meant that he had a higher social status than the stonemasons. But to the administrators of the empire, the skills of those who cut, carved and fitted the blocks that built the city were much more important. By the second century when Sulinus was perhaps busy, the architectural style they worked with was already several hundred years old. Perhaps some thought it to be backward-looking, for in the second century a completely new way and style of building appeared – one that was already old in Rome.

The enclosing walls of the Great Bath are a mix of exposed masonry with large patches of original terracotta-sprinkled plaster and colour-washed panels of Pompeian red. At one end, leaning like a wounded creature, is a section of arch colossal in scale that was craned from the bottom of the pool in 1899. The top edge of this humdrum-looking arch is covered with large clay roofing tiles of the standard Roman size pushed into the wet cement that was still holding them fast. The fragment, several yards long, formed part of a large semicircular *lunette*, or window. Its size suggests the roof it supported would have been by any standard a triumph of engineering.

After about a century of covering the Great Bath, the original timber roof succumbed to the damp, humid atmosphere. It was replaced in the early second or third century with the gigantic barrel vault of clay tiles, the haunches of which rested on the roof vault of the newly reinforced side aisles. This design helped to resist the side thrust created by the spreading load of the roof, which was carried down to the ground through reinforcing piers added to the inner and outer walls of the arcade. The piers lining the steps into the water that once supported the original roof were reinforced by the addition of new bases to the front and back, which can still be seen today. The tiles of the vault were laid in concrete with hollow bricks incorporated into the apex of the vault to reduce its weight. This was one of the first buildings that we know of in Britain to deal with the problem of lateral thrust from masonry used in a roof structure. It is the most westerly example of a new system of building that underpinned Western architecture as it continued to evolve through the Middle Ages and into modern times.

This system could not have worked without an effective glue to stick it all together. An imperial, European-Union type of mortar standardisation was adhered to from the wastes of Hadrian's Wall to the deserts of Syria. In Joseph Gwilt's 1826 translation of *De Architectura*, the Roman architect Vitruvius described it thus:

> There is a species of sand which, naturally, possesses extraordinary qualities.
>
> It is found about Baia and the territory in the neighbourhood of Mount Vesuvius; if mixed with lime and rubble, it hardens as well under water as in ordinary buildings.

It was not until the beginning of the first century that its potential for expressive work was realised. This concrete, in the same way as modern concrete buildings, could be poured into timber shuttering and cast into any shape. Once it had hardened the resulting work was so solid that in some instances the best Roman concrete is better than its modern equivalent, due to the superior way that the lime and volcanic ash (*pozzolana*) bind with sand. These new methods speeded up the construction of the road bridges, aqueducts and bathhouses that expanded infrastructure and advanced civilisation throughout the empire.

Like the walls of brutalist concrete buildings today, only a handful of observers considered the result aesthetically pleasing, so a facing was often applied. Depending on the budget, the choice could be large blocks of ashlar (*opus quadratum*), small squared off blocks (*opus vittatum*), rubble (*opus incertum*) or plaster finished (*opus signinum*). By the second century CE, the Romans came to appreciate brick in its own right. Concrete freed the Roman architect from the restrictions of rectilinear architecture, removing the requirement to build in brick or stone that applied to temples like that of Sulis-Minerva. By my desk, there are dusty shelves and cabinets of old mortars, saved from each job, awaiting a purpose. Many are from around the Roman world – chunks of hardened lime, some mixed with oyster shells, some with crushed bone, and most commonly the beautiful terracotta-speckled *opus signinum*, which is made from lime and tiles broken up into very small pieces at a ratio of 3:1. In volcano-free Britannia this acted as an equally durable replacement pozzolana.

As with the construction of West Kennet Long Barrow, huge quantities of timber would have been required for the scaffolding, shuttering and formwork that acted like a giant mould to support the rooftile-covered vault of large structures such as a great bath. As stages progressed during the building season, the formwork would have been left in place over the winter, until the master mason – architects are a modern concept – decided that the time was right to allow the team to tap out all the folding wedges holding the uprights of the formwork in place. In what must have been a tense moment, they would have been knocked out at the same time to allow the section to drop the couple of inches needed to allow the vault to sustain its own weight, in a way perhaps similar to the Devil's Den and the great cathedral vaults still to come of medieval times.

Despite the success of Roman cement-based building technology, once the Romans left Britain in the fifth century there was a decline in wealth and technical knowledge. As Britain broke away from the central authority of Rome, the administrators of the province lost the ability to undertake the large projects that could only be done with a bureaucracy and proper organisation. With that the practical skills and know-how seem to have disappeared.

Yet many aspects of Roman culture did survive right through the Anglo-Saxon period. In out-of-the-way places, villa life continued precariously for a few generations and as a British-Romano-Saxon way of life evolved, Christian worship may be considered to be the most important element of the earlier culture to have made it through. Around Bath, vaulted roof structures, the use of *opus signinum* and masonry for building work disappeared to be replaced with timber constructions. Perhaps the new abbey, first mentioned in 757, was built from the great free quarry of construction materials in the decaying Roman town lying fallow all around.

★

One April morning, I was to be found crouching among Wiltshire Museum's artefact-filled cabinets. Around me were all kinds of objects: distaffs, spindles and niddy-noddies – spinning and weaving equipment of the women's household separated from the swords, axes, spearheads and blacksmiths' tools – that filled the hessian-backed display cabinets. I had hauled out an unassuming block of stone about half the size of an old-fashioned hay bale. The moss-covered lump, which had been newly loaned to the museum after it had come to light in the grounds of a nearby school, had drawn classicists, art historians and archaeologists from around the country to examine it.

There was much speculation by the assembled experts over the origin of this previously unknown piece of sculpture. Who were the three shadowy figures cut in relief that could be made out under the blanket of moss and why were they pulling on what looked like a rope? Could it be a representation of the three Matres – similar to, but more sophisticated than, the one to be seen in the Roman Baths. Once its condition had been recorded, the moss could be carefully separated from the carved surface. The aim was to get down to the mat of thread-like roots that attached the moss to the substrate. This would be gently removed later back at my workshop with a small steam gun. The process of removal involved nothing more sophisti-cated than wooden spatulas – ice lolly sticks that soon lifted the moss to expose the hidden detailing.

The three figures were dressed in skirts or baggy pantaloons, but the focus of the piece seemed to be the sagging rope two of them were holding from which appendages hung. These seemed vaguely familiar. Glancing over to the display cabinet I was struck by their similarity to the spindle whorls on display, which I pointed out to Professor Martin Henig of Oxford University. He stood up, waved his wooden spatula and made an immediate pronouncement about what we were looking at. This stone, he claimed, was not religious but funereal: two of the three figures were weaving a cord held down by the spindle whorls, while the third figure stood by with a measure, perhaps ready to cut it at the designated time. These were the Fates – the female personifications of destiny known to the Romans as the *Parcae*.

The Parcae were even feared by the gods as they determined the course of each person's life, regardless of their actions. The professor proceeded to name them: to the left, Decima, holding her ruler over her shoulder, waited patiently to measure the thread; Nona, spinning the thread on her spindle, stood in the middle; Morta, on the right, cut the thread and chose the moment of a person's death. To one side of the block clung a tiny smudge of mortar. Looked at through a lens, it was apparent that the lime contained inclusions of red ceramic material, indicating that it had been held in a larger structure, perhaps a built tomb or mausoleum. The layering of fingernail-sized fossils and its creamy appearance showed that the stone had come from a local quarry just off the Roman road to Bath at Hazelbury. Now that all were agreed about the nature of the sculpture, I could set about removing the millimetre-thick layer of matted roots. This was an art rather that a science, and one that required the same disciplined mindset as when cutting a detail into stone. The role of the conservator is to control and slow down the effects of time that, as Sir Thomas Browne put it, 'antiquates Antiquities, and hath an art to make dust of all things'.

After three days of looking into the lens of a jeweller's illuminated magnifying lamp, and gently working through the rootstock to get to the surface, it was a great relief to be able to place the Parcae on display in the museum's Roman gallery. How many hundreds of winters had it spent hidden away under hedges and what had been the mausoleum's story? What lucky thread of fate had allowed this one part to survive the period when civilisation seemed to drift?

People continued to cultivate the land in southern Britain, and to occupy the crumbling villas and maintain the roads, but otherwise the Roman way of life had disappeared before the Anglo-Saxons came in successive waves to settle during the fifth to ninth centuries. The *Anglo-Saxon Chronicle* (*c.*890 CE) records that in 577, after the Battle of Deorham (or Dyrham), the centres of Aquae Sulis (Bath), Glevum (Gloucester) and Corinium (Cirencester) were settled by the West Saxons.

For the rural population, thatched round houses were either replaced or accompanied, for the first time since people settled the land, by rectangular houses, brought by the new settlers. These were simply a pair of thatched 'A' frames connected by a ridge beam, constructed over a board-covered pit. Was the mausoleum that held the Parcae still standing when the first of these settlers tramped this way along the Roman road? Throughout Europe and the British Isles, great masses of people were on the move with their possessions and animals. If they had paused to take a look at the roadside monument, would they have seen a once-grand piece of work as nothing more than a quarry to infill the walls of their new timber-built barn or farmstead? Although they were illiterate, these soldier-farmers and their families may have understood the figurative message that was presented to them, as the idea that our individual destinies were controlled by fate was familiar to the new settlers. One must have seen the figures as a sign in itself, and perhaps removed it to use as an altar. They would have known the three figures as *wyrd* or fate.

In Germanic mythology the Parcae found an equivalent in the Norns, who spun their threads at the foot of Yggdrasil, the tree of the world. Later, the Fates would appear as three witches, or the 'Weird Sisters', in Shakespeare's *Macbeth*. References to *wyrd* can be found in much Old English literature of the tenth century. In *Beowulf*, 'fate often saves an undoomed man when his courage is good'. In *The Wanderer*, the power of *wyrd* is one of its central themes. Written when paganism still flourished, it declares that the only possible refuge from misery and uncertainty caused by the relentless nature of fate is 'to be found in God's grace'. The poem hints at the new force, Christianity, taking over across the land. This was the time when the first churches were going up by the side of Roman roads, in riverside villages and on the outskirts of towns.

An atmospheric account of the devastation of those times survives in 'The Ruin', an Old English poem which conjures up the former splendour of a ruined city, possibly Aquae Sulis, by contrasting its derelict present:

> *Wrætlic is þes wealstan, wyrde gebræcon;*
> *burgstede burston, brosnað enta geweorc.*
> *Hrofas sind gehrorene, hreorge torras,*
> *hrungeat berofen, hrim on lime*
> Wondrous is this wall-stead, wasted by fate.
> Battlements broken, giant's work shattered.
> Roofs are in ruin, towers destroyed,
> Broken the barred gate, rime on the plaster

In this translation by Professor Siân Echard, 'hrim' is interpreted as 'plaster', but by the time of the desolation, midway through the first millennium, the plaster would have gone from the walls. As the poet goes on:

hoary with lichen, red-stained, withstanding the storm,
one reign after another; the high arch has now fallen.
The wall-stone still stands, hacked by weapons,
by grim-ground files.

The phrase 'red stained' may refer to Roman concrete with its red terracotta additive that gave it its strength and so held the 'gaping walls' together, but not the 'high arch', which was perhaps the roof vault section that was to lie beyond the builders' reach at the bottom of the Great Bath in the Roman Baths for the next fifteen hundred years. Over time the hot springs, combined with winter floods from the River Avon, forced water up through this rubble-scape to form hot pools where wilderness took over and marsh fowl reclaimed their place. With sights like this it was hardly surprising that the Saxon poet was moved to record the drama of this ruination in poetry. He clearly had a good eye and understood the building process when he described 'the mason,/ skilled in round-building, bound the wall-base/ wondrously with iron.' The reinforcing of old buildings with blacksmith-forged iron has been common practice since antiquity. Was the round building the speaker saw the *tholos*, strapped in a final attempt to hold the last vestiges of civilisation together?

4

MAUNDY THURSDAY

With our work to the Roman Baths concluded, I decided to paddle *Laughing Water* a few miles upstream to a small yet sophisticated Anglo-Saxon building where the baton of the classical world had been handed on, a place that mingles Germanic and Celtic influences: St Laurence's Church in Bradford-on-Avon.

While most other Saxon churches survive only as fragments – like the few pages of a Saxon manuscript that survive to tantalise scholars – St Laurence's is almost unique in that it is able to be read as a full text. Although once remote, Bradford-on-Avon remained an outpost of the Church, and a place that suggested that the classical world hadn't totally ended with the departure of the Legions.

It was Petrarch, the Italian poet, who considered the post-Roman world as dark and barbaric and who first coined the catchy but now discredited term 'Dark Ages' in the 1330s. But St Laurence's was one of the places where the Middle Ages were illuminated, a beacon of the Saxo-Roman, Christian renaissance, its construction beginning a line of architectural continuity that was only curtailed by the Reformation.

I pushed off from Bath and made slow progress against a strong current and mattresses of waterweed. The accompanying tree canopy became denser and along the riverbank nature was slowly coming into its own.

The first centres of Christian mission from the fifth and sixth centuries were simple preaching crosses; timber churches were then built – *mynsters* – the position of some of which were marked by much later replacement stone bell-towers that lifted as distant landmarks along my route. To the early Saxons, building in stone was anathema; their word *getimber* meant 'to build' and even in stone-rich areas they maintained their carpentry tradition, building their homes, great halls and places of worship in wood. Their towns were generally adjacent (and often separate) to the old Roman ones: Saxon Lundenwic was pitched a mile west of the stone walls of Londonium. Some would certainly have seen the value of reusing the materials of monuments and ruins in the towns and villages the Roman world had left behind.

I paddled past the slopes of Sally in the Wood, so-named after a small fight or 'sally' during the Civil War; the place was laden with boulders the size of houses hidden among the deep cover of a thick yew wood. Many of its gnarled and hollowed-out trees were already thousands of years old when the Viking King Cnut harried his way along the valley under his raven banner in the year 1015 as he ravaged Wessex while the Saxon King Æthelred lay ill in Corsham.

Above, venturing rooks, young and old, ignored the sour-tasting new buds and stole twigs from each other's nests. Marsh marigolds and the green blades of young iris were encroaching on the riverbank. Catkins hung from silver birch and crack willow, their downy coverings pecked apart by foraging bands of goldcrests.

Jagged gaps in the treeline blurred where the old quarries at Ancliffe and Westwood had been worked since Saxon times. Through the green shoots of a field thorn, a pair of thrushes fed on the mistletoe's last miraculous pearls, grown without water or soil. Coming into Bradford-on-Avon, the Barton Farm packhorse bridge, its fourteenth-century structure untouched until we repaired it at the millennium, spanned the slow-moving water, marking the approach to my destination. I tried to imagine the Anglo-Saxon settlement on the small knoll ahead, the cluster of thatched wooden outbuildings enclosed by vineyards that formed a poorly defended enclosure. The church at its heart, thick-walled and windowless, would have provided refuge for the nuns and their relics.

Although harriers and invaders kept life in a state of flux during the first millennium, there was enough stability by this river crossing for a monastic tradition to become established. As Christianity took over, a renaissance in stone construction took place. As with Roman Bath, masons with the right skills and the latest ideas came over from the continent. In the seventh century CE the historian Bede recorded that Benedict, the abbot of Wearmouth in Northumbria, 'crossed the sea into Gaul, and obtained and carried back with him some masons (*cæmentarios*) to build him a church in the Roman style, which he had always admired'. A few select locals might have been schooled abroad as apprentices before they continued as journeymen, working their way back to their homeland where they in turn passed on the new craft and design. Despite the interruptions caused by the great migrations of the early Middle Ages, strong connections with the continental Church and beyond made the rapid spread of knowledge and technology possible.

The arrival in the seventh century of an unusual pair of migrants – Theodore of Tarsus, a Syrian Christian, and Hadrian, a native of North Africa – sparked a golden age of Anglo-Saxon learning. Theodore was archbishop of Canterbury from 669 to 690, assisted by Hadrian who, as the abbot in charge, administered the city's monastery. Here they established a school that taught scripture in both Latin and Greek, and this soon led to the dissemination of Byzantine Christian ideas via their novices to all parts of the country. Their Anglo-Saxon students included Bede and the 'builder of churches', Aldhelm, who was destined to become first bishop to the West Saxons. What the recently converted nation of carpenters made of this Syrian and African Berber as they travelled through their vast island parish is not known, but Bede noted:

> They attracted a large number of students, into whose minds they poured the waters of wholesome knowledge day by day. In addition to instructing them in the Holy Scriptures, they also taught their pupils poetry, astronomy and the calculation of the church calendar – never had there been such happy times as these since the English settled Britain.

By this time the Roman Empire had been split into two parts. Rome itself had become a city of ruins, 'five times conquered', its aqueducts in disrepair, its countryside a wasteland. Now the real capital was that of the 'New Rome' of the Eastern Roman Empire – at Constantinople. The sculptural fragments and architecture left from the churches that came in Theodore's wake testify to the distant pull of Constantinople. There was a surprisingly fertile exchange between the Byzantine and Saxon worlds in the large numbers of mercenaries that left for Constantinople after the Norman Conquest. Many were recruited to protect the Byzantine emperor as members of the Varangian Guard. And Theodore came to Britain partly in flight from the Byzantine–Sasanian (Persian) War of 602–628, and perhaps the Muslim conquests.

I tied up *Laughing Water* by the old Avon Rubber mill, where the springs that have surrounded the little church for millennia run into the river through Victorian culverts. The mill is now quiet but I can remember when the scream of the factory whistle would send the workers home through the small town, past smoke-blackened walls and tall industrial chimneys.

Across the lane from the later Norman church, in its inferior position on the floodplain, is the surprisingly lofty church of St Laurence. It is well placed by the wide ford across the Avon that today is surrounded by fine Tudor, Jacobean and Georgian houses of mill owners and wool merchants. As a backdrop the serried, south-facing ranks of their employees' cottages lift dramatically in terraces to the Cotswold plateau. The sun reflects from dozens of dormer windows, built to light the small looms that once stood inside. In early medieval times a busy town bridge superseded the ford. These bridges are structures I know well as we are often called out to fix them. This example carries the main arterial route for traffic through the county and often falls victim to overlarge lorries and drunk drivers.

Sections of parapet invariably end up in the river after these events, which occasionally means that I will be stood up to my waist in the water, dragging out the masonry sections that have been knocked in.

I sat on the low wall we had built a few summers before, which enclosed the back of the church's small tomb-less grave-yard. The building is comprised of three differently sized boxes that rise to steeply pitched, stone-tiled roofs. The three boxes are all long, tall and narrow, a trait shared with the handful of other complete churches that remain from early medieval times. The most important group can be seen at Monkwearmouth, Jarrow and Escomb in north-east England, where Abbot Benedict brought his masons from the continent to build a Roman church. Although they are of similar design, they are less sophisticated in construction, with rubble masonry mixed with reused material from the Roman world.

It took me a while to see the minor repairs I had done to the north porticus two decades previously. At some distant point the foundation on the west side of the porticus had slipped a little, which had the knock-on effect of loosening some of the corner stones. With the aid of a long pair of ancient crowbars that held the stamp of my great-uncle's initials – RPG – the stones levered out like sliding open a matchbox, which is not usually the case with mortared joints. A familiar smell wafted from the cavity as I wriggled the tail of the first stone out to look at the inside of the wall. Cautiously I leant in and was surprised to encounter the familiar oily funk of the riverbank. The hole was lined with clay that was still as workable as the day it had been smarmed around each stone to act as a bedding mortar. This would have been a far cheaper material than lime, which in any case may have been a technology unfamiliar to the Saxons when they put this place up with clay dug from the riverbank. This was good as I could save on costs by simply knocking up and pounding the clay back into life for reuse and another thousand years of service. After the gaps had been filled with more of the same, dug out of the same part of the riverbank, the hole and stone were given a nice drink of water to help the blocks slide back easily into position.

Each perfectly square block had the tell-tale markings of being cut by an axe or perhaps the similar adze, where the arched blade sits at right angles to the handle. The shallow gouges the tools had made, so well preserved that they could have been cut the day before, ran diagonally across each of the six sides. These stones would have been extracted from the quarry in the winter months using Roman methods, then squared off in the summer, with time set aside to allow the blocks to season. Then they could be carved further during the winter when building work had finished. Fixing of the new work took place in the spring, from Valentine's Day onwards, giving time for the roof structure to go up before winter set in.

For some reason, later Saxon or Norman alterations to the church's fabric were less sophisticated than the original work. On the west face of the porticus the semicircular window had been enlarged by tunnelling out the yard-thick wall and an inconveniently placed decorative moulding was chopped away to leave it truncated in one of the jambs – the window's side stones. Why had they recut the windows? Perhaps they were originally little more than slits, which would give a sombre light to the idea that this was once a shrine to house the sanctified remains of the teenage King Edward the Martyr, who was murdered, perhaps on the instructions of his stepmother, at Corfe Castle in Dorset in 978 CE. The integrity of the external decorations suggests that the church had been carefully built and planned in a single scheme on a cruciform plan (the north porticus once had a twin, and though only its outline on the south wall remains, beneath it archaeologists discovered a chamber where perhaps the Martyr's relics were kept). All was held firmly together by quoins (corner stones) in a way that can be seen in most churches that came in its wake, instead of the distinctive 'long and short work' – normally a Saxon signature – where 'long' horizontal quoins alternate with 'short' verticals.

To break up what would otherwise have been an empty expanse of wall, the Saxon masons introduced pilaster strips that mimic timbers and blind arcading, a decorative element that originated in the Islamic world and spread through early medieval Europe. This detail can also be seen in the seventh-century Baptistery of Saint-Jean at Poitiers, France, where comparison confirms what a sophisticated piece of work St Laurence's is. Poitiers is a crude interpretation of the neoclassical world, with many elements of reused Roman architecture – pediments, capitals and pilasters – placed randomly by the masons who were unaware of their original intention. To paraphrase Eric Morecambe, they were 'laying the right stones, but not necessarily in the right order'.

With lunch finished, I brushed off my hands and crossed into the dark, damp interior through the north porticus. The narrow opening was offset, perhaps to accommodate a baptismal font on one side. In a Roman house, the water source was kept by the front door. Early Christians took on this symbolic meaning, as baptism is the means by which one enters a church and Christian life. To the weary pilgrim who had crossed the nearby ford, having dodged the wolves and bandits that lurked in the great Selwood Forest, the look and feel of the interior would have been very different. Theodore and Hadrian's pupil St Aldhelm recalls in a poem the rich interior of a West Saxon church, dedicated to the Virgin, 'with its lofty structure' and 'where clear light diffuses through the rectangular church'. It feels like a close fit for St Laurence's:

> A golden cloth glistens with its twisted threads and forms a beautiful covering for the sacred altar. And a golden chalice covered with jewels gleams so that it seems to reflect the heavens with their bright stars; and there is a large paten made from silver. Here glistens the metal of the Cross made from burnished gold and adorned at the same time with silver and jewels. Here too a thurible embossed on all sides hangs suspended from on high having vaporous openings from which the Sabaean frankincense emits ambrosia when the priests are asked to perform mass.

All would have been overlooked by a mighty stone representation of the Crucifixion flanked by ministering angels.

Today, stripped of its bling, St Laurence's possesses an austere beauty and one of the most evocative church interiors in Britain. Floating on their chests in the shadows high above the chancel arch, only a pair of flanking angels sculpted in a light linear relief remain of the now long-gone central depiction of the Crucifixion, known to us as a 'rood'. Dating Saxon sculpture can be difficult as so few comparative works survive, but the distinctive style of the Winchester School of sculpture in these angels is clear. Their outlines are recognisable from much contemporary manuscript art. The eleventh-century Hexateuch (the first translation of the Old Testament's six books into Old English) hold, in pen and coloured ink, angels in identical repose, their drapery swirling as they support Christ seated in a mandorla while he dispenses judgement to the damned. Even an inexpert linguist would understand these Old English words when read aloud – *Fæder ure þu þe eart on heofonum* – the first line of the Lord's Prayer. The Winchester School was active from about 950 CE until the Conquest in 1066, and was renowned for its skill in the depiction of animalistic themes combined with foliate forms that well illustrate the hatred of empty space characteristic of religious art at that time.

Beyond St Laurence's narrow chancel arch part of the shaft of a Saxon stone cross was fixed to the east wall of the chancel. It was likely to be one of those that were said to have been placed every seven miles to mark the resting places of the body of St Aldhelm on its journey from Doulting, Somerset, where he died, to his burial place at Malmesbury Abbey. Below the cross fragment there is an assembled altar with a finely carved stone slab turned on its side. Interlaced triangular-shaped knots enclose a finely cut geometric design of stepped interconnecting diamonds with crosslets at their centre. Smaller panels along the side complete this ad hoc altar, cleverly put together after its sections were discovered at the adjacent church of Holy Trinity. These enigmatic fragments are perhaps all that remain of the earlier church, built in the late seventh or early eighth century, that probably stood on the site.

The design of its framework of diaper patterns looked like

a larger version of the jewelled clasps from the Sutton Hoo treasure of King Rædwald of East Anglia, a contemporary of Aldhelm. This was the best sort of work; could it have once formed part of the shrine of Aldhelm or even perhaps another Saxon king? The designs are also reminiscent of a place that was as remote as one could get from gentle Wiltshire, and I thought back to a working visit to the island community of Iona in the Western Isles of Scotland.

The European decline in commerce, learning, cultural life and confidence had been so steep that the sixth-century historian Bishop Gregory of Tours wrote despairingly: 'In the cities of Gaul there could be found no scholar trained in ordered composition that could present a picture in prose or verse of the things that had befallen.' However, not all was lost. On the periphery of the old empire, a few isolated centres of monastic learning kept the flame alive. Skellig Michael, off the west coast of Ireland, lifts like a pair of mountain-sized inverted shark's teeth from the Atlantic that foams around its base. It was used in the *Star Wars* series, the island of the Last Jedi, where Luke Skywalker sought solace. Here a different religious brotherhood settled, their beehive-shaped cells, built dry without mortar with only moss pushed between the joints to keep out the elements, describe without the need for words the ascetic form of monasticism adopted by the monks, whose philosophy had spread west from the deserts of Egypt where monasticism had begun under St Anthony in the fourth century.

Other Atlantic-facing monastic settlements developed in Cornwall, Wales and Ireland where ozonic sea breezes and light combined to create what the Celts knew as 'thin places'. They saw heaven and earth as only three feet apart, but in these thin places the distance felt closer still. This insular culture, which flourished from the sixth to twelfth centuries on either side of the Irish Sea, became known for a religious ideal based around a life of poverty and simplicity, scholarship and a love of nature. By the 800s, converts were coming from the mainland 'to labour and not to seek reward'. Here the culture and civilisation was so sophisticated that the scriptoriums established by the monks to copy and distribute the ancient texts created the finest illuminated manuscripts of the time, including the Book of Kells. The monks roved over the sea-roads in their skin-clad boats to Scotland, Ireland, England and beyond, spreading the Christian message. The heart of this unique Church was the monastic settlement on the Scottish isle of Iona, a place which would have been near impossible to get to overland at that time but was in a central position along the sea lanes.

In my youth I had travelled countrywide for a year, learning skills on site, 'hands on', from other specialist craftspeople and architects repairing old buildings.

At one point on my travels I journeyed to Iona in the Inner Hebrides. As usual I had brought *Laughing Water* along in the back of the pickup. No black clouds were to be seen and although the Atlantic was surging out of the bay, the turquoise waters of the Sound of Iona were calm. I paddled past the inquisitive seals and stepped onto a white, shell-sand beach and thought of St Columba who had landed there in 563 CE to form a monastic community that was to become perhaps the most important in Europe.

The Victorian portside buildings led to ruins and moorland crags which echoed with the rasping call of the corncrake. The atmosphere became more intense on the approach to the abbey along the cobbled path – *Sraid nam Marbh*, 'the way of the dead' – that led to a pair of ancient high crosses, monumental in scale, that fronted the abbey range and the shrine of St Columba, or Colm Cille as he is known in Gaelic. The high crosses acted to imitate the hill of Calvary, as originally there were three at this spot. I wanted to know how it was possible that somewhere as remote as this could have created perhaps the greatest contribution to the sculpture of Europe during the early medieval period. An archaeologist I met went so far as to say that the two hundred crosses remaining across Ireland, Scotland and parts of England were the most significant body of free-standing sculpture to have been created between the collapse of Rome and the Italian Renaissance a thousand years later.

One cross towered up to twice my height. All of its four sides were carved, but apart from the Celtic knotwork that was to become familiar to me at St Laurence's, the panels on the west face were hard to read. I thought they had been blurred by time and the elements, but in running my hand across the surface I could tell that this material was of a stubborn character. The cross, dedicated to St Martin, was cut from a single block of greyish-green epidiorite, brought from Loch Sween, fifty miles by sea from the mainland. Carved between 750 and 800 CE, it was composed of base-plinth, shaft and cross head and was the sole survivor of many dozens, perhaps hundreds, of crosses that were made on the island. It still stands in the spot where it was first put up.

Behind it, closest to the church front, the larger St John's Cross is a skilled copy in concrete. The east face of St Martin's

Cross is highly decorated with motifs that would have conveyed a lot of Christian messages in its small space. The hemispherical boss at the centre of the cross is thought to be a representation of God, the arms connected by a circle of stone in the Celtic way that represents the universe revolving around Him. The decorative imagery is then controlled by yet more bosses from where spirals and interwoven serpents spring. In the shedding of their skin, the snakes represent the rebirth into a new life upon the viewer's acceptance of Christ. Like plaited hair, panels of interlace are symbolic of an endless journey, eternal life, and are interposed with the symbol of Christ's majesty, the lion. The sides of the cross are just as elaborately decorated with vines and ornamental circles.

The west face is a less interesting mix of scenes cut in relief from the Gospels and strapwork decoration. At the centre of the crosshead is Mary with the infant Jesus. Down the shaft are biblical scenes, standard stuff – Daniel flanked by a pair of lions in a cosy-looking den, then a small figure, with sword raised: perhaps Abraham about to sacrifice his son Isaac. Next comes King David playing the harp, followed by two pairs of unknown figures. The arms of the cross are decorated with more lions.

When finished, as with the Sulis-Minerva Roman temple in Bath and most other medieval sculpture to come, they were probably covered with a layer of carefully modelled plaster and painted to render biblical events in Technicolor. These were examples of the Iona school of masonry, whose influence can still be seen spread throughout the churchyards of Ireland and Scotland. On the Irish mainland, in the town of Kells in County Meath, five high crosses are spread around the precinct of an abbey, re-founded by the community of monks from Iona in 804 in a bid to avoid the depredations of the Vikings. One, which looks as if the sculptor has just walked away for a minute, is under the shadow of the monastery's thin round tower. It is interesting to see that the job was undertaken in situ, perhaps from a small scaffold. These working methods are a surprise as the patterns of interlacing on the ring of the crosshead were finished first. The carving for the central crucifixion scene is almost complete but the series of projecting blocks that would be filled with figurative work are all unfinished; either the Vikings took the mason away or he simply ran out of the zeal needed for a job that would have taken a good few weeks. This and its siblings had all been cut with great geometric accuracy, as with the contents of the most important illuminated manuscript from the early medieval period, and especially the book of extraordinary beauty that was kept inside the adjacent abbey, the eponymously titled Book of Kells. It was created on Iona, before it was taken away for safekeeping, perhaps after a Viking raid in 806 when sixty-eight monks were slaughtered.

Easily transportable illuminated Bibles like the Book of Kells influenced the design of not only the high crosses but also other church work, jewellery and reliquaries. From the Atlantic coast, this influence permeated the British Isles, mingling with the ornamental style of southern England to create the Hiberno-Saxon style that I could see back in Wiltshire and St Laurence's Church. It was tantalising to think that ornamentation from this Celtic culture had been translated into the shrine of a sainted English king in a church associated with the most Anglo-Saxon of saints, Aldhelm.

Around the time that Iona was becoming the most important

place of Christian mission in the British Isles, St Aldhelm was born. His strong association with Wessex, as a driving force in the building of convents and churches as well as new monasteries at Malmesbury and my home town of Frome, is still evident today. He was known as Britain's first man of letters. Among his many influential poetic texts is a book of a hundred riddles, *The Aenigmata*, which can be found in an early manuscript written in about 697. Accompanying it, and written perhaps with the same hand, is one of the first non-liturgical Latin texts to arrive in the Anglo-Saxon world, the *Psychomachia* or War of the Soul. This fifth-century text was written originally by Prudentius, a late-antique Spanish poet, and it profoundly influenced not only Aldhelm and his Anglo-Saxon contemporaries, but also poets and storytellers in word and stone throughout the later medieval world. Besides the riddles and songs on sacred subjects, sung in their own Saxon tongue, the crowds he drew would perhaps have relished his interpretation of the *Psychomachia*, in which the personified virtues and vices take to the field in action-packed clashes for possession of the human soul, no doubt all in gory detail.

I decided to try Aldhelm's riddles out on the other visitors to the chapel. Apart from a solid and suspicious Australian couple, a succession of curious day-trippers were happy to mull over the saint's many offerings, such as this:

> Spawned without seed, produced in ways of wonder,
> I load my sweetened breast with floral plunder;
> Kings' honeyed fare grows gilded through my flair.
> Sharp spears of fearsome war are what I bear,
> And I beat − handless! − craftsmen's metalware.

St Laurence's disappeared from the record for a millennium and in that time was used variously as a school and 'skull house' for the storage of bones, until in the nineteenth century Canon Jones of Holy Trinity Church found reference to it in the *Gesta Pontificum* of 1125 written by the foremost English historian of that time, William of Malmesbury. He spotted the sentence: 'To this day at that place there exists a little church, which Aldhelm is said to have built to the name of the most blessed Laurence.' The church is now thought to have been built about three hundred years on from the time of Aldhelm, sometime in the tenth or eleventh centuries, during the reign of King Æthelred II, better known as 'the Unready'.

In 1001, King Æthelred gave land in Bradford-on-Avon to the nuns of Shaftesbury Abbey, where the mortal remains of his half-brother Edward the Martyr had been buried. A record of a diploma in the name of Æthelred survives. The next year the massacre of Norse settlers instigated by Æthelred brought on the invasion of Sweden's King Sweyn Forkbeard, seeking revenge for the St Brice's Day massacre of 13 November 1002. By 1012 England was in a state of emergency as Forkbeard's army systematically harried and burned their way across the country. It's not hard to imagine the locals praying for salvation from the followers of Thor and Odin within St Laurence's interior.

The *Anglo-Saxon Chronicle* lists the failures of Æthelred's government. It tells us that the decline of leadership even led to a sudden descent into paganism. Enchanters, shadow men and spell workers stalked the land, and in 1013 the Anglo-Saxon world fell apart when Ælfheah, the archbishop of Canterbury, was beaten to death by the Danes with animal bones. Silver pennies were minted for the first time with the image of the Agnus Dei – the Lamb of God – instead of the king as a divine talisman.

With a couple of hours of light left, I returned to the canoe and left Bradford-on-Avon in my thin wake, paddling back the way I had come and enjoying the far quicker and relatively effortless journey downstream to Bath.

Today, the geographical boundary of our work seems defined by Aldhelm's Wessex bishopric that encompassed his abbeys of Sherborne and Malmesbury. Before his death in 1697, John Aubrey recorded the tradition that attributed to St Aldhelm the founding of the nearby limestone quarry at Hazelbury:

> Hazebury quarre is not to be forgot. It is the eminentest free-stone quarry in the West of England, Malmesbury and all around the County of it.
>
> The old men's story is that St Aldelme, riding over there, threw down his glove, and bade them digge and they should find great treasure, meaning the quarrey.

St Aldhelm's gauntlet can be seen in old photos stencilled onto freshly extracted blocks as the trademark of the quarry. As the stone from Hazelbury hardens, it becomes a creamy white that, as atmospheric pollution and lichen growth take their toll, shifts to an unsatisfactory grey. Aubrey described the stone as 'the most eminent for freestone in the western parts before the discovery of the Portland quarry, which was but about anno 1600'.

The intense period of church building that took place after the Norman Conquest made good use of the geographical position of the quarry. To the east of Hazelbury the landscape gently drops away towards the Vale of Pewsey, easy cartage distance to the new pair of churches and vast castle that went up in Devizes, while stone for the new abbey at Malmesbury could have been transported north by raft via the Bybrook and Avon rivers. After 1066, William the Bastard, as the *Anglo-Saxon Chronicle* called him, appointed a new archbishop of Canterbury to oversee the reformation of the English Church. Under the reforms of Archbishop Lanfranc, Anglo-Saxon clergy were replaced with Norman. Within a decade or two a more sophisticated Anglo-Norman form of church began to appear, a strategy that led to the demolition or incorporation of those that had been erected by Saxon noblemen and women.

Finds from Holy Trinity across the lane from St Laurence's indicate the success of this scorched earth policy. The walls and footings of the replacement minster reflect the story of other pre-Conquest churches that have been found packed with broken-up Anglo-Saxon tomb slabs, sculpture and architectural carvings. Bradford is about the only place in the land where the jostle for power between Saxon and Norman is still quietly played out, with most church visitors electing to visit Holy Trinity's elder sibling first.

Elsewhere in Wessex, evidence of the erasure of the Saxon aristocracy can be seen in the conflation of Saxon place names with those of the new landowners. The common 'Easton' for 'east farm' often acquired the supplement of the new lord – for example Bassett, Grey or Percy – and 'Wootton' for 'the woodland farm' can be found with the appellation Bassett, as well as with Fitzpaine and Glanville. During this cultural cleansing the names of natural features tended to be left alone. The

Saxon capital of Wilton, built as part of King Alfred's defensive chain of burghs during the Danish wars and from where the county took its name, had a defensive weakness. It had been burned to the ground by King Sweyn in 1003, and that weakness was soon recognised by the Conqueror. He consolidated the ramparts of the nearby Iron Age hill fort of Old Sarum, a couple of miles north of modern Salisbury, where within three years of the Conquest, he threw up a motte and huge outer earthworks to protect his royal castle upon which a web of roads, Roman and older, already focused. Consolidation was one of the Conqueror's key tactics and the bishop's seat was moved from Aldhelm's Sherborne in about 1075 to Old Sarum with its bustling settlement, garrison and royal mint.

Old Sarum possesses great landscape drama. Its naturally elevated position over the Wylye and Avon valleys mean that people have taken advantage of its defensive potential since prehistoric times. Its perfectly circular earthen rampart, twenty yards deep, encloses the low flint walls of what was once a busy urban centre with the old cathedral now outlined in the turf. From the keep of the motte and bailey one can see across the new city, beyond the Wylye and Nadder river valleys to a secret wood that at the start of my time at Salisbury Cathedral had become a home of sorts.

During the first faltering steps of life as a journeyman, earning potential is minimal. The reality of a below living-wage income at the cathedral meant we were obliged to squat in a long-abandoned Victorian warehouse. In the ultra-conservative, heavily policed, walled fiefdom of a former Conservative prime minister, we were quickly moved on and so formed an encampment at Great Yews, a downland wood enclosed by the impenetrable stands of an overgrown chestnut coppice. Planted during medieval times to provide yew for long bows, this was a place so secret that its only building, avoided by us, was rumoured to have been a government safe house, one of many where the author Salman Rushdie was reputed to have hidden away during his fatwa.

Our trespass in the magnificent seventy-acre grove remained undiscovered. The locals knew it as Witches Wood, a place best avoided and through which the prehistoric Grim's Ditch passed. Made otherworldly by the orange light thrown into the enveloping darkness by our small campfire, twisted yews of gigantic growth and great age formed a roof over our kraal. Looking up from my deep bed of soft needles I wondered if the cathedral builders had enjoyed the same view of the conjoined canopy vault imitated by the man-made equivalent in stone across the downs. Every morning, I would cycle the few miles to the cathedral, turning to enter the precinct under the Exeter Street gatehouse, dedicated to St Ann, the only gap in the high wall designed to keep the ruder elements of the city away from the quiet, contemplative world within.

As the weeks passed, I came to appreciate how quirky the wall was, built with a mixture of carved stones that had been brought in from elsewhere, placed in an ad-hoc way that made their stylistic origins difficult to distinguish at first. Could this have been Anglo-Saxon work? I had learned that their relief-carving tended to be more of an embellishment once construction was completed, but that Norman sculpture was a more integral part of a building with architectural decoration that depended on the repetition of patterns, with regional variations. The penny dropped when I began to notice many more examples of these motifs hidden in the shadows of the tucked-away areas of the new cathedral, such as in the roof space of the nave. The bronze plaque by St Ann's Gate confirmed this direction of thought: the wall to which it was affixed was built with stones carted from Old Sarum in the fourteenth century.

About one hundred and fifty years after its founding, Bishop Jocelyn tired of the problems of life in the garrison and the lack of water in Old Sarum's repurposed Iron Age hill fort. Around 1220 work started on the new cathedral, the location of which folklore says was chosen by the distance of an arrow fired by a longbow from the ramparts towards more amiable surroundings amid the water meadows.

Even though the Exeter Street wall was blurred by pollution, I was managing to fill up my notebook with sketches that showed a broad variety of motifs and designs. Among the chevrons and billets, nail heads and other hallmarks of Norman architecture, time and again there was a curious motif of unknown symbolism – a circular medallion that looked like the top of a pie crust with four of its sides turned in to the centre. These were paterae, in imitation of the shallow dish upon which bread is offered during Mass. I had no idea then that recording this detail's strange, stand-out form was to act as a waymarker, revealing routes of cultural transmission across early medieval Europe and the exotic origins of Norman art and architecture.

PART THREE
MARBLE

5

ARMAGEDDON

It was May Day, the old pagan festival of Beltane, and the workers' holiday. But I was cycling to an urgent site visit with a church architect who had phoned with worrying news about the carving surrounding the north doorway of All Saints' in Lullington. The church was hidden in semi-retirement behind hedgerows, midway between the Norman citadels of Old Sarum and Bristol. A pair of neo-Gothic gatehouses marked the start of the long ride through a private estate and all around were the last remnants of the once great Selwood Forest. There was a long drag past the pheasant pens and cottages of the gamekeepers. The narrow tarmac twisted its way between lone oaks and hornbeams, while sand bunkers marked out ancient parkland that had been golf-coursed. The trees had remained protected, while vast stands of unimproved pasture, thick with bee, spider and pyramidal orchid, had been ploughed out of this former paradise. Over the way, new barbed-wire fencing contained walkers and channelled them away from the lake with the rotting boathouse where we used to mess about.

Although early, it was already warm. The house martins twittered as they closed in on a condensing insect swarm above the tower's battlements and I listened out for the long scream of swifts, still on their way back from Africa. Nell, my work-mate, said to make sure I washed my face in the May morning dew and I did so under the watchful eyes of a be-draped figure of a Norman Christ who sat in Majesty over the doorway.

John the architect arrived with a shoebox of stone fragments, more granules than pieces, which he had collected from the grass over the past few months. The porch door was ajar and its font was unmissable. Cut from Hazelbury limestone, the large lead-lined, plinth-mounted bucket was divided into four decorative bands. At the base an arcade of intersecting or blind arches supported a ring of chrysanthemum-type flowers. Above that, the inscription cut into the font – *hoc fontis sacro pereunt delicta lavacro*, in the sacred washing of this font are sins cleansed – seemed appropriate for my dewy facewash. The font's top layer of carving was formed by a ring of simple-looking dogs, cats and green men who spewed entwined foliage from the sides of their biting mouths. The topmost sections were concerned with what was to become a familiar representation of the ever-present conflict between good and evil. These themes can be seen played out repeatedly in Norman and later churches, church sculpture being used as a method of instruction for illiterate parishioners. This continued throughout the medieval period up to the Reformation, each lesson generally ending with 'Let this be a warning to you.'

Much of this allegorical sculpture depicting the battle of good versus evil was based on the 'War of the Soul', as portrayed in the poem *Psychomachia* that St Aldhem used to instruct his flock. Sometimes, where the Virtues triumph over the contrary Vices for possession of the human soul, the names beneath the depictions of their characters are often cut in backwards mirror-writing as an indication of their wickedness. Although charismatic, by any reckoning, the font looked like freelance pre-Conquest Saxon work. It was a surprise to read on the ping-pong-bat guide that it had been carved in the 1150s. I like to think it was the creation of a Saxon workshop that had somehow managed to maintain the local font-making franchise. By contrast, a very different hand had designed the external north doorway. This was the place we had come to inspect, the work executed by one who was more experienced, sophisticated – and perhaps even a foreigner.

John's box of fragments was from a continuous row of carved blocks that projected from just below the level of the eaves, a giveaway Norman feature known as a 'corbel table'. The addition of corbels helped to reinforce the topmost courses and accommodate the heavy timbers of a pitched roof and the corresponding outward thrust exerted on the wall. These blocks projected forwards from the face every few feet and presented a further opportunity for carving, with an assortment of decorative motifs and grotesques, both sacred and profane. All were rather tired, smoke-blackened, blistered, and worn away by acid rain, but with treatment it would be possible to slow down the damaging effects of pollution. We picked a few more bits from the grass underneath that were all clearly beyond help.

One of the most striking corbels was that of a king crowned with a mane of stylised hair. I had met similar characteristics many years before when, during my training, I was tasked with copy-carving one of the few figurative corbels to have survived from the cathedral at Old Sarum. The corbels were now stored in a cabinet in Salisbury Museum. Surveying the options –

corbels that stared forlornly back, their eyes elsewhere – I chose a lion with a luxuriant and stylised mane. I translated the sketches to a rectangular block of Chilmark stone of similar size, about eighteen inches long and nine deep. Its back half would be built into the wall and so remained untouched. On the front and sides, once the profile of the brow, nose, lips and beard of the beast were pencilled in, it could be scribed in deeper with a metal point so as to not lose the pencil outline in the dust.

The old masons each had their own preference for the wood that their mallets were turned out of: apple, cherry, lignum vitae, even yew. Tools were passed down to son or daughter and maybe further. Although considered a male occupation, there would have been journeywomen as well. In 1408, documents from York's Corpus Christi Guild noted that an apprentice 'had to obey, the Master or Dame or any other Freemason'.

Some of my heavyweight hammers and chisels are over eighty years old, inherited from a carver from Dorset's Isle of Purbeck, but my favourite is my modern dense white nylon mallet; after thirty years of use it has hefted itself to my hand more than any other tool. It's quite indestructible and has helped to pay the rent pretty much every day since leaving college. The biggest fear is that it will be lost or not be returned by an apprentice. It propelled the one-inch-wide steel claw chisel across the face of the soft stone to create a roughed-out profile covered in tiny furrows. Now I was ready to cut the detailing into the lion's face. For this the mallet-headed claw chisel worked well. I worked from the centre to round away the sides, removing the stone that wasn't nose-shaped and slowly the haughty profile began to reveal itself.

A finer chisel with a flat head and fire-sharpened edge then took away the furrows left by the claw tool to form eyelids, brows and moustache. This is driven by a little lead-alloy mallet known as a 'dummy', the head of which is 60 per cent lead and 40 per cent zinc – the ideal mix for weight and durability. The dummy is the typical tool used for detailed work or letter cutting.

I started to focus on one of the master's hallmarks. His rendering of eyes was particularly distinctive – the top eyelid overlaps a lower that encloses a protruding eyeball; then the indented forehead and snarling lips that surround a letterbox mouth, more Wallace than Gromit, which I filled with teeth as repeat work, cut into tiny daggers. More work followed on his mane, which rolled down both sides in small icicle-like shards ending with a tiny sphere to give the impression of curls. A finishing touch was the careful drilling out of the nostrils and pupils of the eyes which, when broadened out slightly – in imitation of the original's sideways direction of view – with the curved edge of a gouge, were only a quarter-inch wide.

With the chisel laid down at last, the beast fixed into position and viewed from below, I noticed how intensely he stared, something not apparent with the original in his cabinet.

Beneath All Saints' corbel table, our attention turned to the extravagant north doorway, which in a small way gives the best idea as to what Old Sarum, once the most significant Norman building in the West Country, looked like. One chevroned and one barley-sugar-twist shaft lift from the turf to a pair of somewhat weathered capitals. These in turn support a carved semicircular tympanum a yard or so wide at the base that was a feature comparable in importance to the triangular pediment of a Roman temple, like that of old Sulis-Minerva. Cut in a now-faded low relief onto its face, a griffin and a lion tug on the branches of a tree of life, its trunk decorated with a line of beads.

Like the arcs of a rainbow, three courses of strange decoration radiated out from the tympanum to form an archway. The first band was made up of nine of the unusual paterae – the motifs that I noticed had been reused from Old Sarum on New Sarum's precinct wall. So many familiar elements followed in the next bands that this felt surely to have been translated by the same hand. Next came an arc of chevrons that held at the apex an odd mistake. Each arrowed segment is cut from a block of similar size, but the topmost is much larger, twice the size of the others. It is all so well set out that I can't believe this was not done deliberately. Perhaps the mason was not only keen to demonstrate humility but also the impossibility of creating perfection under the eyes of God.

The wide arch concluded with an array of grimacing, horned creatures, known as 'beakheads', which project a degree of malevolence towards the viewer. The beaks, perhaps developed from the chevron ornament, are found in most late-Norman churches and are more commonly seen in the British Isles than Europe. This would have been good piecework for the maker as they accentuate and add depth and richness to door surrounds, arches, doorways, windows and rib vaults. Gouge out a pair of eyes in the broad base of an individual chevron and you have a form that approaches a beakhead.

However, all this bravado work was merely a frame for the most important part – the narrow pediment with the enthroned figure of Christ in Majesty looking down over all. The Old Sarum style was heavily influenced by the latest developments of the time in central France. Bishop Roger of Sarum, who put it up in the 1130s, was perhaps the most prolific builder of the early Middle Ages. His dark grey tomb slab rests in the nave of Salisbury Cathedral. Roger was far more than a churchman. He was a courtier who ran England for the first King Henry, a man typical of his time – ambitious, acquisitive and ostentatious, to judge by the number of castles he built in his diocese, which stretched for fifty miles from the Cotswold Hills south to Dorset, incorporating the abbeys of Malmesbury and Sherborne. Today, decay and destruction conspire to disguise Roger's true status as the greatest builder of his age as very little of his work survives above ground. His grip on the country was so complete that his two nephews were appointed bishops of Lincoln and Ely.

We finished our inspection and John left the box of bits and a note expressing his concern on the vestry table. Bishop Roger's hugely influential style can be seen throughout the churches and cathedrals that went up in Old Sarum's wake, one of which, in the nearby market town of Devizes, possesses what may be the earliest example in England of the greatest innovation in the history of architecture.

A short while after the Lullington visit I was to be found a hundred feet above Devizes painting a flagpole on the rectangular Norman tower of St John's Church. Stood on my ladder, clinging onto the pole that vibrated like a ship's mast, I looked down into the landscaped gardens of the adjacent castle whose needs the church had been built to serve. Today's castle is but a sham – a Victorian Gothic folly in imitation of Bishop Roger's original, which had been slighted during the English Civil War. A sea of red-tiled roofs spread away to St John's Anglo-Norman twin of St Mary's. Leaning over the parapet's east face, I looked down past the semicircular Norman-arched windows and saw plenty of evidence that the church had also received a battering during the Civil War. The long drop of lichen-encrusted stone quarried in Hazelbury was covered with hundreds of unhealed scars from different types of artillery. Single cannonball-shaped dents from which cracks still radiated contrasted with a dense area that had been pockmarked with canister and grapeshot, designed to take down cavalry and infantry, and the even smaller imprints of musketry.

The town had developed around the marketplace at the foot of a castle that sat at the division of two boundaries – *ad divisas* – from which it took its name. This was one of a chain of castles that Roger built along with Malmesbury and Sherborne, which allowed him to control the eastern approaches to his West Country powerbase. Below me the graveyard surrounding the church was filled with the regular users of God's acre. Many had been drawn by the free lunch in the adjacent parish hall's drop-in centre. Smoking crack with a Special Brew chaser seemed the chosen pastime for some, either in the porch or behind the mound of grass cuttings or the green corrugated shed where the lawnmower was kept. They were always friendly, even more so when bits of our kit went missing.

With their giros cashed they would get their act together and have a grand cook up. The burgers and sausages smelt good as they seared on a pair of disposable barbecues, their table groaning with buns, relish and cans of Scrumpy Jack. On occasions like these, my trembling whippet feared for her life as their unruly dogs became even more boisterous in the fight over scraps. My admiration of their resilience and ingenuity changed to unease when I noticed the searing heat of their tin tray barbecues focused on the ledger slab of a Georgian box tomb. As the North family and their five children who were the tomb's residents were not in a position to complain, I intervened on their behalf. But when my overtures, asking them to move their kitchen, were met with a friendly invitation to join them, I gave in.

In St Mary's graveyard on the other side of town, a stone table easily mistaken for a box tomb leans at an alarming angle. It is in fact a medieval alms table for the distribution of dole – bread and ale to the needy. One of the side panels had fallen and contained a reminder that these people were perhaps the authentic residents of this place. The space inside had been used as a bin and stuffed with dozens of plastic cider bottles. These were of a different order of homeless to the old types we used to see: the once-institutionalised mad, the war veterans and apparent aristocrats who tramped parish to parish in search of alms and shelter. I reflected that these unfortunates had the same tales to tell, ruined by circumstance and by austerity, but finished off by the methamphetamine that had replaced the methylated spirit.

With the flagpole freshly decorated, I descended the spiral staircase and quietly entered the church to undertake the next job on the list. In the dark chancel, the aluminium click of the tall stepladder echoed about the walls as I climbed the creaking steps heavenwards to check on the gridded plastic strips – tell-tales – that had been fitted a few months before to the stone vaulted ceiling. The previous year's long wet summer had provoked movement in the footings. The knock-on effect was a corresponding shift in the walls that led to the vault's ongoing deflection.

The ceiling's faded blue background still held the ghost of its original decoration – once gilded constellations of dusty stars would have shone out of the sombre gloom. On the European mainland the end wall of the chancel would be curved to form an apse, but in Anglo-Norman England, the tradition still followed that of earlier churches such as St Laurence's. A blind arcade made its way around three sides of the chancel's box to enclose the original altar of grey Purbeck marble that sits on thickset legs. Here the Normans had abandoned the idea of wooden vaulted ceilings, which were not only prone to combustion but limited the scale of their buildings. To overcome this they reinvented the idea of a continuous semicircular Roman roof vault.

St John's chancel reflects the next step of the form – where another vault meets the continuous vault at a right angle. This intersection formed a cross, known as a groin vault, as the ribs meet to form a V. This quadripartite system was first used at Durham Cathedral (constructed between 1093 and 1132), where the clerk of works had told me of the legend that Arab masons, brought as prisoners from the Holy Land after the First Crusade of 1095, had first brought the technology to north-east England. Their innovation was to guide all the weight of the roof vault down onto just four points at the corners of each bay through hefty piers that support the corners like table legs. Greater loads could be handled with the addition of external buttresses against the springing point where the arch meets the piers, an innovation known as a *tas-de-charge*. This system allowed the construction of buildings of great ambition, the first in Britain since the Roman Baths over nine hundred years earlier.

Equally, this innovation could have been adapted from a part of the Islamic world that was closer to home: the Bab Mardum Mosque in Toledo, Spain, which was built around the year 1000. Its domed roof structure sits on square walls, supported centrally by four columns that carry horseshoe arches, which define its nine ceiling bays. These square compartments are subdivided by supporting ribs, some intersecting each other to create a basic quadripartite ribbed vault. As the taking of prisoners was commonplace during the First Crusade to the Holy Land, and the *reconquista* of Spain from the Moors that lasted from 718 until 1492 was slow, surely the presence of Moors helps to explain the rapid improvement in the quality of building work from the Norman Conquest and onwards through the course of the twelfth century? The growing sophistication of church building would only have been possible by masons developing an enhanced geometrical knowledge and much greater precision of measurement and setting-out. These requirements came about as a consequence of the influence of Islam, but via a different route with the rediscovery of the Greek mathematician Euclid, whose work had profound implications for the development of many churches and cathedrals.

It was Adelard of Bath who first translated Euclid's *The Elements* from the Arabic into Latin and brought it back to Bath around 1130, as the Norman building boom got into its stride. Adelard (1080–1152) is perhaps the most important citizen the city has produced. Schooled at Bath Abbey when there would still have been Roman ruins around, he went on to study and teach in France, before travelling for several years through the 'lands of the Crusades'. Upon his return to Bath he was one of the first to introduce the Arabic numbering system into Europe.

At St John's, with the measurements from the sanctuary vault collated, I was relieved to see that there had been no more movement since my last visit. I stopped on my way out under the rectangular tower and turned to admire the crossing space. Here, where the transepts meet the crossing, the fact that the side arches are pointed would not normally warrant any comment, but this relatively unregarded church could well be the first time in England that the pointed arch was used, and so marks a turning point in the history of architecture. Changing the centre point from a curve to a point where the two halves brace each other meant a reduced amount of outward pressure being placed on adjacent walls. It is possible that pointed arches existed in the east end of Old Sarum, which was completed around 1125, predating by nearly twenty years its development on the Île-de-France at the Cathedral of St Denis that is reckoned to be the world's first Gothic church.

I have an idea that this may also have been influenced by the skill and knowledge of a Muslim. A Welsh chronicle of 1130 records a captive 'from the land of Canaan, of the name of Lalys [who] was a man eminent in the art of masonry who constructed the most celebrated monasteries, castles, and churches in the country . . . and taught the art to many of the Welsh and English'. Later he rose to become royal architect for Roger's patron, King Henry I.

If it hadn't come from a mason who was a follower of the Prophet Muhammad, then the Normans had at least learned from their opponents the building methods and techniques that were to create the solid and cohesive style better known on the continent as the Romanesque. The pointed arch reached England via France where it had been used for some time at Cluny Abbey in Burgundy, which until the building of St Peter's Basilica in Rome (consecrated 1626) was the largest church in Christendom. Knowledge at that time would have been disseminated along the network of pilgrimage routes that pass through France. They cross the Pyrenees through one of two passes that converged in northern Spain to send a single movement of pilgrims west along deep-rutted paths and byways to the shrine of St James the Apostle at distant Santiago de Compostela in northern Galicia. The Romanesque architecture and carving that is to be found along the Camino or 'Way', as it is better known, acts as a sort of human catnip to me and so, before the heat of summer kicked in, I was setting off as usual to France to explore the churches, abbeys and chapels that lined that part of the Way.

The pilgrims' motives were the same as those that gathered at Chaucer's Tabard Inn in Southwark at the start of *The Canterbury Tales*. Many simply wanted to see new places with the benefit of some heavenly credit; some, to fulfil a vow or search for a cure or blessing, but most were keen simply to enjoy following the Way and explore the many wayside chapels.

The city of Autun has been a place of pilgrimage since the cathedral was consecrated in the first half of the twelfth century. It was built to house the relics of Lazarus, whom Jesus restored to life four days after his death. As is the confusing way of relics, though, Autun houses the bones of someone else in this grand shrine: those of Bishop Lazarus of Aix, who died in the fifth century.

It is common enough to encounter the Christ figure, sitting in judgement above the entrance to a wayside church, but the western portico of Autun Cathedral has a sculpture of Christ in Majesty that was of a different order entirely to that at tiny Lullington. The design starts gently, the outer orders of arches framed by signs of the zodiac and carved foliage that encloses horn-blowing angels heralding the Day of Judgement. Flanked by the Virgin and Apostles, and supported by angels, Christ sits directing the apocalyptic goings on below him. For the few that could read it, the tone was set with the Latin inscription cut into the margin of the almond-shaped mandorla that encloses the Christ figure: 'I alone dispose of all things and crown merit. Those who are led by crime will be judged and chastised by me.'

On the left side of Christ are the worthy people – pilgrims, bishops and a crusading knight – who have been gathered by angels and sent on their way to heaven, where St Peter awaits the resurrected, who sport chainmail, bishops' mitres and pilgrimage attire in contrast with the naked damned on the right. The Latin inscription above the unfortunates reads: 'May terror cover those who are in bondage on account of earthly error' and the horror of this scene shows them their lot. Against a maelstrom of elongated demons, the Archangel Michael weighs the souls of the damned.

Immediately beneath Christ's right foot, in the place that would normally carry the name of the patron, are cut the words '*Giselbertus hoc fecit*', 'Giselbertus made this'. Could the individual immediately below, stood in the queue for judgement, his hands lifted up as if in ecstasy, be a self-portrait of the sculptor on his own work? Giselbertus's tympanum marks the revival of truly monumental sculpture, driven by the surge in confidence and relief at having survived the Last Judgement, which many had expected during the year 1000.

The doors into the nave were open, its giant piers crowned with capitals just about low enough to allow their detailing to be made out. Sculpted capitals were, along with wall paintings and the tympanum, the three main vehicles used in the early medieval church to tell a story, or sequence of stories, from the Bible or the life of a saint. Autun is also home to an entire scheme of the finest narrative carving, also thought to be the creation of Giselbertus.

One sequence telling the story of the three Magi and their visit to the manger concludes with the Holy Family's flight into Egypt and the Magi's dream. The rectangular panel, only a couple of feet wide and eighteen inches deep, had its relief design made in the workshop and inserted into a space cut into the face of the capital. Even though they share a single pillow and are still wearing their crowns, the kings appear to have slept soundly, tucked in with a stylised semicircular counterpane the shape of a Cornish pasty, its drapes edged with rich embroidery. Another sequence shows a basilisk – a demonic half-cockerel, half-snake – being attacked by naked men wearing only helmets, an assault illustrative of the eternal battle between good and evil. It was a surprise to see the beast's clawed foot resting on that circular pie-crust motif I recognised from Old Sarum and Lullington, and I saw again how connected the early medieval church was.

Once the discipline and repetition of working yard after yard of architectural moulding had been mastered, a jobbing mason might perhaps struggle with the carving of freehand drapery. Some more highly skilled, such as Giselbertus, would have soon chosen to specialise as carvers. It was clear from the sophisticated way the joints and blocks of the judgement tympanum interlocked into the surrounding architecture that the sculptor had begun his career as a mason at the Benedictine Abbey of Cluny, which is three days' walk away. Cluny had a profound influence on Romanesque figurative carving and architecture, which was spread via sister churches in Europe. The Benedictines encouraged instructive images of faith, and its daughter houses along the pilgrimage routes throughout Burgundy, western France, Spain and England were once adorned with sculpture. The main themes of this new style were drawn from the empires of Islam and Byzantium, which were, as Sir Kenneth Clark put it in *Civilisation*, 'like two beasts pulling at the carcass of the Roman Empire'. Many British pilgrims would have returned home from Santiago de Compostela via the port city of Bristol that would have had a harbourside teeming with returning pilgrims, merchants and craftspeople full of new ideas and fashions. A few of these artisans made the two days' journey across the Cotswold Hills through flat cornfields to Malmesbury – the oldest borough in England.

I too had come to Malmesbury upon my return from France. Andy and I knew the ancient borough well, having conserved many of its buildings, defensive walls and pack-horse bridges.

The top of the market cross is possibly the best vantage point to understand the town. Now Nell and I were sat on beer crates upon the lead roof working on a pre-Reformation likeness of

St Peter who, stood tight in his niche, had been watching the comings and goings of the citizenry to the abbey and market-place for several centuries. The scale of the adjacent abbey's walls felt quite overbearing. The ruination that boxed in the east and west ends was on an epic scale. Thick clumps of devil's beard, also known as red valerian, and buddleia rampaged through the open core of a wall, a hundred feet high, that was not designed to be exposed. How was it that these artificial cliff faces continued to defy gravity?

The abbey was one of the last Norman buildings to be built, of which the roofed rump of the nave's six bays, where today's church mission is concentrated, is all that remains of what was once the tallest church in England. Its Gothic spire, 27 feet higher than Salisbury's at 431 feet, fell after a storm in the mid-sixteenth century, destroying much of the church and leaving it in the state that we could see from the top of the market cross.

The abbey had flourished during the time of William of Malmesbury, when it became a major centre of learning with one of the finest libraries in England. In later years the library was scattered and destroyed. John Aubrey recorded the fate of some of the manuscripts in their use by the grandson of a wealthy clothier, William Stumpe, who had bought the abbey from Cromwell and gifted the nave to the town as the parish church: 'Stumpe was a proper man and a good fellow; and when he brewed a barrel of his special ale his use was to stop the bunghole, under the clay, with a sheet of manuscript; he said nothing did it so well, which me thought did grieve me much to see.'

When I noticed that the space either side of the clerestory

windows that filled the upper part of the nave was covered in a series of the decorative roundels seen in association with the patera motif at Lullington, I downed tools and wandered over to the abbey to take a closer look. This would have been one of the last times that the hallmarks of the Old Sarum workshop would have been used, and I wondered if there were any more awaiting discovery.

The churchyard path headed towards the rather grand south porch, which in common with many other West Country churches faces the town as the main entrance. Most visitors pause to take in the carved scheme of biblical scenes before passing through the porch's large semicircular mouth and into the cool nave. Britain never achieved the same scale of monumental glories seen in mid-twelfth-century France, but in front of me survived a piece of work that suggested that those who had put it up had also felt the influence of Autun, the vineyards of Burgundy and perhaps their contemporary Giselbertus.

I sat down on the stone bench lining both sides of the porch with a slab of local lardy cake and a flask of tea. An old boy took off his hat and joined me. 'You'll be one of the masons working on the market cross,' he stated. Nodding, I asked if he knew who the life-size characters were carved on the wall above us. 'Haven't a clue. I've not set foot inside the church for sixty years.' I thought better than to ask the reason why. He got up to leave, slipping on his bicycle clips. He gave the carved stonework a hollow sounding parting knock as he passed through the portal. I asked if he was one of the town's commoners – a member of the old corporation, a tradition of common land allotment and ownership handed down to married men from father to son since the Saxon king Athelstan in 934 CE. He puffed out his chest. 'My family have never left the town. I am one of the two hundred and sixty who can trace ancestry back over a thousand years,' he said. It is unusual to meet someone so rooted to their place and I wondered how many of his ancestors had tapped the stone out of habit in the same way. Turning back he said, 'You'll be interested to know, my cousin sweeps up a good amount of stone dust at the foot of the arch every day. It's much worse since they treated it with that, what was it, Bostik?'

I wandered over and touched its surface. It felt sealed as if by plastic and looking up I could see blisters baring open-pored stone, as under a newly picked scab. Elsewhere, obscured by dirty cobwebs, suffocating clusters of salt crystals sprouted from a fine lozenge-shaped carving. The arch had been impregnated only a few years before with an irreversible wonder chemical that should have been used only as a last resort. Today it looked as if the surface crust was becoming detached and the greatest work of Norman England would soon, perhaps, be lost.

Over the narrow entrance doorway into the nave the Christ figure sits on a rainbow within a mandorla held by a pair of supporting angels. In the other two semicircles, supported at head height on blind arcades, twelve life-sized figures – six in each – sit on thrones in a schematic room on both sidewalls. A life-sized angel, not dissimilar to those at St Laurence's in Bradford-on-Avon, passes over the heads of the rather animated Apostles. They converse in pairs, feet crossed, their hands lively. Their robes drape and cling to their bodies like wet cloth in a style known as 'damp' or 'bandage-fold', a hallmark of the English Romanesque art found in the south-west in the mid–twelfth century. The solitary end figures sit opposite each other. St Peter with his key stares ahead while a balding St Paul seems distracted, leaning back with a stiff neck as if in surprise at the likeness of Christ that sits above the entrance to the abbey. The architectural historian Pevsner thought the Apostles and the arrangement of the tympanum 'purely Burgundian in origin'. There is certainly a similarity with the elongated style of Autun, and although the Malmesbury work is handled with great sensitivity, it seems a little too naive and rustic to have been that of a team of French carvers. The execution of the outer porch carving, however, is technically superior to what I could see inside. Had it been done by two separate teams, one local and one brought over from France? Clearly, the inner crew had the ability and potential to improve and would have learned on the job.

Inside the abbey, erected five hundred years after his demise is the tomb of King Athelstan, Alfred the Great's grandson and first king of the English from 927 until his death in 939, cryptic brasses, and some good Victorian glass. The nave indicated that the move away from the Romanesque semicircular arch to the pointed style was nearly complete and a big step from the first signs of change that appeared at the chancel crossing at Devizes.

This was where the rump of Roger's masons ended up when their patron was imprisoned in disgrace after the death of King Henry I. The style of their workshop was everywhere: paterae, chevroned hood mouldings, wolves' heads carved in the same tradition with the stylised eyes and hair finishing in tiny volutes; but it was clear that they were being steered by a new hand with the latest European knowledge. Many of the

crew would have been quite mature when the work started
and I wondered how well they got on with the new regime.
As in the Roman Baths, and with every generation of practi-
tioners of any craft since, the absorption of the new style and
its rapid dissemination happened quickest through the malleable
apprentices as the baton was handed on.

With the damage to the market cross rectified, we packed
up our kit, gave a few moments' thought to our Anglo-
Norman predecessors – thanks be to them – whose work
had given us our own. Now I needed to satisfy myself as to
the message that the Apostles and the Christ figure wished
to share with the citizenry who entered the church by the
porch. The key to this mystery was to be found in the village
of Kempley thirty miles to the west.

Like the upturned ribcage of a beached whale, Kempley's
silvered oak porch offered welcome shelter from the elements.
I turned the ring latch and pushed at the surprisingly light
door – three planks wide and held together with staples made
by a long ago blacksmith. Stepping down into the nave I first
detected the aroma of oak pews and damp plaster and then
my eyes adjusted to the dark interior when the walls started
to glow in intensity. Every surface seemed to be covered in
painted decoration on a monumental scale. Red is the palette
here. Flagstones, plaster, and paint from ground earth pigments
lend the place an exotic quality unexpected from the outside.
Scarlet chequer-work fills the window splays, and the walls of
the nave are covered with imagery from the fourteenth-century
Biblia Pauperum or 'Poor Man's Bible'. These include a mixed
bag of warning scenes – St Michael and the Virgin Mary

weighing souls, a large Wheel of Life, along with depictions of St Christopher and the murder of St Thomas à Becket.

I have walked into many chancels. This was the first time I felt I had stepped into another world. Spread across the barrel-vaulted ceiling and walls was a complete scheme of images from the Book of Revelation. The church guide said these were frescoes, meaning that the colours had been swiftly painted onto wet plaster to fuse with the surface, whilst those in the nave were an albumen tempera, where the pigments were mixed with egg white and painted onto plaster that had already dried.

The ghostly but familiar outline of the twelve Apostles were depicted in a similar way to their near contemporaries at Malmesbury. Their hands are held up in delight as they receive the benediction from the Christ figure sat on a rainbow within a triple mandorla supported by angels along the curved apex of the vault. In the twelfth century, the Apostles were considered co-assessors at the Day of Judgement. I was whisked back nine centuries, and understood how dramatic the sculpture of Malmesbury's porch would have seemed to the congregation. I pictured them, their clogs dragging on the Pennant flagstones as they processed from their drab, cruck-framed homes to an all-night vigil at the abbey. The entrance, its interior lit bright with candles against the black sky, must have looked like the gate of heaven, with the Apostles and Christ figure brought alive to them. His mandorla, held by a pair of supporting angels, their wings overlapping the margin of the tympanum, presented the illusion that they were approaching from the heavens. All that passed underneath into the comfort of the church would have understood that soon 'the quick and the dead' would be judged, a powerful reminder that after death there was a new life in paradise to be had for those who maintained their faith.

Once nearly every parish church would have been filled with colour and dramatic imagery on the same scale as this, before one by one they fell prey to the actions of iconoclasts, vandals and restorers, to leave us just scraps.

6

WHITSUNTIDE

I was standing on the rampart edge of a ruined citadel from where a limestone crag plunged down to rough, ferny moorland. Carreg Cennen Castle felt out of place among the surrounding fields and moors, but this was hardly surprising as the castle laid out in front of me, in this Welsh-speaking heartland of the Celts, had its origin in the Middle East during the time of Saladin and Richard the Lionheart.

I had ventured deep into South Wales, where in the castle's shadow I had been labouring to extract a rare stone type once freely available from many quarries around Bristol and South Wales. The fortress, which still seemed impenetrable, protected the crossing point of the River Cennen and the northern approach to the important medieval port of Swansea. It had been built in the mid to latter part of the thirteenth century to keep the English at bay. This turned out to have been a huge waste of labour and materials – it was soon captured and enhanced to enforce the authority of Edward I, the English king. Edward is known as the hammer of the Scots, but after his invasion of 1277 when Carreg Cennen was incorporated into the ring of castles he had constructed to secure the Welsh border, it was clear that he had made his mark on the people of Wales as well.

A low early morning mist emanated from the Cennen river covering the tops of the hedgerows that define the surrounding farmland. An outcrop in the middle distance that peeked through the mist indicated where I had been extracting blue Pennant, a type of sandstone once widely used around the west of England for paving, headstones and ledgers. It is an endangered resource with no supplies available on the south side of the Severn estuary. The unadvertised quarry is little more than a shallow scrape in the ground known as a 'delve'. The farmer is happy to open the gate and allow the extraction of a few blocks or slabs for cash in hand.

Lower beds yield ashlar block or freestone. I work a different part of the delve where the beds are thinner and split well, parallel to the bed. This means that I can lift what I need with only a long lever of the type used by rail-track gangers, some metal wedges and a sledgehammer. My orange petrol angle grinder soon cuts the Pennant into the sizes needed. A couple of hours' work fills the pickup with about twelve square yards, which is worth a few hundred pounds and will only need dressing before it can be laid down for paving or walling work. This is probably one of the last of this type of small-scale quarry, where the topsoil is scraped away to expose the stone: holes in the ground that would once have been commonplace across Britain, supplying the raw material for more or less every homestead, church, castle or bridge in medieval times. It would be easier to get what I needed elsewhere in border country, but even in the drizzle it is an enjoyable place to share with the wild creatures that have adapted to these semi-abandoned

havens. The reedy pool in the corner was full of newts. A tree
creeper scooted across the exposed stone face. In the marginal
woodland that camouflaged us from the nearby lane, a motion-
less tawny owl sat watching for the entire time I laboured.
When done and loaded, I made the usual long precipitous
clamber up to the black walls that crowned the castle's rocky
crag.

Leaning against the rampart tower, the remoteness of its
situation and its glossary of belvederes, berms and breastworks,
donjons, loopholes and oubliettes reminded me that this castle
architecture was used by both the Crusaders who had gone to
the Holy Land as well as its Muslim defenders whom they had
gone to conquer. There, instead of the Norman square keep,
like the White Tower at the Tower of London, the Crusaders
encountered fortified keeps protected by concentric walls with
bastions that worked as a castle within a castle. This technology
transfer from the east could be seen in Carreg Cennen's concentric walls that break down into walled cells. The rectangular
outer ward, filled with the ruined walls of limekilns, stables
and workshops, was a killing zone designed to trap intruders.
From the colossal tower of death the defenders could fire
projectiles, hurl missiles and tip burning liquids from the loop
and murder holes above. If this formidable series of obstacles
was overcome, opponents were then forced to storm the narrow
walkway across drawbridges that could be lifted to leave an
unassailable chasm.

Here an aristocracy of Celtic, French, Scandinavian and
Anglo-Saxon origin used military technology that had been
taken over from the Romans by Arab generals. This knowledge
had in turn been used to oppress the last of the Keltoi, the

descendants of the Britons who were recorded by Julius Caesar in 55 BCE and who had been pushed west over many centuries.

Having loaded the truck and left Wales behind, I followed the ancient road south in the wake of those nameless old hands from Malmesbury to the city of Wells where, within the span of their working life, the world of the Romanesque disappeared.

At the point on the road where it seems to pause before tipping over the edge of the escarpment of the Mendip Hills, I pulled over to take in the flatlands that spread far into the distance. The Somerset Levels look watery, gridded out with drainage ditches and rivers and interrupted by mumps and tors – small hills that break up the peaty monotony. However, the eye is drawn to the compact, low-slung city gathered around a pair of church towers at the foot of the ridge. At one end of town is St Cuthbert's, tall, slender and pinnacled, the perfect foil for the wide and tall central tower of its overbearing relative: the Cathedral Church of St Andrew.

Reversing under the Bishop's Eye, the gatehouse where the authorities could keep a watchful eye across the marketplace, I entered the precinct of the cathedral and the moated Bishop's Palace where we had already brought some of our kit of gantry, mixer and formwork. The palace is a big rambling complex of halls, rooms and chapels that enclose the skeletal ruins of the earlier roofless great hall surrounded by a walled and moated garden of old-fashioned beauty.

There has always been plenty of work to be done in the city. This time our main task, apart from laying the new pavers, was to span a gap in the battlemented walls of purple conglomerate and old red sandstone with a new arched gateway. I was pleased to be back as the carvings of the cathedral's north porch would help guide my design for a local church, where the foliage detailing of one of its capitals had eroded so much that there was little left to steer the making of its replacement. I wanted to seek the inspiration and guidance of a predecessor from nine centuries earlier, and recreate a very particular style of medieval carving that I had not yet attempted.

A network of culverts feed the moat that encircle the palace from a springhead that perpetually gushes forth. They are the source of the city's origins and gave the place its Saxon name of 'Wella'. Sink a spade into the ground and the hole soon fills with water to within a few inches of the surface. On that morning the spring bubbled up, in a different mood from usual, churning out silt in an aggressive way after a cloudburst on the hills above.

It is easy to imagine ancient people making offerings to the deity that resided here. I wondered if, as at Aquae Sulis, the Romans ever tossed lead curses and prayers into the spring. We once repaired a damaged child's stone coffin, recently vandalised in the cathedral's cloisters, that had been excavated next to the spring, one of many found around the foundation of what was a mausoleum or shrine, Roman in origin.

A Saxon community continued the settlement of Wells around its spring. Around 705 CE, during St Aldhelm's time, a 'mynster' church dedicated to St Andrew was built next to a holy well. It seemed appropriate that the great flank of the cathedral that filled the skyline should be moored comfortably in the centre of so much wateriness, as the word 'nave' comes from the Latin for ship. I tossed a coin into the well, paying my respects to whatever forces were at work in the spring, before heading back to the palace.

Studying the adjacent transept I was pleased to see the familiar but fading handiwork of a team of masons who may have come down from Malmesbury. The clues were in the prevalence of arches built without capitals, where the moulding passed up and over the windows without a break, and in the panels of blind arcading that were also free of capitals. Here the pointed style is embraced in the earliest type of truly Gothic arch. Proportionally very acute – narrow by comparison to height – these openings, 'lancets', took their name from their resemblance to the head of a spear or lance. The cathedral was built in stages, perhaps as resources allowed. The first phase of construction from about 1175 created the main body and the lower parts of the tower and transepts. The topmost part of the nave wall, the clerestory, was filled with slightly later pointed windows that had broadened out as fashion changed.

This was known as the 'French style' until nicknamed 'Gothic' by the Florentine writer Vasari at the time of the Renaissance as a disparaging description of an architectural style that he considered to be barbaric. It was not until Thomas Rickman published *An Attempt to Discriminate the Styles of English Architecture from the Conquest to the Reformation* in 1817 that English medieval architecture was systematically classified and subdivided into three main periods: Early English (*c.*1175–1275), Decorated (*c.*1275–1380) and Perpendicular (*c.*1380–1520). The ubiquity of the Gothic style and its later plundering by the Victorians for new churches, railway stations and town halls means it's a style we take for granted today, but in the years 1175 through to 1220 it must have felt as if something supernatural had seized the earth. This was a time where art and science combined to advance building technology and engineering in a cultural revolution that was to last until the Dissolution of the Monasteries in 1539.

When Bishop Reginald Fitz Jocelyn and his unknown architect laid the foundation stone at the east end of Wells Cathedral in 1175, they must have known that they were taking a risk, moving away from the previous vogue for dark, massive interiors with small windows that the local masons knew how to build. A degree of trial and error must have come into play as they interpreted the new theologically driven taste for church walls to be built solely to support glass windows.

Fitz Jocelyn was in the thick of the events that gave rise to one of the biggest cultural and social changes yet seen in the British Isles, following the murder of the Archbishop of Canterbury Thomas à Becket in 1170. As penance, King Henry II sponsored many new churches in the latest fashion, funded by pilgrimage and taxation. Fitz Jocelyn had studied in Paris in the early 1160s and, in common with every other churchman of that time, had been enormously influenced by the completion of the most revolutionary building project of the early Middle Ages. The dedication of the new east end and choir of the Royal Basilica of Saint-Denis on 11 June 1144 marked the completion of a structure that had been built in an entirely new way.

Abbot Suger is generally credited as the creative force behind the new choir, designed to improve access for the crowds of pilgrims drawn to the shrine of its eponymous martyr, and so provide a greater income for the cathedral. Suger couldn't have done it without the unknown master who responded to his dramatic vision. Suger thought that radiant light was the manifestation of the creator, and he had a strong desire to engineer ways of allowing new light to shine through larger windows into the space where Norman darkness once prevailed. The unknown master mason responded by drawing together and engineering in a completely new way the latest advances of ribbed vault, as well as the pointed arch and window. This was the first architecture where the masonry emphasis was thrust upwards in a way that seemed to ignore gravity. This new style appreciated that the connection between architecture and its purpose should be manifest; Gothic churches were thus not only filled with symbolism, but became symbols themselves.

Heavy columns were replaced with a central shaft of reduced diameter, surrounded by bunches of slender columns that flowed freely upwards into a seemingly weightless vaulted arch. The patterns of light and shadow, good and evil, were at the heart of the new style. Suger intended his church to be a physical embodiment of the belief that God could be approached by the beauty and harmony of a building's structure.

Although Suger was a statesman and friend of Louis VI – nicknamed 'the Fat' – he was not right about everything. Such as his famous pronouncement that 'The English are destined by moral and natural law to be subjected to the French, and not contrariwise'.

The outside walls of Wells might have looked inert and stable, but the old Muslim saying 'the arch never sleeps' allowed me to visualise them enclosed in a glow where colossal amounts of energy and force drained down to the ground around either side of each arch. The inclination of the cathedral's walls is to push out sideways and here the eternal structural game of thrust and counter-thrust was won, in the same way as at Saint-Denis. Necessity led to the most marvellous and beautiful of structural concepts, without which the Gothic world would have never got off the ground: the flying buttress.

I realised that the nave's flying buttresses remained hidden, covered by the lean-to roof of the aisles, almost as an embarrassment, unlike its contemporaries elsewhere. At Wells' near cousin, Salisbury Cathedral, the flying buttresses are clearly seen to be doing their job as they rise above the aisles. One of my first tasks while training at Salisbury was to help repair one. From the scaffolding that enclosed each upright section, one could sense the dynamic importance of the flying buttresses, as via a half-arch they channelled the outward thrust from the base of the central tower. A large square pinnacle, eroded and worn down to a witch's hat, its outer surface turned to loose sand by acid rain and great age, topped off the structure. Although severely decayed, it still managed to act as a dead weight to direct the stresses down via the aisle's thick walls.

This development away from the groin and round-arched rib vault allowed the creation of a more elegant interior, open and lighter, as supporting walls no longer needed to be so strong and to some extent could be replaced with glass. Walls with windows became windows with walls. This also made it possible to span greater distances between columns that had become thinner. To reduce weight further, the vault webs – the infill area between the ribs – were packed with tufa, a porous lightweight rock.

The formidable strength of this vaulting system can be seen in St Andrew's near contemporary, the Cathedral of Notre-Dame de Paris. In the aftermath of the fire of 2019, many tons of burning roof timbers and molten lead that once protected the nave collapsed onto the vault below, which, apart from two sections, somehow held. Some put this down to a miracle, but instead I suggest that prayers are said for the souls of the unknown masters, masons and labourers who put together the interlocking system of pointed arches, ribbed vaulting and flying buttresses.

Crossing back over the drawbridge into the Bishop's Palace, I stood in front of the gap in the precinct wall, five yards wide, which the new semi-circular archway was to span. The arch was a simple affair built with giant blocks. The architect's concept had been interpreted and the springing point – the place where the underside of the arch rises from the supporting wall – had been calculated. Its segmented, or Syrian arch, as it is also known, was a simple task to set out. All that was required was to bridge the opening with an arch that was less than 180 degrees of a semicircle.

Cutting the masonry would be straightforward enough – the difficult part would be raising the huge sections to span the gap. Normally work like this would be done by hand, but to save time the sawyers at the quarry had removed most of the waste from the car engine-sized blocks before their final dressing. Working on one's knees, the first step is to transpose the architect's design into a one-to-one scale drawing with a thick carpenter's pencil. Then, unrolling a large plastic sheet of template material a yard deep across the drawing, the lines could be inked onto the transparent plastic with a Chinagraph pencil. Just to make sure the drawings were accurate I took them to the palace to offer them up in situ. With one end temporarily fixed to the wall with batten and screws, pulled tight across the gap and fixed the other side, I stepped back and looked to see if it would all come together.

The design would then be divided into its sections, and the template profile cut to suit each individual block. The method for cutting arch stones such as these remains pretty much the same whatever the profile or shape of the arch. With the profile marked along the front and back faces, the unrequired parts could then be scooped away. The masonry process is based on the simple act of roughing out waste material: the giant nail-like tungsten-tipped waster, a type of punch, is the most efficient tool for the job. With it in my left hand and the power unit, the trusty four-pound hammer that is just an extension of my arm in my right, I am ready. The impact of hammer on punch is a controlled act of violence that is repeated time and again across the width of the block.

With the waste removed to reveal a rough arc, I go over it with a claw chisel. Then it is ready for some finessing. Changing from hammer to mallet, all my concentration is focused on the broad edge of the chisel as I send it zipping along the surface to leave a smooth finish. Getting this right is all about practice. Each repetitive blow quickly blends into a natural rhythm. Time passes quickly while mind and body coordinate subconsciously with the application of accuracy and fine judgement in the endless repetition of an operation. If interrupted and the autopilot is disengaged, inevitably it is human nature to think too hard about the task in hand and, on returning, be more likely to make a mistake. To get back on track, Technotronic's 'Pump Up the Jam' is a useful earworm to call up; its rhythm of 125 beats per minute matches perfectly with my own natural pace of mallet on chisel.

When finished, the blocks were delivered to the palace, where a robust wooden formwork was waiting to support the arch from underneath. Each was too big to lift manually, so a hire crane that crawled across the croquet lawn on caterpillar tracks did the heavy lifting using the Lewis-pin method. From left to right they were dropped into position with only the usual thin wipe of lime putty between each joint.

A few days later, when it had all settled, Andy and I returned to take away the timber formwork. A nimble cock wren trilled its sharp way around the yew tree and other ancient plantings as we braced ourselves to knock the folding wedges away from the foot of the formwork. We hailed Mary and in unison popped the wedges loose. The wooden frame wobbled for what seemed like moments. The cock wren shut up, silence filled the air and breaths were held before each of us let out a silent whistle of relief as the formwork dropped and the arch supported itself. All that was left to do then, apart from sweetening-in the inevitable slight overlap between the joints, was to rebuild the crenellations with the Pennant sandstone from Carreg Cennen Castle.

A couple of days later, I strode away over the cobbles and Pennant flagstones toward the cathedral's north porch to do some preparatory sketches of its foliate capitals. This route is only a few hundred yards, but it gives a glimpse of the England that vanished as a consequence of the Reformation. It was Whit Wednesday and the marketplace was bustling with traders and their customers. Yet again, it became the secular focal point of the city as it had done weekly over the ages. The leat that eased its way down the high street from the Holy Well would, I imagined, once have been useful to wash the blood and offal away at the end of the day.

I squeezed through the crowds and paused under Penniless Porch, a vaulted medieval gateway where the profane world of the marketplace was left behind as one entered the sacred liberty of St Andrew – the walled precinct that encloses the cathedral. The porch provides an oblique view of one of the great sights of England, the cathedral's West Front that at first glance could be taken for a grandstand, populated with hundreds of life-sized stone figures. These characters, however, were not looking down on us but had been designed for us to look up at them, as its series of platforms recorded the complete history of man's salvation from Creation to the Apocalypse.

In contrast with Malmesbury and developments in France, where the focus was around the doorways, here things were quite different. The facade was simply a rectangle laid on its side as a double square from which lifted two low towers at either end. Its three diminutive entrances were overwhelmed by the theatrical scale of the great man-made cliff face that towered over them. In the thirteenth century there had clearly been a tectonic shift, not only in aesthetics but also in funding and administration to undertake this enormous project that would have drawn masons and carvers from all over Europe. As the art historian Nikolaus Pevsner observed:

When compared to French and German sculpture at the time, the individual quality could be found wanting in places, but there is little in Europe to compare with the quantity of figures that survive at Wells, where about half of the three hundred and forty or so originals [can] still be seen.

I thought the best way to appreciate this history of man's redemption was to lie down on the warm flagstones and look up. With the aid of binoculars I sought out one figure in particular, that of Athelstan, the first Saxon king of all England who was rightly situated in an elevated position, with deeply folded drapery covering his legs and throne. Damp-folds had been replaced by loops of cloth, in a style unique to Wells. Up high, the life-sized figure seemed well proportioned, but I thought back to the plaster cast of Athelstan in the city's museum, where he presented a very different pose when viewed up close. His shortened thighs contrasted with an unrealistic torso from which the hands of overlong arms pushed forward to rest on his knees in an awkward way, elbows up. This distortion of Athelstan's body to present a natural pose to the viewer on the ground is known as fore-shortening and indicated that the sculptors had been schooled in the classical tradition. The success of this effect would have been difficult to judge as it was carved in the workshop, so the carver would have placed the block on a platform tilted backwards on a solid trestle. This meant that as the figure was released from inside, all the sculptor had to do was crouch down at its foot to check whether the right effect had been achieved.

Still on my back, I directed the binoculars to the broad rectangular panel, which sat at the apex of all this wonderment, and covers what would otherwise be the exposed gable end of the nave roof. This contains the Christ figure flanked by seraphim seated in judgement within a mandorla. One hand is raised in blessing, with the other low in welcome. His feet bear the puncture wounds of the Crucifixion.

Below, standing dutifully under cusped canopies, is an Apostles gallery of fifteenth-century date, supported by angels; next a row of very worn out angels, and then, at last, Judgement Day, where naked figures haul themselves out of open coffins, some joyful, others pulling their hair out in despair. The middle-tier niches, which contain stories from the Creation to the Ascension, are interrupted by three pairs of buttresses that prevent this cliff face from falling forward. Life-sized figures sit and stand in the niches, martyred virgins to the left, martyred kings to the right. They mix in with a rough lot of knights just back from the Second Crusade, then more kings, courtiers and ecclesiastics, both male and female, from the history of the Church. Below the second drip-course quatrefoil are half-length angels floating on clouds, arms outstretched to fill the space. Biblical scenes, such as the tale of Jesus among the doctors, are enlivened with donkeys. The sculpture wraps itself around the north tower, where it is best preserved. One individual who seems to have dropped his trousers is in fact Moses wading across a rippling calf-deep Red Sea.

The homogeneity of it all is striking. Whoever was in charge had exerted such an enormous amount of stylistic control that it would have been unsustainable over a long period. From about 1220, when its building commenced, the whole scheme took a little over twenty years to complete. Standardisation helped speed things along. Blocks of the same size and profile would have been produced on the equivalent of a medieval production line that led to increased efficiency and time saving. As at Stonehenge, we can look in vain for a continuation of the work that this team created, which was among the best in Europe at the time, but it seems they just slipped away, a few at a time, on to the next job as different phases were completed.

The quarry for Wells was only a few miles away at Doulting, the village where the saintly Aldhelm had died. I wondered if he had also thrown his gauntlet down there, as he had at Hazelbury. Doulting is a variant of Bath stone, known in geological circles as an inferior oolite. This does not mean that it is worse than other Bath stones, but that the generic Bath stones of the great oolite group overlie it. It is denser and richer in fossilised organic material, which makes it harder to work, but it cuts cleanly rather than crumbling like some other variants of Bath Stone.

But as well as its art and architecture, the West Front is important for its ground-breaking programme of work to conserve the sculpture during the late 1970s and early 1980s. It created a philosophy of work that guides the hand of the mason-conservator to this day. The solution up until then for the conservation of friable stone sculpture was to pump them with wonder-chemical consolidants that tended to seal the surface and accelerate decay in the same way as I had noticed at Malmesbury's south porch. Architectural detailing was replaced with new stone or damaging, cement-based mortars. Burt Wheeler, the then clerk of works at Wells, experimented with more traditional ways by following a course of minimum intervention, using lime-based mortars and protective coatings. Stone replacement was kept to a minimum. At a recent conference to explore how the experimental work has weathered after three decades of exposure, these techniques were found to be doing their job in a steady way, indicating that with softer lime mortars there is strength in weakness.

★

When the bells of the cathedral started a slow toll, echoing off the secular medieval buildings that bordered the other three sides of the cathedral green, I understood that this place had been designed not only with architecture but music in mind. Here the two worked in harmony with their surroundings to flavour the city. No busker in Penniless Porch could hope to compete with the biggest peal of bells in the country, once it started its slow mathematical build-up. A solitary trombone joined in from the cathedral school's music room. All that was needed was a roll of thunder to conclude the abstract performance, which after ten minutes stopped abruptly. The air seemed to grey as the bells' huge forces dissipated, and it was easy to imagine how important the music would have been that accompanied the processions and outdoor services.

The use of this space increased in frequency over the spring and summer when people had more time on their hands between the time of ploughing, sowing and making hay. The church year is comprised of six seasons – Lent, Easter, Pentecost, Trinity, with a gap to Advent and Christmas – and we were here at its midpoint. In the Middle Ages, Pentecost was the second biggest festival after Easter and thought more important even than Christmas and the principal holiday of the year. The business of outdoor worship and processing would have been unrelenting at that time. It was recorded that the rituals relating to the movable feast of Corpus Christi were performed outside the newly completed West Front at the end of May 1311. The laity would have made the most of the opportunity to have a good time at the many feasts and church ales, games, fairs and markets that took place under the 'bishop's eye'.

The West Front really came into its own on Palm or Yew

Sunday. (In Somerset, as palms were thin on the ground in the thirteenth century, yews, which are easy to find in a churchyard, were handy replacements for the congregation and a contrast with the richness of the procession.) The clergy, clad in their finery, led the way with crosses held aloft as censers were swung to create clouds of incense while they processed from the cloisters to the West Front's closed door. They would have been accompanied by the chanting of 'Gloria, laus et honor' by choristers hidden away in the concealed gallery that was built into the facade and pierced with invisible openings to give the impression of the singing of angels to those in the procession. Those outside would have repeated the 'Gloria' as a chorus. A translation of the first couplet written by St Theodolf of Orleans, from the late eighth or early ninth century, goes:

> All glory, laud, and honour
> To Thee, Redeemer, King,
> To whom the lips of children
> Made sweet hosannas ring.

As the subdeacon struck the door with the staff of his crozier, to allow access into the sacred interior, the hymn ceased. With the opening of the doors, trumpets blazed from the nine mystery openings at the base of the gable and the procession crossed the threshold into the church. At this point the pilgrims re-enacted the triumphal Palm Sunday entrance into Jerusalem at the start of the Passion, with the west doors becoming the gate into the heavenly city.

Time was pressing and I got up from the flagstones, dusted

myself down and turned past 'Kill Canon Corner', where earlier decaying stonework once fell, to the north porch and its marvellous group of instructive capitals that decorate the entrance arches' springing point. Read from left to right, it tells a dramatic narrative in four scenes of the martyrdom of St Edmund who in the Middle Ages was the patron saint of England before St George. The events take place within a forest of stylised foliage known as stiff leaf. The central focus is on Edmund tied to a tree shortly after his capture by Vikings. Confronted with his refusal to renounce his faith, their archers shoot the king through from either side until the arrows stick out of him like a porcupine's quills. Next the saintly king is bent double, a sad figure, head in his hands and about to be beheaded by an axe-wielding Dane with a pudding-bowl haircut, as he refuses to abandon Christ despite his previous ordeal.

In the penultimate scene, a wolf – looking more like a pantomime crocodile – discovers his head, which has been thrown into the forest. The beast recognises him and so guards him until the king's men arrive and discover the severed head. The final scene has his head miraculously rejoined to the body within the royal tomb, and Edmund coming back to life – although much of this capital is now missing.

Oddly, there is no equivalent instructive scheme on the other side of the arch, where the capitals are enriched solely with more stiff-leaf foliage that is anything but stiff. I sketched the lush and lively bulging lobes in clusters of three, deeply undercut to cast shadows, which sprout from stalks that give the form its name. The stiff-leaf capital is an English invention indicative of the new naturalism of the early thirteenth century and is seen to its best advantage on the tops of piers in the choir, nave and transepts. The design is perhaps a conflation of an acanthus oak leaf and a vine leaf that was intended to speak to the viewer of the miraculous transformation of a dead twig into a thing of spring buds and fresh young leaves. In doing so, each foliate capital shares the message of the Resurrection and the promise of eternal life. It is a bridge to earlier pagan beliefs, where the cycle of life, death and rebirth was also represented by the green foliage that sprouts from the mouth and nose of Jack in the Green and the green man.

It was exciting to enter their designer's mind as I tried to work out how the stiff leaf had come together. I had already cut out three quarters of a cylinder on the top part of the stone laid on the bench, a handspan deep. At its base was a smaller cylinder that would later marry up with the shaft, six inches in diameter, upon which the capital was to rest. I then cut the two parts to form the rough shape of an upturned bell, but one with a flat back as, when finished, it was destined to sit against a wall. Normally a job like this would first be modelled in clay – a maquette for the approval of the architect and parishioners. Judging by some of the subject matter woven through the foliage on the work inside Wells, carvers had been allowed a free hand as long as the church was filled with the right sort of images of saints and Bible stories.

With the dummy light in my right hand and a small letter-cutting chisel in my left, I plunged in, following the course of the leafy outlines drawn on the bell. Then with it all set up, I brought a punch into play and removed the waste. It was difficult to visualise the foliage that was hidden within, as I needed to see the different layers within the stone. It was good to be released from the regular beat of the heavier tools, the mallet and claw chisel that I had used to cut the arches. Teasing out the first lobe is the most satisfying moment of all and from then on it all seemed to flow. Electricity courses through my veins as what is locked away within the stone is released. From the first lobe, fronds and stems seem to sprout and unfurl as in real life. The tempo changes and so does the amount of elasticity required of my wrists, the chisel twisting and turning at speed. The dead stone is slowly forced through a man-made metamorphosis into something which when finished will look as if it had been frozen by the same chill wind of the originals from eight centuries before. I work outside to see how the natural light falls on the undercutting as the fronds get deeper and fulfil the need for chiaroscuro.

With the job done, I looked at my sketches and wondered if the secret room above the cathedral's north porch had been used for setting out the rest of the sculpture and stiff leaf, as it retains a remarkable floor where the more experienced masons had once calculated and drawn their designs. I remembered my first visit here as a novice with our tutor, who had worked on the repair scheme to the West Front in the 1980s and was the perfect guide. As he shone his torch across the surface of the floor, its secrets were revealed. Faint scratches in the plaster showed a palimpsest of ogees, radiuses and arcs. When calculations were finished, the drawings would have been obscured by a simple brushing over, and newly scratched lines would show up crisp and white. Over time the floor was covered with disconnected patterns of arcs and lines, recording in the plaster numerous thought processes illustrative of the craft's procedures. The setter-outer, who worked in this surprisingly dark space, made good use of the complex manipulation of just three shapes – the circle, square and equilateral triangle – to create all the various parts of the cathedral.

Only two rooms like this exist in England. The other, at York Minster, is a rather more comfortable place than this garret, with a fireplace and toilet. Why had they chosen to use this space – so ill-lit, out of the way and difficult to get to? Were they not allowed their own space in the workshop? On the other hand, this out-of-the-way-ness meant they would have been undisturbed and I understood that this was a space for thinking and theorising, with the real setting-out taking place on the workshop floor.

From the smallest profile for a hood moulding to establishing the size and bays of the nave, a knowledge was needed of not only proportion, ratio and symmetry, but also geometry – earth-measuring – as recorded by Euclid. In Germany, the Masonic craft guilds of different cathedrals felt the need to create a series of regulations to protect their methods of training. It is recorded in the ordinances of the city of Regensburg that a mason should be able to take the elevation from a ground plan. To do this all that was needed was a large square, a pair of compasses and a single unit of measurement or dimension that would have been set out on the most important measuring instrument, with a variety of names – a pole, perch or rod – that was used for the main dimensions. There was no standardisation at that time and the rod, blacksmith-made and square in section, was about 16½ feet long. A large square was also used to create a method of measurement in a process known as constructive geometry, which was based on its diagonal subdivision known as a quadrature or *ad quadratum* and which could be used to produce other structures including cross-sections.

In common with most large medieval buildings, the simple ratio of one to the square root of two formed the basis for setting out the entire space. Modern researchers waste too much time looking for a Dan Brown-influenced mystical truth when all masons knew in the Middle Ages was how to create the sublime by a few simple calculations. It is as easy to create this ratio on paper, as it would have been in the cathedral's cloisters with just a set square, ruler or even a length of rope. To a square, add a diagonal line between two of its corners. The relationship between the length of this line and the side of the square form the vital square root of two proportions – scale this up and its patterns can be seen in every aspect of the cathedral's design.

Knowledge of Euclid's *Elements* had disappeared from the West until the diligent work of Muslim scholars reintroduced it via Adelard of Bath's translation early in the twelfth century. Its rediscovery helped to spark the Gothic architectural revolution. I pondered over Euclid's forty-seventh problem – also known as the Egyptian string trick – useful when the set square is left at home. By marking out twelve knots as units of measurement onto a piece of string – feet, inches, yards or centimetres, to suit one's needs – and joining the two ends, it is easy to create a triangle. With the knots pegged at points 3:4:5, a moment of epiphany will reveal that the angle between the 3 units and the 4 units is, of necessity, a right angle. But it is proposition eleven in book one that is perhaps most essential for understanding Gothic design. It explains the importance of bisection in the construction of angles and shows that where a pair of identical circles intersect at their midpoints, a *vesica piscis* becomes evident – a lens shape familiar as the mandorla that encloses the Christ figures at Malmesbury and Autun. By coincidence, the bisection (a straight line drawn from top to bottom of the *vesica*) will have a square root of the Holy Trinity – the magic number three. By drawing a line between the midpoints of the circles, a perfect equilateral triangle can be constructed with the top of the *vesica* as its pinnacle. From this it is straightforward to set out many other aspects, including the conventional pointed Gothic arch that only uses two centres to construct its arcs.

Behind a wooden door marked 'Private', a stone spiral stairway leads to the triforium gallery, so called as it has three openings onto the nave, where a walkway above the aisle vaulting leads to the west end. This is the place to come and lean on a column and try to understand the cathedral. The long nave stretches away to create a long open vista that would have continued to the high altar. Compared with what had come before, the interior space looked light and graceful, filled with the 'superessential light' that Abbot Suger believed was the essence of the Creator.

As we stood there as novices, our tutor suggested that we imagine away the great strainer arches that today interrupt the view through the tower crossing. The interior architecture is plain but with a greater horizontal emphasis when compared to French cathedrals of the time. The stiff-leaf capitals that decorate each pier enrich it. When painted, the nave would have had the feeling of a tree-lined avenue.

Instead of going back to the palace via the West Front and

marketplace, I cut across the nave to the transept to exit through the cloisters and a door to the palace grounds. As with the north porch carvings of St Edmund's demise, more instructive cartoons could be followed on the capitals of the south transept. A man pulls his mouth down on one side, miserable with toothache, his gaze directed to the floor, which may be a reference to the thirteenth-century effigy of Bishop William Bytton who still rests in the south choir aisle and whose likeness is incised into the flat slab of blue lias stone.

Blue lias, which derives its name from the Somerset dialect for 'layers', is a limestone extracted in thin beds in a few low quarries around Glastonbury and the Polden Hills. It is a smoky grey colour and contains interesting fossils. Once when splitting slabs for paving at Muchelney Abbey I opened a split paver as carefully as a book, only to reveal the shoulder blade of a young plesiosaur, a long-necked carnivorous marine reptile that died out about 65 million years ago.

William Bytton would have stood out in a crowd in the Middle Ages as he had a full set of teeth. After he died, pilgrims suffering from toothache would come to Wells to touch his stone, and his effigy is particularly pitted and worn around his remarkable teeth. His tomb became such a popular attraction that throughout the later Middle Ages Bishop Bytton brought in the greatest amount of offerings, second only to those dedicated to the Virgin.

Another story is told on four capitals that enclose one of the transept piers. The fruit-stealers' story, a warning about the wages of sin, starts with a pair of thieves who have crept into an orchard and filled their basket. One looks guiltily over his shoulder towards the second capital. They are spotted by a wood-cutting neighbour, axe in hand, who tells the owner by pointing at the scrumpers with one outsized finger. One has fled the scene in the third capital, and the farmer has grabbed the other. In the fourth, he hits the miscreant so vigorously with his pitchfork that the thief's hat jumps off behind his head as his apples spill out of their basket.

I slipped past the foot of the cathedral's library and went out of the cloisters on my way back to the Bishop's Palace to pack away our gear, tackle and trim, and prepare for the next job. It was a pity to leave behind the sparse but fresh spring of the Early English, but I was looking forward to the summer warmth that came with the next iteration of Gothic style, known as the Decorated. This was a period when the austere pointed lancet window would give place to something altogether more evolved and naturalistic, as a result of evolution rather than revolution such as had come before.

INTERLUDE

SUMMER SOLSTICE

I returned to Stonehenge on the eve of the longest day. I had come to see if the astronomical alignment marking the position of the winter solstice sunrise would continue to where the sun set when viewed from the megalith's opposite face on midsummer's eve. Could it be possible that the monument, far better known for its alignment with the summer solstice sunrise, also marked the point when the Neolithic astronomer-priests would know the exact moment when solstice eve began?

It was around 8 p.m. and Violet, my daughter, and I watched the sun glower low over the copse of Robin Hood's Ball, where a small stone circle lay hidden on the south-western horizon. We squeezed through the excited throng gathering within the horseshoe setting of trilithons and stood beneath the same stone – number 56. This time I held Vi up so her nose touched the opposite south-eastern corner of the stone and she cast her eye westward along its perfectly flat plane. As the sun slowly lowered toward a solitary outlying boulder, my pulse quickened as our star touched its top and slowly disappeared, exactly as anticipated.

We sat down on stone fifty-five. I told Vi about my own

small-scale experiences with the sarsen upright in our garden, and then scaled up the tale to accommodate the entire ancient community involved. I tried to describe the huge physical effort that would have been involved in the transportation of the thirty-odd-ton obelisk, how the faces would have been dressed with nothing more than mauls, and it would have been articulated into the carefully considered position it still occupies.

She jabbed me in the arm with an index finger. 'Yes, but what's it for?' I had a crack at explaining the part that was almost beyond comprehension, that all we could see about us had been conceived as a functioning scientific instrument. Normally, scientific instruments require some sort of mechanism and moving parts, but here (I waved my arm around in an arc) this function would have been fulfilled by the priests themselves, using observation to aid the computation of the calendar to guide the forthcoming agricultural year and connect in some way with their gods.

We dozed fitfully over the short night atop an outlying round barrow covered in a few nettles, tall grasses and the brown stems of knapweed broomrape, a parasitic wild flower. We could sense, even through the low mist, the crowd's anticipation growing as they waited for the sunrise.

With dawn beginning to warm the horizon we turned our back on the stones and stumbled away in the dark across the sheep-cropped turf. We had decided to approach the place along the processional Avenue towards the henge's main entrance. At each step forward the distant monument's inky silhouette rose higher against the star-flecked southern sky while behind us the horizon's orange fuzz indicated that the rays of the solstice would soon pass this way as well. We stopped by the Heel Stone, which marks where the Avenue enters the henge earthwork, and were made aware of the solstice moment by twenty thousand smart-phones flashing into life in front of us, a spectacle that was almost more awesome to witness than the sun, which had begun its ascent into the sky over our shoulders.

Tired after tramping about all night, we drove home exhausted and slept for the rest of the morning. The following day it was work as normal, and the tying up of a few loose ends at an old job. I made the short journey from home to the now-deserted medieval village of Old Dilton, where the church, dedicated to St Mary, had somehow survived. I arrived as the sun was rising and, with my head full of the events of the morning before, the possibility suddenly dawned on me that the position of medieval churches such as this one could have likewise been determined by solar observation.

As the daylight increased, the Westbury White Horse – a chalk figure cut into the escarpment of Salisbury Plain a couple of miles distant – was revealed. As the eastern horizon could not be seen from the church, I wanted to know how accurately it had been set out. Did it face due east or not?

I wondered if St Mary's orientation could have been achieved with the aid of a rudimentary compass. The early builders were known to have used a naturally magnetised piece of magnetite, which when hung from a string will rotate to indicate north. This lodestone, which was christened 'the finger of God', was used surprisingly often to determine true east. This would have been the first act before the site was pegged out in the direction of Jerusalem, which would have determined the orientation of the church. It was the same principle that Muslims had developed with the compass to determine the accurate direction of Mecca.

The word 'lodestone' comes from the Middle English for 'course stone' or 'leading stone', from the now-obsolete meaning of lode as a journey or way. At Old Dilton, which was established in the 1300s, the compass bearing was, I discovered, a few degrees south of east, something that seems to be a pattern with some other churches, such as the abbeys of Sherborne and Malmesbury, also established around this time and likewise dedicated to the Virgin. The discrepancy may be explained by the wandering nature of the North Pole and the earth's magnetic field, or by churches being aligned towards sunrise on the feast day of the patron saint. I guess that topography, the direction of an adjacent stream or the line of a low hill where the place is situated, may equally have determined the orientation.

West Kennet Long Barrow, the temples of the Roman Baths and the cathedral of St Denis in Paris were all erected with the same intention: to act as a catalyst for religion by placing the worshipper in the direction relevant to their God. All share a common bearing, found in the etymology of the word 'orientation' which comes from the Latin *oriens* meaning 'the rising sun, the East', a direction of influence that was to continue to refine the sinews of English Gothic architecture's next change of style.

The main reason that I had come to Old Dilton was that the church's porch needed a final coat of limewash to release the last payment of what had been a long on-and-off sort of job where a damp summer had meant that the multiple coats of lime plaster we had applied had taken longer to set. It is a place I know intimately, as over the years we have spent many hours keeping its fabric together – preventing the ingress of water and keeping an eye on its walls which were prone to brown rot and weevil infestations.

This church has a bit of everything about it, history having touched it lightly but regularly over the centuries with the techniques, materials and architectural fashions of the time. From its foundations laid in the thirteenth century it evolved in stages – withstanding the fundamentalism of the Reformation and the English civil war – until Victorian times.

The story of St Mary's is typical of the mixed bag of styles that can be seen in small-town and village churches throughout Britain. A railway track and lush pasture drop into the dell that hides it from the outside world. In his *Guide to English Parish Churches* Sir John Betjeman describes it as one of the most atmospheric in Wiltshire. The village was abandoned and its houses and mills were taken down to build a new village that developed around the railway halt a few fields away. A slender iron cross projects like a television aerial from above the walnut grove that cosseted its once-failing walls. Its silhouetted spirelet with its flute-like openings rose from the edge of the Biss brook, a feeder for the River Avon whose waters drove the three long-gone mills where the county's renowned broadcloth was manufactured.

Drowsy wasps gathered among the ivy that covered the fourteenth-century rubble walls, where past neglect meant the masonry had been stitched together by the ivy stems. Over the years they had increased their sinuous grip on the little church, rendering its walls invisible to a passer-by in the dark, until we had cut the stumps at the base of the wall and peeled it away like a thick green carpet.

Passing under the high gable of the chancel's east end, my head was occupied with thoughts of what pigment to add to the limewash, as well as breakfast. I took a note of the church's orientation and turned the corner to the priest's door. Behind loomed an eighteenth-century box tomb, made from finely cut Bath stone. Four of its five surfaces had been carved with twisting stems of acanthus that hid gurning, flute-blowing cherubs with shepherd-boy faces. The lid provided a dedication and description of those who were not allowed to rest inside the church, such as the farmers and tradespeople of the parish. Here they lay with their kin, piled one atop the other beneath their carved stone box in the black earth.

Working the heavy old blacksmith-made key into the sticky Tudor lock, my mind adrift, I noticed a heavy oily smell, rich, like a newly cleared ditch, that was accompanied by an almost imperceptible groan coming from the small adjacent porch. I increased my wrist pressure on the stuck key and stared at the bat guano, sprinkled like hundreds and thousands over that left by the swallows which nested in the eaves. Through the gloaming my light-adjusting eyes slowly made out what I took to be a low box tomb, before focusing on a figure slowly raising itself onto an elbow. The man sighed deeply, breaking the silence as he cleared his tubes with a window-rattling hawk. Trembling cupped hands lit a roll-up that illuminated natty dreadlocks and a Guy Fawkes beard. My heart racing, I breathed out in relief and went over to lean against the porch's arch, where I noticed a small, clay-covered bundle on the stone bench beside him. My new acquaintance inclined his head to the bundle and said, 'If you want to cook the hotchi-witch, first drop him in a trough and kill him, makes him easier to cook, see.' Leaning forward, the finest example of a vagabond I was ever likely to encounter rummaged around in his old hessian sack. His serious demeanour brightened and he rose for the day, snapping open a can of Scrumpy Jack. After plunging half of it down his neck, he continued, 'But you have to be careful to avoid his poisonous bite.'

I could only nod in dumb agreement until I found the courage to speak. 'Er, OK. Will you be staying here long?' It was now obvious that he had moved into the newly plastered porch that was awaiting its last coat of limewash. 'Does it taste of chicken?' I ventured, nodding in the direction of the bundle. He fixed me with the rose-tinted gaze that only damaged capillaries can provide, and responded as if talking to a child, 'No, you daft'un, it tastes of hedgehog.' I decided to cut my losses, and get on with another task inside.

Going through the priest's door, one is greeted by a school-room balcony squeezed into a floor over the vestry. The fireplace it contains is the church's only nod to modernity or comfort; this was a place free from electricity and with its occasional services held by candlelight. Bleached oak and elm, whitewash and a strong feeling of Dissenter spirit predominated. At some point in the distant past a communion table had replaced the altar, reinforcing the idea that this was more a house for meeting than for devotion.

Its walls went up as part of an ecclesiastical building boom, a dividend of the monies that poured in as a consequence of the slaughter of Thomas à Becket in 1170. They looked like they had not been decorated since the Puritans painted out the medieval saints and testaments at the time of the Commonwealth. St Mary's, it seems, missed out on the innovations that came from France, which were to become the defining features of the Gothic style's next phase. Little else had been attempted since the eighteenth century, when the rest of the church was crowded out by box pews from the time of the Georges. Although St Mary's is now redundant, services only taking place on special days, the ramblers, locals and ancestor-seekers who come here understand that this is a place where prayer has the power to be acknowledged.

Sat in a pew, listening to the sermon from its triple-decker pulpit in the candlelit dusk of a harvest festival service, one feels St Mary's come into its own. My mother, who would accompany me to these festivals, would always ask the same question: 'How old is this place?' I would explain that although a foundation stone would have been laid sometime in the 1300s, it is like most other rural churches, a mixture of dates and styles. If there was a Saxon minster or a Norman establishment here, then the physical evidence is slim. An earlier church may have existed but, as with St Laurence's in nearby Bradford-on-Avon, the original structure could have been demolished and re-incorporated into the walls of the new building. The leaf-shaped heads of the windows are the features that allow the building to be properly dated. These foils (derived from the Latin for leaf, *folium*) are so named from the number of cusps (small arcs projecting inwards that form the outline of the leaf design). If three-lobed or trefoil they are of the Early English style (thirteenth century); four-lobed or quatrefoil Decorated (fourteenth century); five-lobed cinquefoils (fifteenth century). When the north aisle was added in the fifteenth century, to accommodate the growing congregation, its window design culminated in the Tudor square window head, a style that remained in vogue for a couple of hundred years.

This is a place that feels as if it has been left behind. Elsewhere church window openings grew larger and cusped heads became unfashionable, but in St Mary's the stone roof vault that would have spread the weight of the arch in a more elegant way is missing; the ceiling is made from wooden lath and plaster. Elsewhere, apart from the pointed arches of the north aisle arcade that leans at a ridiculous angle, the Gothic movement seems to have had limited impact on the interior – it doesn't even have a chancel arch. Its interior, dressed not in stone but timber, is what moves this place into a different class.

Benches were a form of furniture common to most English churches and became increasingly popular with the rise of the sermon as the main act of worship during the Georgian era. The economy-minded congregants at Old Dilton had consolidated their stock of old medieval benches, enclosing them with boxes: here, a section of ancient rood screen; there, carved work saved from some local manor house. The oak panels with elm seats and floorboards formed a truly harmonious concoction. Doors with locks – the keys having long since disappeared – bore witness to their installation at the expense of the parishioners.

Climbing the steps to the triple-decker pulpit and its tester – a sounding board designed to deflect the sermon down to those below – I imagined hectoring the Puritan parishioners, sat stolidly in their pews below. Testing the tester, I announced, 'Here endeth the lesson', and the echoes sniggered briefly through what I thought was an empty church. Then I noticed the vagabond in one of the box pews. He unexpectedly lifted up his arms in devotion and recited a line that I have never heard or seen written in any book: 'As we were unable to remain holy in Thy presence, we wouldst cloister ourselves from thee.'

Old Dilton suffers from the usual range of problems we have

encountered over the years. The diamond-hard cement was picked out from the walls and replaced with something more sympathetic – the secret mortar recipe from Avebury's Nonconformist chapel with its soft chalk/lime mixture. We reduced the level of the damp soil beneath the floorboards so as to take away the food source for the brown rot's fruiting bodies. I sieved each shovelful for interest and found much evidence of past parishioners. Lost between the floorboards and slipped under the pews I found various treasures: pins, marbles, clay candle-holders, musket balls, desiccated rats, more pins, buttons, teeth, one copper groat of Charles I, sections of clay pipe, bits of pot, nails, one shark's tooth and an ammonite suture. Pins were commonly used from the fourteenth to the seventeenth centuries to secure ruffs, skirts, veils and partlets; they were handmade and expensive, so their loss for the woman concerned – as well as the dapper chap whose ruff unwrapped – would have been awkward and annoying.

This was also a place of graffiti but not of the defacing type. The oak pews and rough limewashed stone provided a base for short messages, curious cartoons, masons' marks and autographs. The work of more modern artists could also be seen: an American soldier, Harold Cypher, and some of his pals had pencilled their names above a door arch just a couple of weeks before D-Day in May 1944. I hoped he had survived the landings in Normandy.

That the interior of St Mary's had survived at all was down to fashion, or rather the lack of it. Electricity and the railway had bypassed the hamlet. Even the other buildings had been taken down stone by stone to go back up again around the new halt. The sudden disappearance of its parishioners, who a key-holder told me were noted for 'singing in a primitive style', and the mothballing of the church saved it from the worst excesses of the Victorian restorers.

This 'backwardness' can be seen in the local nature of the materials from which it was built. St Mary's would have been a building typical of the pre-industrial age, its style a product of the underlying geology. The bedrock it stands on reveals its existence not only in the soil and the plants and animals but in the local buildings themselves. It gives them a particular contextual *terroir*, as the French put it so well. These subtly differing characteristics are things that can be seen and sensed across Britain, from inside the West Kennet Long Barrow, around the high crosses of Iona and even within the Roman Baths, where the *genius loci* – the spirit of the place – is perhaps strongest of all.

As the Early English style took hold across the country, the local flavour of cathedrals, abbeys and churches became diluted. Suddenly special materials were being brought in from elsewhere. In particular a kind of stone drawn from the Dorset cliffs would be disseminated along the east and west coasts of Britain and then along the Thames, Humber and Wear, the Severn and Avon to create the frame from which many of the greatest early Gothic cathedrals were built.

7

THE FEAST OF THE TRANSFIGURATION

The clerk of works and I were waiting quietly within the triforium gallery for the service in the chapel below to end. Wafts of incense and the last murmurs of Holy Communion that observed the feast day of Christ's Transfiguration found their way up to us. In the dark-floored space behind where we were stood, the plaster casts of near life-sized medieval statuary looked as if they were ready to play a game of 'Grandmother's footsteps'. This part of Westminster Abbey was an unnerving place to be.

I was shadowing him on his rounds as part of my fellowship training. I had to stifle a squeak when we leant out from the opening and looked down at the straight drop to the swirling thirteenth-century Cosmati pavement, a geometric mosaic of semi-precious stones, Egyptian porphyry and Italian marble, seventy feet below. Behind the high altar is the shrine of Edward the Confessor, monarch and saint, accompanied by the tombs of most of the Plantagenet kings and queens including Henry III, who laid the foundation stone in 1245.

The clerk pointed down to the windows of the old east end of Edward the Confessor's Chapel and suggested that this had been a place of transfiguration in itself. Here the abbey had gone through a complete change of form and appearance when the Norman monastery that once stood on this site was swept away in the mid-thirteenth century and replaced with something more beautiful and spiritual.

It was at this period that the bar tracery window – a more refined form of the simple pair of lancet-shaped windows with an oculus sitting between their pointed arches – was introduced to England from France. Here the central mullion was more delicately cut, with the load on the window from the wall above reduced by strainer arches. These new developments helped to create a French-influenced Gothic church that allowed the use of plain and coloured glass on a bigger scale, lighting interior naves of greater height. At 102 feet tall, Westminster was taller than Wells Cathedral by 35 feet. Elsewhere in the abbey, the nave and transepts are distinguished by the two distinct varieties of marble that give this place much of its character. A couple of hundred years of dust covered the bewigged heads and shoulders of the standing likenesses of eighteenth- and nineteenth-century statesmen, soldiers, priests, heroes and rogues, all sculpted in Italian Carrara marble, a material that was a perfect foil to the deep blue of the polished Purbeck 'marble' columns of the arcade.

London is not blessed with a good choice of local building stone. It has had to put up with a poor lot: the not very durable Reigate and Kentish rag stones. This meant that the stone used to shoulder the burden of the abbey's nave piers and crossing had to be shipped in at great expense from Caen in Normandy and along the coast in Dorset. By the time of the early Plantagenets, transportation by sea of large quantities of building stone to London had become the norm. In 1375, the sailing ketch *Margarite* was listed as having made a trip to London from the Saxon port of Wareham, its consignment of super-dense Purbeck marble used to reinforce and beautify the capital.

Purbeck marble is characterised by densely packed shells of water snails – viviparous creatures which, like the viper or adder, give birth to live young – compressed and solidified during the Jurassic period into a building material that defined the Middle Ages. A process of metamorphosis forms the crystalline character of a true marble when limestone is exposed to great heat or pressure deep within the earth's crust. Purbeck, by contrast, cannot be classified as a true marble as it is simply a densely fossiliferous limestone that can take a polish.

The supply from Dorset to London became an unparalleled logistical operation and one that lingered after Purbeck had gone out of fashion. The churches constructed with Purbeck can be plotted along the east and west coasts and it crops up in places surprisingly distant from its source. Purbeck marble columns were shipped over four hundred nautical miles to their place of work via the River Wear to the Galilee Chapel of Durham Cathedral, which was built around 1175.

Whenever I visit Purbeck to pick up a load of its greatest natural resource, I am reminded how much it appealed to 1930s surrealists such as Paul Nash: the rectangular mass of 'the Isle that is not' is surrounded only on three sides by sea. Symmetry rules Purbeck's landscape, which is divided by a central ridge-line, twelve miles long, that splits the isle in two. The top half is chalk and heathland; the bottom is defined by pale limestone.

At a strategic pivot midway along the ridge, Corfe's great unmissable Tolkienesque fortress commands all approaches. The ridgeway terminates dramatically at cliff faces, its fall punctuated by the great 'tout' – or lookout – of Worbarrow, a mound of beds of Portland and Purbeck stone that projects into the sea at the head of a sweeping bay. Worbarrow holds a rich cache of alabaster, the softest and most water-soluble of stones, which by the fifteenth century had replaced marble for fashionable internal work. It was mainly quarried around Nottinghamshire and was the only stone valued for aesthetic over utilitarian reasons in medieval times. The quality of detail possible when carving alabaster meant that English sculpture and altarpiece panels were well regarded in Europe and exported in huge numbers.

From the dock, a boat could be loaded with creamy Purbeck limestone quarried from the adjacent cliff face and carefully lowered onto the waiting vessels via a special type of wooden crane, known as a 'whim'. This 'marble' made its way to Salisbury Cathedral via a slipway in Wareham or Poole Harbour.

The Isle of Purbeck is home to the finest of public houses: the Square and Compass, where, in common with other local pubs, a good-sized dressed paving could be exchanged for a pint by a quarryman up until the 1930s. The landlord would stockpile this cache before taking it to the stone markets in Swanage.

After my time was done at Westminster, I got to know Purbeck 'marble' more closely at Salisbury Cathedral while working as part of a team that repaired some of the cloisters' unglazed traceried openings. The openings face in to frame the noble

pair of Lebanese cedars that preside over the enclosed quad-
rangle. During our lunch breaks we tried to figure out how
to play the tic-tac-toe and three men's morris boards that had
been cut long ago into the top of the low wall that had been
used as seating by the monks. They would have leant on the
clusters of drainpipe-like Purbeck shafts, made as a single unit
without any joints, that sprouted to support tracery of a style
copied from the east end of Westminster Abbey.

We found each shaft in a sorry state. Cracks running from
top to bottom made us question their ability to support the
two pairs of lancet windows with a central large oculus between
them, all enclosed by a broad arch. This cracking was the curse
of the marble. Sedimentary rocks are laid down in horizontal
layers, 'beds', and should be placed in a building in relation to
this natural bedding plane. The shafts had been put in the
building with their beds in a vertical plane.

Inside, Salisbury shares its emphasis on horizontality with Wells
Cathedral, an accent enhanced by the way the piers of the nave
arcade continue upwards, flush with the wall until interrupted
by a foot-thick horizontal band of projecting stone, the string
course, that draws the eye towards the altar. The triforium arcade
is of the same design as the openings in the cloisters and sits as
a layer that in turn supports the upper part of the nave, pierced
by windows, the clerestory. Here the English peculiarity of
square-end transepts and chancels, an idea taken from the floor
plan of Saxon churches such as St Laurence's in Bradford-on-
Avon, continued to evolve. But the connection with Wells may
be said to end there, for the capitals on the piers at Salisbury
don't have that quantity of embellishment that might 'glut the
eye', as Wren appreciated during his repair survey of 1668. There

is no stiff-leaf carving. Salisbury was the most unified and pure cathedral of Gothic times, and a pause for thought, perhaps, before the onslaught of decoration that was about to gain traction with the masons.

I stood on the off-centre brass dot that indicates the position of the top of the spire if a plumb line is dropped, and looked up. Four piers clad in ornamental shafts of Purbeck marble reached up to the springing point of the fan vaulting, and it was no surprise to see that they had buckled inwards due to the settlement of the shallow foundations on the river gravels and the sidewards thrust of the nave and choir walls.

During tea breaks I would assist the verger as he checked the groundwater levels beneath the tower crossing. Hidden in a Purbeck floor slab, a small cover lifted to reveal a drainpipe that headed down into dark peaty water. With a giant dipstick we ascertained how many feet beneath the floor the water table lay, which was on average only about eighteen inches. The Purbeck shafts often take the credit for bearing the vaulting, but they obscure the great piers of Chilmark limestone that are doing the real work. All this movement in the structure at Salisbury has a knock-on effect and so it was time for the tell-tales (plastic strips stuck over the cracks) that had been fitted throughout the tower to be checked.

Looking up, I imagined the fine fan vault of the tower removed. Its original view would have revealed the pairs of large window openings that created a giant lantern and formed a crown of light. Today's view, which is interrupted by the vault, hides subsequent floors, which provide useful spaces: a belfry and a high-level workshop and store for our tools and materials, and even a loo with perhaps the longest of drops.

We climbed up the hidden spiral staircases passing from floor to floor, with frequent stops to record the movement, or otherwise, of the tower's many cracks. Above us the internal scaffolding of the spire lifted into the darkness. Looking down from the top of the ladder, the octagonal base of the spire rose from the square tower with the aid of a purely Middle Eastern invention from the third century CE. The sight took me back vividly to the road trip where I had last encountered this simple engineering innovation – the squinch – at its point of origin in Fars province in Iran.

At Tehran Airport, Ahmad, the taxi driver, after lengthy negotiation, agreed to take me on an itinerary of early mosques, mausoleums and madrasahs. Everywhere we visited seemed to have some geometric wall design, arch shape or cusped window that I could see were features common to both Islamic and Christian cultures, much of which would not have been out of place in the country churches and cathedrals of south-west England.

The Sassanid Persian Empire of Zoroastrian fire worshippers yielded to the wave of Islamised Arabs in their expansion in the mid-seventh century. Their buildings were to have a profound influence – more than any other – on the architecture of Islam. A key example of this is the citadel that overlooks old, deserted Firuzabad, the capital city of Ardashir the Great, the Sassanian king. I observed how its streets radiated away from the ruined temples at its centre and past city walls that had been set out in an enormous circle. This plan was reflected in the design of Baghdad five centuries later when it became the capital of the new Islamic empire under the Abbasids.

After a tramp through cornfields from the old town to a dry treeless gorge, I paused by a collapsed bridge from the time of the Sassanians that held the curiosity of a five-centred pointed arch.

I found shelter in the custodian's shack. The ancient, fez-sporting Qashqai shared sweet tea, even sweeter pistachio cake and his hubble-bubble pipe. He motioned with a ballpoint towards the visitor's book, which showed only one other weekday signature: that of another Englishman, Neil MacGregor, at that time director of the British Museum.

After my rest, I took in the palaces, noting their well-chosen strategic and defensive position. Protected on three sides by dun-coloured precipices, it was a scramble over low ruined walls towards two prototypes for ancient Persia's most important contribution to architecture. In front, facing out towards an open courtyard, was a great arch, or *iwan*, a form that guides the faithful to the sanctuary and so the correct bearing to Mecca and which characterises the early mosques. Behind it is a dome-capped chamber, its massive walls acting as buttresses. Unlike earlier Roman domes such as the Pantheon, which were built on a cylinder, here for the first time a square space supported a circle, to create a watershed from which sprang two watercourses that over the centuries trickled down to two religions and cultures – medieval Persian and Byzantine Romanesque. The squinch here was simply formed by a pair of quarter-circles that acted as an arch and which drew together the corners of the square. This simple engineering innovation, a dusty landmark in architecture, allowed the transition from square to octagon that in time would allow the development of not only the dome, but also the spire.

The Persians, influenced by Indian culture, had moved mathematics forward to the point where structures such as window tracery and complex decorative motifs could be developed using geometric techniques of great sophistication. These motifs were to catch on throughout the Islamic world. Designs in Spain, such as at the Great Mosque of Córdoba, with its arches, interlaced, branched and full of multifaceted layers, are a close cousin of the cusped openwork of a Gothic tracery window.

Once the tower work at Salisbury was concluded, Andy and I set up shop on our own, learning on the job and earning pretty much nothing as a result. Over time the nature of our work became more complicated, with one of the most challenging of all arriving by pager. I found a phone box and rang the number. 'Would you be so kind as to come along and take a look at a window that we have a problem with?' When I responded that I had a busy programme that day, the normally reticent churchwarden insisted that I drop what I was doing as 'it had fallen out'. Picturing one of its lancets, I headed over 'drectly' with rubble sacks and an Acrow prop.

An hour later, as I drove down Holmstoke's short high street, what I saw almost made me turn around and head home. A black window-shaped void towered above a twisted pile of rubble the size of a small car, from which protruded vaguely recognisable bits of masonry. Mullions, the legs that once held up the arch with its infill tracery, were mixed in with the smashed glass of a window in the Decorated style. According to the churchwarden, the window had blown out in a ferocious storm that I had no recollection of. *Some storm*, I thought, while separating glass from stone, assessing what was reusable and what was destined for the skip. A glazing conservator took care of what was left of the leaded lights.

To prevent the west end of the church collapsing, the yawning cavity was soon shored up with scaffolding and timber. The once-great window, based on a standard design from the 1270s, had illustrated the next logical stage in the development of bar tracery similar to that in the Salisbury cloisters, but more substantial. Here a central rosette or rose (as it is better known) window was supported on either side by a pair of pointed arches that in turn rested on two pairs of long mullions containing five lancets. In France, the rose can be seen in many west ends but in Britain, with the exception of Old St Paul's that burned to the ground during the Great Fire of 1666, rose windows were confined to the north or south ends of a transept. These windows were notoriously unstable, with sudden collapses occurring through the centuries on a regular basis. Normally these were down to stone fatigue or the corrosion of iron fixings that sometimes held the wheel together. Here, I suspected that there was another story.

Andy and I had never tackled a job as ambitious as this and recognised it as an opportunity that we were not likely to encounter again. All of the salvageable elements were taken back to the workshop where they were laid out like a jigsaw on the floor of the setting-out space. The mullions were unable to support their own weight and beyond repair, but provided templates to guide the manufacture of the four new mullion sections, each about five yards long. Much of the tracery was also useless, so we glued the retrieved smashed sections together and from these were able to create 1:1 scale drawings of the gaps between the bits that could be reused. What was spread out on the floor allowed all involved an appreciation of the thirteenth-century masons' work. They had created some of the most free-spirited art in Britain.

By experimenting with nothing more than a pair of dividers, the tracery flowed from the double continuous S-shape of an ogee moulding to create a mesh of complex curves that were simply a framework to support the largest possible area of glass. I thought back to Holmstoke church, its walls supported by flying buttresses, which in turn took the stresses of the ceiling vault to the ground. The apex of this vault was further steadied by a ridge rib, a purely English innovation that ran the length of the nave. Other ribs, known as liernes – from the Norman French for the liana, a luxuriant vine that climbs tree trunks – spread like innumerable matchsticks between the main ribs to form ornamental star shapes where the interfaces were filled with keystones and bosses. These were decorated with a multitude of curvaceous foliage, stiff leaf – but by then less stiff – acanthus, ivy and oak, which bunched out where the ribs met. Strange faces and birds peered out from what had become the realm of the green man, leaves debouching from their grinning, choking mouths, as symbols of rebirth and the cycle of life.

This naturalism continued across the church's exterior walls with the regularly spaced leitmotif of the Decorated style, where three petals of a cupped flower are folded across cricket-ball sized motifs: the ball-flower. The horrible faces of the gargoyles crowded along the parapet and tower, leering down.

Once set up in the workshop the team was able to inscribe the complex profiles of the many templates onto the differing faces of sawn rectangular limestone blocks. One section template would go on the side to show a profile, a bed template on top, two different templates for the bottom, and one on the face that showed the shape of the stone when viewed from the front. With the one-yard-square and foot-thick block laid on its side, it was difficult to visualise the lightness and cleverness of the design that would be reached at the end of the process.

I find it most satisfying doing smaller masonry jobs with hand tools, using the nylon or cherry-wood mallet to propel the chisel along. This, however, was not a job to be done without the help of power. Speed was of the essence, as the price had been based on the creation of each part taking a given amount of time, a method of payment that will be familiar to most craftspeople. The masons who originally created this work were artists, but to us it was more of a job to be done. Creativity was impossible when all of one's energy was focused on keeping a systematic process on track.

We used the modern equivalent of the mallet and chisel – the air-powered, or pneumatic, chisel – to remove the waste that hadn't been drilled in careful and considered sections until just the abstract-looking outline was left. Using power tools may appear to reflect a lack of skill, but to a stonemason it makes no difference as the focus is still at the point where the blade touches the surface. This is the place where, apart from breathing, all that matters is complete commitment to the requirements of the job.

For as well as being more efficient, the pneumatic chisel is gentler on the stone, with each percussive blow being far lighter than that rendered by a mallet, and thus quicker, less damaging and intrusive. Having followed the scribed outlines and hollowed out the stone between what was to become the symbolic ogeed forms of the tracery's ribs, the end was in sight. All that was left was detailing. When each section was completed the tracery was laid out on the workshop floor. The sections were hoisted one by one onto the scaffold, and each part was hefted and lowered into place with only a thin wipe of mortar between where each stone came together.

As the window went up, the joints of the side walls were packed with oyster shells from the collapsed rubble. These, the probable remains of the original mason's lunch, were pushed in between the stones as a useful packer. A few days later, with the scaffold down, the grass raked over for debris one last time and the interior vacuumed, we could observe our work in situ – which is always an odd feeling after many months of staring intently at each component part.

The geometric rose window is not an unusual feature in the churches of the West Country. With Holmstoke finished I was looking forward to seeing an even grander example at the Lord Mayor's Chapel across the College Green from our next job at Bristol's medieval cathedral. As we arrived I was distracted by the cathedral's crenulated and pinnacled silhouette. Why was it not accompanied by the expected flying buttresses around its eastern parts? How were the high vaults inside supported? This was a clue to the unique interior that is as impressive as that to be found at Wells.

The cathedral has two lady chapels. Just off the north transept, the Elder Lady Chapel dates from the early thirteenth century. There is a clear connection to Wells Cathedral. I wondered if they had used the same templates, particularly in the arcading that lined both walls and in the spandrels which are filled with entertaining sculptures, many in the form of animals and stiff-leaf carving. One of the most prominent was a monkey playing that most popular of instruments for medieval musicians – judging by how many adorn church buildings – the bagpipe.

Our interest however was with the Eastern Lady Chapel, which had been built into the east end of the choir and was younger by eighty years. Part of its floor of inscribed stone tablets and rectangular slabs had collapsed into a void. A few days of work with the archaeologist later, the paving was lifted to reveal the eighteenth-century brick vaults that were the origin of the problem. Their walls had collapsed onto the remains of long-departed Bristolians that were piled up beneath. Under the marble ledger stones, inscribed with the names of local merchants and plantation owners from the West Indies, the substrate of the floor was made of local red sand and bone mixed with lime to form a sort of 'bonecrete'. Behind a screen put up to shield the remains from public view, the archaeologist carefully lifted out the human bones that lay around the remains of collapsed coffins, which had originally been laid on top of each other. The coffin edges were regularly dotted with the verdigris of the old studs that held in place swags of perished, tasselled leather. Once these were cleared, we were in a position to rebuild the brick walls and carefully reinter the human remains, after a few words of blessing from the dean.

One advantage of our low position within the dark red crypt was a new appreciation of the grand space above. The square east wall lifted to a remarkable reredos of painted, cusped and ogeed arches, that hid gilded diapered panels and a frieze of big heads that grinned down, all with the Bee-Gee-like hair that had last been in fashion in the mid-fourteenth century. On the chapel's side walls, thin shafts of Purbeck marble lifted to ribs that spread equally up to the vault, where instead of meeting at the apex the liernes changed to form a series of kite-like shapes that ran the length of the chapel and chancel. Stretch out both of your thumbs and forefingers and connect them together and you will see the form I mean. These panels were cusped, like rose thorns, to create a stellar effect in the choir, but were plain in their continuation over the Eastern Lady Chapel, otherwise the most adorned part of the cathedral. Here, the kite-shaped ribs interacted perfectly with the east window tracery, its glass casting a rainbow that dazzled across the floor brasses and marble plaques. When I turned around to take in the chancel vault, I realised that Bristol Cathedral is a true one-off. Its master mason had designed an internal space that was one of the highest achievements of Decorated Gothic.

The lights of the clerestory that you would expect to see lining a nave had been done away with to allow the normally covered aisle space to open up in a completely new way. High-level internal stone bridges act like the missing flying buttresses at the same height as the nave, choir and Lady Chapel, and created a hall church by transferring the vault's weight. This gives the interior an impression of generous width and spaciousness and allows in far more light than previous forms of vault. This design, probably influenced by domestic or monastic great halls, was used extensively in the later Gothic architecture of Germany. Why did its marvellous spaciousness never catch on in Britain? Perhaps the great experiment was too much of a distraction. Normally in a church or cathedral the sight line is deliberately drawn only in two directions – towards the altar and up to the stained glass. At Bristol, one is encouraged to look around the entire space.

Every day at the same time we stopped work for the services which have been held there since Saxon times despite the inconveniences of the Norman invasion, the Black Death, fire, riot and the Blitz. Sitting in on Holy Communion, I was enthralled by the cathedral's greatest treasure – a battered candelabrum hanging from the centre of a star vault. Stylised square leaves sprouted from around a central statue of the Virgin and Child, which crowned a rather casual St George, running the dragon through with his sword. This fifteenth-century example of good triumphing over evil had a special modern resonance: it had been pulled from the wreckage of the city's Temple Church that had been bombed during the Blitz.

Later, with the burial vaults rebuilt, and as the last slab of inscribed marble was dropped into place, I suddenly wondered whether any of the bones we had been handling were from the great pestilence that started in 1348 and killed most of the city's population – and I went off to give my hands another good scrub.

Across the river, the most prodigious of Bristol's churches sat in competition with the cathedral for the attentions of returning seafarers, though it was St Mary Redcliffe that became the more dramatic point of welcome. John Cabot, who returned on the flood tide through the Avon Gorge from Newfoundland in 1497, brought a strange offering for his safe return in his little ship, the *Matthew*: a whalebone rib now stapled to one of the crossing piers. A hovering verger proudly informed me that Cabot had named the unknown land after the city's principal customs official and sheriff, Richard Amerike.

But whoever set out the design for the porch had given the church its greatest treasure, and one that had been brought a long way. Inside, a shrine dedicated to Our Lady of Redcliffe channelled the influence from many different cultures to produce what Nikolaus Pevsner felt might have been the first case of '*orientalisme*' in Western architecture. Four exotic doorways allowed pilgrims access through the large hexagonal box that contained the shrine to the Virgin, but it was the design of the central doorway that would have been a jaw-dropper. The carving and figurative work that encompasses the door today is a business-like Victorian replacement, the original having succumbed to the pollution of the nearby glass kilns that once fired the red sands of the cliff below to create the city's famous blue glass.

Outside, the walls are divided horizontally by a run of deep crocketed zigzags that acted as canopies over deep niches. Corbels that might have supported images of the kings of England and holy men were instead carved sensitively with likenesses of the ordinary-looking people of the city, crippled and malnourished churls, burgesses and tradesmen. Gone from here it seemed were the tales of light and dark, good and evil. The seven-cusped curve and counter-curve of an ogee arch drew the sides up and over the door opening. Tiny, ecstatic figures swooned down from between the cusps of each spandrel. The master mason, perhaps well travelled himself, drew together a composite interpretation of geometrical forms from not only the south-west of England but across the Islamic world. There was a touch of the Persian prayer niche, as well as a sprinkling of Mughal Indian style. The orientalist who commissioned the works was most probably a successful merchant with strong trading links with Portugal and the Moorish Islamic world of the south. The Crusades drawing to a stalemate proved a good thing for medieval trade. China and India reconnected to European markets overland via the Mediterranean, and merchants and even clergy made good use of the potential these new links offered – it seemed the whole world was on the move. Walking down the steps from the porch, I could feel that change was in the air: a chill wind was coming in from the East and summer was drawing to a close.

8
AUTUMNAL EQUINOX

The gales of autumn had come early, and it had been raining heavily since we fixed the last voussoirs (arch stones) into the fourteenth-century packhorse bridge. I was back in Bradford-on-Avon, the Saxon church a few hundred yards upstream. The water meadows that only a couple of weeks previously had been parched and straw-brown after a long dry summer were now hidden under a choppy lake. I wondered how the newly fixed stone was coping with the battering. The handrail that ran along the top, which was all that was visible of the bridge, was bent at 45 degrees by tree trunks in the heavy flow. Tyres and large metal drums, washed downstream from the Avon Rubber factory, had been drawn into a liquid vortex under the vault of the central arch.

The bridge connected the route down from the fertile corn-fields of the Cotswold plateau to Barton Farm Grange with its stone-tiled tithe barn. The problem of a winter crossing had been overcome from Norman times onwards by the stand-ardisation of bridge design. The masons who built the bridge had similar ideas for the technology of infrastructure to those who had built the fourth-century bridge abutment with its pointed arch that I had seen in Iran. These were concepts that would allow the crossing of Himalayan torrents, the great rivers of the Levant and Danubian tributaries.

As England developed into a centralised state it needed a national road system to handle the shift away from pack animals and ox-drawn wagons to horse-drawn carts that struggled to cross the fords used previously. Apart from royal grants, all sorts of people and institutions came together to pay for this work, from religious and charitable donations to those who managed the royal grant of pontage, the toll levied specifically for the building of bridges: it was the avoidance of that toll that was the principal consideration at Barton Farm Grange.

The farm and its buildings were part of a huge estate owned by the abbess of Shaftesbury, whose lands spread across much of the West Country. She would have taken a 'tithe', or a tenth, of cereal from her tenants and this grain would have been collected and stored at the stone barn built from the local quarries and forests she owned. Her tithe barn is so vast it almost feels like a sacred structure, a cathedral built on land taxation. Its size illustrates that the quantities of grain being collected would have been so large that the abbess would have anticipated a huge saving in bypassing the existing town bridge toll, even after the expenditure of building a new bridge.

The bridge structure was so beaten by the weather that it cried out for some compassion, something it had not received since it was built in about 1320. The wonder was that apart from a few inappropriate attempts at renovation it remained in its original state, having never been adapted for use for vehicular traffic. Spanning the river with four pointed arches, the three cutwaters added upstream in the fifteenth century deflected water pressure away from the arches. In summer the river level dropped, exposing more of the bridge than at any other time, which allowed an opportunity for repair.

Work on the pointed barrel vaults could only begin once the resident Daubenton's bats had fledged and dispersed to mating roosts in the surrounding poplar trees. Known also as the water or fishing bat, these creatures have turned up in the deep cracks of every medieval bridge I have worked on. Instead of scaffolding, a floating pontoon allowed enjoyment of long evenings with the local bat expert while he sealed roost holes and fractures, to stop any of the bats returning before we opened the structure up. Our torches attracted both the local drunks and constabulary, while midges and mosquitoes sought nourishment on our bare skin. Night was when the river really came to life; the large bat population fed well on the invertebrates that lived just above the river, which by the time dawn came were replaced by squadrons of damsel and dragonflies.

Later, we created new roosts deep in the arches, hollowed out from large blocks with access slits cut into the front. After the floods had subsided, we inspected the cavity with an endoscope and found more than sixty bats resident, with females and young clinging on within a space only eighteen inches square.

We removed a few modern stones, fixed in hard cement by brave council workers who had done the work from a rubber dinghy in the 1970s. Then we took down the semi-pyramidal cutwaters damaged by the jacking action of elder and willow root growth and spread them out on the pontoon. Picking it apart, the great surprise was, as with St Laurence's a few hundred feet upstream, the lack of mortar used to hold it all together. Although the surface joints had been packed with lime to a depth of an inch or so, I guessed the builders thought they needn't bother with the rest when they had a material conveniently to hand on the riverbank.

To build the piers of the bridge, the river would have been dammed and diverted in an arc around the line of work that still exists. In digging out the cutting they discovered a supply of the raw clay that only needed to be beaten to make it softer and more usable as a material to glue stones together. The equal spread of axe marks across the vault indicated that lots of original stonework survived, quarried either from the mines that pepper the valley, or from the wood cliff face that overlooked it. Timber formwork supported the vault while we replaced the failed voussoirs with limestone from the Limpley Stoke mine, only a short journey downstream. Dense plumes of dust blew over our shoulders as we cut and dressed each wedge shape into the replacements with air and power tools. Once these were in place, joints were filled with a heavy-duty lime to deal with winter's challenges from floodwater and frosts. The last job was to scrape away the tarmac carriageway that had been laid down in the 1940s and replace it with hydraulic lime concrete to create a durable surface, which allowed the evaporation of trapped water when the bridge became saturated.

Most bridges like this were built in the period from 1250, until the arrival of the plague a century later saw the end of three centuries of population growth when all investment in infrastructure stopped. Edward III's primary focus was what was to become the Hundred Years' War, which began in 1337 over the right to rule France. Edward assumed the title of king of France, and in July 1346 landed in Normandy. His decisive victory at the battle of Crécy dispersed the French army. The Black Death was first recorded as arriving in Weymouth in 1348, when its first wave cut down about a third of the population. The annual campaigning was paused as a consequence of the plague in 1355 and thereafter English influence in France declined.

For a good while building work almost stopped and where it was maintained, curves, showiness and extravagance in elements such as vaulting and window tracery were considered inappropriate. The straightening of lines created a new style: the Perpendicular. Those dead from the plague bequeathed millions, which led to a spate of church rebuilding, and it was to one of the many from this time that we were to journey next, to a place that grew out of the shadow of the Black Death and where the sadness of that time can still be felt.

We were deep in Hardy country, near the old Roman Road that leads to Weymouth. Nell, Mike and I unwrapped the splash protections we had laid around various monuments and features that populated the interior of the little church we had just finished limewashing. This was a quiet place, where sunlight filtered at an angle through clear windows, picking up a soup of lazy motes.

Nell lifted a drape from the top of the Victorian pulpit to uncover the Gothic lettering hidden away underneath. She touched one of the cut letters with a single finger and read out the words 'TAKE YE HEED WHAT YE HEAR'. A pause, then a sudden combination of loud raps issued forth from the other side of the porch door. We three hung a moment in surprise and then Mike and I dashed out to see who was on the other side. I expected to run into the pyjama-clad lord of the manor who lived next door but was greeted only by stillness and insect song. We exchanged looks, and I wondered if we had stood on the edge of the looking glass.

Coming back inside I was distracted by the painted alabaster monument fixed to the wall by the grey oak door. A Shakespearian-looking knight in armour knelt facing his second wife and their seven children. Behind him, clad also in black, knelt his first wife in front of a heap of infants wrapped in red swaddling clothes. The plagues which had continued to occur every twenty years or so, by then took mainly the weakest, which was backed up by the inscription: [with his first wife] 'FILLIP . . . HEE HAD YSSVE 4 CHILDREN AND BEE DEAD'. The sense of loss from the Black Death is not only in the art on the walls and windows; in some places it feels perceptible in the walls themselves.

The masons, builders and labourers that were left behind were much in demand. The practice of 'shop' work emerged where the less complicated and ambitious designs were carved or roughed-out at the quarry by less skilled masons, as uniformity of design, especially in window mullions, became the norm. The new generation that filled the shoes of the older craftspeople did not have the time to train as carvers, becoming instead skilled production workers, and the chain of connection all the way back to Old Sarum was abruptly severed. Gothic became pared down to its essentials and English architecture became simpler. Regimented straight lines, due to the new shift towards austerity, replaced the flamboyance of the Decorated style, and the eye was drawn upwards, either to the fan vault, or outside to the tops of the new towers that were to dominate the late medieval landscape.

Women became more empowered through inheritance and necessity. In the 1350s one Agnes Ramsey ran her father's London workshop. Agnes was so successful that she designed and made the (now destroyed) tomb for Queen Isabella, the widow of King Edward II, whose earlier regicide at Berkeley Castle was to be another factor in the architectural shift taking place. The creation of his royal shrine in the 1330s at Gloucester Abbey, which was commissioned by his son who was to become King Edward III, was only a decade or so after the respective scaffolds had been struck to reveal the Decorated Gothic of Bristol Cathedral's new east end and the north porch of St Mary Redcliffe.

With the Hundred Years' War, England became detached from developments in Europe and French architectural influence waned; but the royal mason brought to Gloucester from London was full of ideas for an entirely new patriotic style. I had once been lucky enough to visit the cathedral and the tomb. As well as the king's likeness, I had come to see Clare, my wife, who was part of the team conserving the shrine. I could see her, busy in blue overalls, working on the canopy that crowned the recumbent alabaster effigy of the king. A French tour guide had just passed by, pronouncing that the king had been '*horriblement tué*'. The guide had left the notorious story (involving a red-hot iron) hanging in the air for his party to research for themselves. The shrine was squeezed under an ochre-red Norman arch, between the thick piers of the ambulatory that had been cut away to an ogee-headed niche to allow pilgrims to pass all the way around what was really a freestanding building, an aedicule or tabernacle that gave importance to its contents.

The royal reliquary lay beneath two tiers of arches that seemed to have been pulled up by an unseen hand to three high peaks, each crowded with crockets in among a forest of small pinnacles. The Cotswold Painswick limestone worked harmoniously with height and light to create a structure that has an acute Perpendicular emphasis. The tomb, which had been much knocked about, had been repaired in the eighteenth century with plaster of Paris. Clare and her colleagues were busy refixing the many tiny loose crockets and remodelling missing parts. All this was supported by a framework of slim mullions and buttresses, which enabled troubled limbs to be passed through into the miraculous space above the king's effigy.

From Clare's work platform, the bright translucent repose of the king could best be seen. Laid out on a Purbeck marble-clad tomb chest he holds a sceptre in his right hand and an orb in his left, with his one remaining foot – the other is missing – resting on a sleeping lion. A pair of angels support his alabaster head and strawberry crown, from where wavy Plantagenet-styled hair falls to a cushion to meet a beard that concludes with three dense corkscrews. The skin-like translucence of the alabaster and the skill of its carving have created an effigy that looks all too real. With a bottom lip that seems ready to pronounce the letter 'V', the king stares eternally heavenwards through disturbing H-shaped cataracts, roughly cut into each open eye, perhaps by bored choirboys. Proof of miraculous cures were soon ratified, and the monies started to flow in. This familiar formula was used to fund the rapid construction of a new choir and crossing in the canopy's new style.

Augustus Pugin, the greatest of nineteenth-century Gothic architects, thought that 'the history of architecture is the history of the world'. This was reflected in the buildings put up by a society that was radically changing both economically as well as politically in the wake of the plague. As with agricultural workers and farmers, skills and labour shortages meant that those who had survived the pestilence were better off. For the first time, masons could dictate their terms and in a break with the old way of doing things clients came to *them* (cap in hand). Suddenly the ordinary people who had become more entre-preneurial were the beneficiaries of the great disaster and found themselves with spare cash. Along with the money bequeathed by the dead, they became the patrons of a new wave of church rebuilding as a response to the feeling that death was now perpetually peering over their shoulder.

Many parishes already had churches that were in good order, so to compete with their neighbours the solution was often to extend the west end upwards, creating a landmark tower that would carry the sound of bells across the fields they commanded. The uniquely English resonance of the bells, along with the height of the towers, skilful construction and decoration, was to become one of the great contributions to late medieval European art and architecture. Western bell-towers were uncommon before the mid-fourteenth century, as they had always been centrally placed between the transepts, nave and chancel as proclamation of the building's high status. Regional differences of wealth and geology created many local variants of the Perpendicular bell-tower. I have worked on many churches from the time after the plague, but for me the north aisle and tower of the Church of St Peter and St Paul in Kilmersdon stands out. In my mind's eye the typical Somerset west tower punches up from low on the moors. Kilmersdon is differently situated at the bottom of a narrow, wooded valley approached on the road from the west where the flagpole on the top of the tower is almost at eye level. The road drops with the sudden plunge of a ski slope to the churchyard yews and redwoods.

The scaffolding had just gone up at St Peter and St Paul, and as the team was due to start work here the following week, I had come to see what exactly we had let ourselves in for. The north aisle was lined with a menagerie of strange stone animals, sat on their hunkers below the parapet. These are known as grotesques, and in Somerset-speak as 'hunky punks'.

Unlike gargoyles (*gargouille* is the old French word for throat), which were designed to channel and throw water away from the roof through their open mouths, these medieval weirdos are purely decorative. Looking up from the churchyard I think the faithful would have seen the grotesques as representing the stark choice between good and evil in the same way that Harry Potter might have anticipated a visit from the dementors. Their grim features would have acted as a reminder of the torments that awaited those who knew their souls were unworthy as they elevated towards the heavenly angels on Judgement Day. Grotesques normally scowl over the parish to avert evil influence or ill luck, but at Kilmersdon the beasts had a different role to play. They formed a scheme that could be followed, with each of the interesting cast of characters warranting attention. On the corner overlooking the little square in front of the tower where church ales would have been enjoyed, a bagpipe-playing hunk, with the usual Plantagenet fringe and cheery disposition, looked as if he would have been the heart and soul of proceedings.

The rest of the punks were designed as a memorial to be seen from the main approach down the hill. Six of the eight creatures represented heraldic beasts of the Botreaux family, barons who had long owned large tracts of the West Country, reflecting the family's long service to Edward III, Richard II and through Henrys IV and V, under whom William de Botreaux survived Agincourt. William was the third Baron Botreaux. He had been born in the village in early 1380 and died in 1462 at North Cadbury where he and his wife still lie within their fine tomb. He was most likely the benefactor of the works at St Peter and St Paul, which stylistically dates from after his demise.

It was important to draw and record the condition of the beasts before repairing them as it was the only way to truly see an object and note its condition. The bagpipe-playing grotesque was over five hundred years old and the most exposed of all – drawing it had allowed a true reading of the man. Removing the damage caused by pollution and acid rain was the priority before repairing the painful-looking blisters that covered him, where the stone's outer skin was curling away from the surface of its blackened underbelly like burnt bacon. Of the six heraldic beasts of the Botreaux family, the first was thought to resemble a toad, as 'botereau' or 'boterel' signifies a little toad in old French dialect. Perhaps from ground level he is a little toad-like; we however saw him differently. Peeling away the poultice we had applied to draw out the pollutants revealed features that were more mammalian than reptile. Obviously, the carvers had never seen what they sought to create, but the eroded but still stylised mane and threatening claws gave it away as the beast of kings: crouched, ready to pounce, with open eyes and a tufted swooshing tail. He would have been recognisable to the medieval scribe of a 'book of beasts', or bestiary, which used a description of exotic creatures as a basis for allegorical teaching. He was sited next to the beast of the Botreaux family, a griffin that looks proud of its place beside another royal creature – a chained white hart, the personal emblem of Richard II.

Then, a completely inexplicable upright beast: beaky, with chimpanzee ears, seemingly intent on listening-in to the conversations of its neighbours down the line, who I always thought were passing their time at the east end by chattering away, their heads craned towards the goings-on in the square as they kept us company while we worked away on the scaffolding. Traces of umber limewash with a fleshy tone over the palate and tongue could be seen in their open mouths, which indicated that the figures had previously been decorated.

With work completed to the punks, we climbed for the first of hundreds of times the spiral staircase to the top of the tower to look at not only the fraying structure, but also things happening in the village. For a nosey parker, it is an interesting job. From the crenellations, Kilmersdon is a busy place, and behind high garden fences, life went on unseen: possibly shady hydroponic activity in greenhouses, rabbit-hutch cleaning, and the crafty painter heading to the inn while the Dulux dried. In a now grassless orchard a woman gathered eggs in the mud, with a quartet of terriers tied in a knot at her heels.

The incessant wind abrades the four large pinnacles, buttressed on each side by two smaller pinnacles that form the corners of the tower. Lichens spreading across the tower's north face like painted Chinese silk covered a multitude of problems; the foremost being the alarming lean of the tower that, when we dropped a plumb line down to the ground, was found to have shifted more than a yard over the length of the drop. I imagined the sleepless nights the builders must have endured as it started to shift while they built the second of the tower's four stages, fifty feet above the graveyard. To compensate, they simply changed the coursing of the adjacent walls that had deflected downwards to tie the discrepancy in and continued to send it upwards. Reinforcing the timber floor in what is now the ringing chamber must have helped, but it was an imperfect solution. It was obvious that the corner buttresses needed some bolstering.

Samantha and John, the masons who did the heavy work, extracted the stones that were fracturing and under stress. Removal by percussive means was out of the question as the buttress supported a pinnacle of several tons in weight. The sudden removal of a block without propping might have brought it all down. Cutting away a few small slices with an angle grinder allows the insertion of the blade of a Strongboy, which when used with a tubular steel Acrow prop acts as a temporary support and so allows the removal of the masonry beneath. This was a nasty job in full face mask, goggles and hard hat; a cloud of dust was created that drifted away over the village to cover surrounding cars with a thin layer. The measurements that we then took were far from standard, as the massive new blocks that Samantha cut to shape in the churchyard had to suit the eccentric, not very square, emergency codge-up from six centuries ago. Chaucer even describes this sort of event in

'The Knight's Tale' – 'the fallynge of the toures and walles' was a regular event in those days – but somehow this tower had managed to stay up, in spite of the additional challenge of containing the huge sheering forces exerted on the walls by its ring of eight bells.

The bells themselves had developed their own problems. The tenor had lost its bearing during ringing practice, when it collided into a compatriot and then smashed through the floor past the terrified ringers below. Convinced they were about to die, they threw themselves down the narrow spiral stairway in a heap. But the bell miraculously wedged itself between the securing tie beams, and they retired next door to the Jolliffe Arms to reflect on their salvation, with no more than a couple of broken ribs and some nasty bruises to show for it. I had arrived in the wake of these events. The damage created by the ton-weight bell as it whirled around in a black hole of destructive energy was something to behold.

When the medieval mason's lodge was set up, building work on the church would have started around Easter and be finished by mid-October, with the winter spent sawing, adzing, chopping and carving the package of stone ready for the next building season. Contracts survive where the terms of employment are clearly defined, with the design left to the master who led only a small team of five or six, supplemented by labour freely supplied by the village, often in an act of devotion, over the four or five seasons it would take to construct.

As our project got into gear, we found that the grotesques and gargoyles were very badly decayed. One in particular, clinging to the tower by its horns and hoofed feet, had a body that had been shorn of detail by the elements. Enough was left to remind me of another beast cut in exactly the same way on a distant church on the other side of Somerset, which we had worked on many years before. It was so strikingly similar that the churches must have been connected in some way, perhaps by the same band of roving carvers. I telephoned the churchwarden to see if I could use it to guide our team on its design for the wings, beaks and feathered breast of our own creature. 'Best bring your wellies and a boat, as we are cut off by the floods,' were the churchwarden's closing words, which was the only excuse I needed to load up *Laughing Water* and take the unique opportunity to see the landscape in its true state, almost as nature intended.

On the drive across the Mendip Hills to St Mary's at Chedzoy I passed unregarded henge monuments, barrows and the soft green 'gruffy' ground of Velvet Bottom's old workings that supplied the lead for the Roman Baths. Pulling in to look at the usual dramatic view west to distant Exmoor, where tree-covered cliffs could be made out as they drop to the sea, I could see that the rains had indeed done their worst. The flatlands cut with rivers had burst their banks to create a vast, brown inland sea where only the lines of hedgerow trees and telegraph poles identified the presence of fields and roads. Distant medieval settlements, normally enclosed by open fields, now sat on low islands around which deep water flowed fast in currents and eddies: a dangerous barrier to overcome for those marooned in their remote farmhouses and villages. Many of the local village names finished with the suffix *ney* – the Saxon for island – and it was easy to see why.

Once through Glastonbury I pulled over in the lee of

Glastonbury's Tor. Floodwaters lapped gently against the tarmac. *Laughing Water* slipped easily into the field where the normally inoffensive River Sheppey had muscled up to create a lake that spread away to the west where it drained into the Severn estuary. It was a calm push off towards the deserted island of Fenny Castle with its tree-crowned motte and bailey. The flooded village of Godney led to the River Brue that passed by the familiar sight of Meare Manor, another old job of ours that was once the summer residence of the abbots of Glastonbury. Its faded roof of terracotta tiles contrasted with the lichenous rusty-orange of Hamstone dressings and courses of steely blue lias to form the colour scheme that defines the old buildings of this place.

Paddling on, I realised that the flooding had resurrected the great Meare Pool itself. This body of water held the fishponds that supplied the monastic estate with great quantities of eel and perch, and was the origin of the village's name. Human activity had somehow inadvertently turned the land back in on itself; rivers, normally twenty metres wide, had spread to a width of many large fields, their channelling embankments submerged all the way to the sea. The landscape had rediscovered some of its prehistoric self. I imagined the shallow lakes criss-crossed with planked trackways built on wooden stakes hammered into the peat; one such, known as the Sweet Track – from the early fourth millennium BCE – that connected the lake villages together through the reedy swamp, has been excavated. Later, in the Iron Age, dugout canoes were used instead of the trackways to get about; some were still usable when dried out after they were discovered by archaeologists, proving that ancient people could move as easily as I could through the flooded moor.

I paddled parallel with the long finger of the Polden Hills along the ancient route connecting Glastonbury and Bridgwater. On its far side – after I had dragged the canoe up through sodden fields – lay my first destination. Ahead was the vast King's Sedgemoor drain, which drained no more. It was a slog across noticeably choppier waters towards the beacon-like tower of St Mary's on what the Saxons knew as 'Cedd's Island', or Chedzoy – the 'zoy' part of the name being a corruption of the Saxon 'Sowy' – raised land in an area prone to flooding.

From among broad, pollarded willows, their withies drawn skyward waiting to be trimmed, the island elevated the embattled western tower of St Mary's Church into iron-shaped clouds that controlled the sky. The dressed stone – quoins, windows and copings – had been brought here by boat from Ham Hill, at the distant end of the River Parrett, which flowed by unnoticed a few fields away. This tower was one of the last to be built in the West Country in the Perpendicular Gothic style, fifty years or so after Kilmersdon, with which it shares not only a hunky-punk design, but also a similar pattern of general development. Unlike at Kilmersdon, the work on St Mary's was not funded by an aristocratic family but by common people. Money came from the new gentry, merchants and the lower classes to create a monument that, as John Leland said of St Andrew's Church in Mells, a couple of miles from Kilmersdon, was built 'yn tyme of mynde by the hole parish'. Incredibly a will survives from 1539 where Thomas Harburfield of the village left 'to the building of the tower of Chardseye £3'. A decade previously our team discovered that much of the original stonework at St Mary's had survived and we had managed to keep every loose chunk in place, which maintained the archaeological integrity of the differing phases of its construction and most importantly its patina of age.

Passing the great porch, the radial marks of the mass dial would not be telling the tides on the grey overcast day. The hidden tower key opened the oak door to the spiral staircase that led up to the roof. My hand ran up the newel post, thick with the usual dedicatory crosses, atropopaic marks, daisy wheels and slashed VVs to invoke the protection of the Virgin Mary. Unlatching the door to the outside, I was surprised to see the lead roof covered with the outlines of Victorian and earlier shoe prints, some with hobnails scratched into its soft surface. Leaning right out over the parapet, using calipers to help with the measurements, I recorded as much of the cousin of Kilmersdon's hunky punks as I dared.

Viewed from over the topmost quatrefoil-pierced crenellations, the inundated flatlands stretched away to the far distant Dorset hills. There was nothing new under the sun: in 1505 it was recorded that 'in the winter season the medewes be so filled and replenysshed with water, that the bootes may go over at every place'. The moor from here to Westonzoyland's fine tower marked where the last battle on English soil took place during the Monmouth Rebellion on 6 July 1685. I remembered prising musket balls out of the joints between the stones. These were carefully replaced. The locals drew an account of the battle on parchment that still hangs on the vestry wall.

Back on *Laughing Water* it was difficult to see where the path of the River Parrett meandered. I noticed that the power cables crossing the fields gave the only clue; to prevent swans and geese from flying into the cables, the electricity board had thoughtfully hung orange markers over them.

Alfred the Great's island retreat from the Danes, Athelney – the Island of Princes – was now visible in the distance. The river cut the county in two and was once the natural boundary between Saxon Wessex and the native Dumnonia, as the Romans knew Devon and Cornwall. When the wind died down to create a still, brown lake, its ghastliness became apparent. The surface was covered with a rainbow film of fuel oil, mixed with plastic garden chairs, children's toys and the contents of cesspits, all bobbing slowly to the sea.

My cruise took me past some of the finest towers in Somerset: Middlezoy, Othery and Aller, where King Alfred baptised the conquered King Guthrum in a font that still exists; and Langport, where the tower was well out of it, high on the hill. Surrounding fields narrowed to orchards and mistletoe-draped fruit trees clung on somehow in the faster moving flow. Huish Episcopi, Muchelney with its abbey, Kingsbury Episcopi and Martock were all places where the church was not only morally but also physically elevated, unlike my wet backside in the canoe. The succession of golden towers came to an end at the point where navigation by barge would have been no longer possible. By then I understood that, by virtue of their ambitious scale, and their design and styling, the towers were unique in the history of English art.

I had brought along a cutting list for the quarry master at Ham Hill to price for an upcoming summer project at the nearby parish church of Hinton St George. It had been a long enough journey for one day and I covered *Laughing Water* over in the corner of a sodden field and curled up, dog-tired in my bivvy bag, on a deep bed of fallen pine needles under a solitary redwood tree that stood sentinel at an ancient crossroads.

The following morning, I made my way up the steep incline lined with terraced houses built from the stone that has been extracted locally since Saxon times. The hill's wooded flanks were surrounded on two sides by what looked like marshy levels formed by the rivers Parrett and Yeo and which in a few weeks' time would have drained back to pasture and meadow. The delves of old quarries were still visible, softened by time and nature within a vast Iron Age fortress, its bank and ditch enclosing the flat summit for three miles.

The scene in the orange-stained stone yard, if the mechanical saws, diggers and cranes were removed, would have been much the same in medieval times. Workshops ran along a muddy track, with piles of orders waiting on pallets for transportation on one side, and waste on the other.

Hidden behind a bund, covered in lime trees and wasted buddleia, the iron-coloured quarry the size of several football pitches would once have been the domain of many dozens of workers. Engaged in deep excavation, these men would have shovelled away the sand to lever out mattress-sized slabs of stone, each no more than a couple of feet thick. Today, the place played host to a solitary man in his yellow JCB who spooked the skylarks and foraging woodpeckers as he trundled by. The club-sandwich-like cross-section of the quarry face told the story of extraction. A mansion-sized scree slope of overburden, broken up and laid down during successive ice ages, was good for walling stone. Larger slabs were lined up waiting for a dumper-truck to take them up the greasy track to the workshop for processing by a circular saw.

From the edge of the rampart, two distant church towers caught my eye. To the left our nation's flag flicked from a flagpole over East Coker Church, where the ashes of the poet T. S. Eliot are interred. To the right the drabness of the damp bare trees was momentarily relieved by the glint of Hinton St George's golden cockerel as it pivoted in the wind.

Both churches may have been built from the best-looking stone in the country, but as a material it has a flaw. The beds are riven with seams of rusty iron and brown clay that grow tired with age; it was to Hinton St George that our team was heading once Kilmersdon was completed to resolve this problem.

I left the hill and headed back down to the canoe and a lift home along the incline, following the route that the gargoyles at Hinton would have made by cart nearly eight centuries earlier.

A few weeks later we started on the late-fifteenth-century tower of Hinton St George. The joints between its stones had been nibbled out in the usual way by time and weather. The same number of storeys as at Kilmersdon lifted to emphasise similar window tracery with crocketed pinnacles on three of the tower's four corners, the pinnacles differing only in that the central one was taller and larger. From the pinnacles' bases, squared shafts dropped to buttress the tower's corners, from where a pair of grotesques sprouted out awkwardly, accompanying a central gargoyle at the base of the battlements. Their puffed-out cheeks and satchel mouths waited on standby to blow water away from the tower roof with yard-long lead tongues.

There was nothing aristocratic about these hunky punks. They crouched, these child-sized caricatures, their cows' bodies fronted by faces of cartoonish simplicity with cat-like ears, bulging eyes and protruding tongues. For what purpose were these devils carved – the nefarious monkeys, the serpents with retracted wings, some with curly hair, some straight, some feathered? Why did that beak come with shark's teeth? A villein in a short tunic leant perilously forward at forty-five degrees, as if doing the *Rocky Horror* 'Time Warp', hands on hips, crouched, ready to jump. These golden beasts reflected a tradition when the church allowed the masons to cater for parishioners who saw Jack-in-the-Green and will-o'-the-wisps behind each trunk and rock.

Looking up from the graveyard it dawned on me that I had encountered some of these creatures before, not in inert stone, but alive, and in this place. The dusky light came and went as I climbed the endless winding stairway, lit every thirty steps by a slit in the wall. I sensed that the many pairs of shiny black pinpricks I had noticed in the dark corners were studying me. In the confined space my eyes slowly adjusted to the gloom. From tiny feet that grasped the underside of a spiral step hung a twitching Christmas bauble, but of fur, fang and membrane. Cat-like ears quivered as its winged cape slowly opened. This pipistrelle, I could see, would have been the inspiration for the corner gargoyle with which it shared the same physiology, the bone ridges of its wing membrane radiating across each side. Suddenly it let go of the inverted perch and flew in rapid circles about my head, the beat of its tiny wings puffing on my face.

This profane crew of grotesques made uncomfortable bedfellows with the church's other images of Christ and his family, the saints and the Passion, and by the time the last of the

Somerset towers were built, reform was in the air. The Black Death had led to a decrease in belief and faith. Many had turned their back on a Church that had failed to help the suffering or come up with solutions for the catastrophe. The Gothic style had reached its autumn even as the first seeds were sown that were to lead to the biggest change the Church had seen – the wintry arrival of the Reformation.

9

MICHAELMAS

The daylight that I could see through the vault indicated that all was not well with one of Britain's most magnificent late-medieval church interiors. The ribs that spread like golden boughs across the underside of the ceiling vault's tree-like canopy were in receipt of some urgent propping, pinning and gap-filling, to allow Sherborne's Abbey Church of St Mary – known to some as the 'Cathedral of Dorset' – to carry on doing its job.

It was 'Pack' Monday, the first Monday after 10 October, which was the old Michaelmas Day – the feast of St Michael the Archangel: weigher of souls, protector of the faithful against the forces of evil, and across the West Country the guardian of high places. Although warm and sunny it was the beginning of autumn. Outside a street fair was in full swing. I asked one of the vergers how long this tradition had been going on for? 'Since time immemorial,' he replied.

The fan vaulting that soared overhead was a mixture of great beauty and advanced engineering that pushed the boundary of what had been possible. The scaffolding soared to the ceiling of the dimly lit south transept and the crossing space of the tower, giving us access to repair the walls and the timber frame of the coffered ceiling. From here we could also get to the lower aisle vault that was buckling at the crossing end, as the colossal weight of the central tower continued its slow downward spread through the buttresses and aisle walls. That the joints between the ribs and webs were open and that some had even come loose suggested it had already been moving in an alarming way.

However, as we removed hundreds of years' worth of soot from the ribs and the cobweb-filled cracks and gaps, it was apparent that it had continued to move since the Victorians had last tackled the problem. Then, they had pumped the tower full of concrete and tunnelled out its core to introduce large adjustable steels designed to stem the spread.

Once our work was done, the top side of the nave vault required a further assessment, which meant the breathless trudge up the tower, hauling on the black plastic water pipe that performed an admirable job as a handrail as it wound up the curved wall. It was my turn to repay my debt of education to the next generation, so I was accompanied by a handful of trainee craftspeople to help with the inspection. We made our way on hands and knees through the thick walls of the tower and the hidden Victorian engineering that was keeping the place together.

The internal Norman predecessor survived, its blind arcade entombed and left behind within the rubble core as the tower was heightened and the lower walls strengthened in the fifteenth century. Crawling in the torch-lit darkness, accompanied by the usual thrill of entering one of those special places where few people go, we waited for our eyes to adjust to the dark. Under the steep internal nave roof, amid medieval timbers that gave off the aroma of oak seeded a millenia ago, pine resin and tallow candles, this was the business end and top side of the nave's fan vault, terminating at a gable end with a 'suicide door' that opened to more than a hundred-foot drop to the car park below.

This was a good way to allow the students a true understanding of the huge forces at work, as we inspected the open semicircular mouths of rubble-filled trumpets, each the size of mini roundabouts, an inverted half conoid (a cone that opens from a concave curve) of the fan that ran along each outer wall. They might have been less keen had they pictured the long drop to the nave floor from the cones that, unlike in the choir, were self-supporting with no need for buttressing or, apart from the walls, any other support. From the cones, liernes arched away as a web to connect with the rickety-looking central rib and the top side of the ceiling bosses, given away by their exposed Lewis holes. Superficially, it all looked as if it had been chucked together in a slapdash way, with plenty of evidence of the lava-like quicklime that had been poured over it all.

As usual, the constructing masons had worked closely with carpenters to create what would have been the most complicated piece of formwork they had attempted. A negative impression of the fan would have been required to support the carved stones that had been carefully placed in position from above, onto wet joints that if too big were quickly filled with the usual debris from the masons' lunch – oyster shells – to induce compression and support.

I noticed that the vault had developed a subtle vibration and put my ear to its curving face to hear the muffled opening strains of William Walton's rousing 'Crown Imperial' played out on the great Victorian organ below. As we crawled back out, the tenor bell struck the hour. Cowed by the reverberations of the colossal weight of iron that resounded heavily around the ringing chamber, I suddenly remembered the inscription cast into its skirting that reflected the events of the English Reformation: *By Wolsey's gift I measure time for all. To Mirth : To Grieffe : To Church : I serve to call.*

Back on the ground, we entered the abbey through the great west door and stood for a few minutes, taking in the astonishing fan vault. The masons had used the original semicircle of the Norman arch over the crossing to guide the new vaulting scheme. I recognised the bulging eyes and snaggled teeth of the beast cut into the keystone as well as an accompanying run of paterae as the work of Old Sarum masons, with its cousins in Cluny and Malmesbury Abbey.

Light panned down from the high clerestory windows to light up the golden Hamstone columns which burst into a fountain that dispersed into liernes and bosses. Pushing along the trolleyed mirror to view the ceiling revealed a record of pre-Reformation theological thinking with a mixture of themes and motifs cut into the bosses. Most were floral or foliate incorporating the three types of green man, rich with the varying theme of virulent nature as foliage, flowers and grapes spewed from the mouths and noses of hapless souls. The coat of arms of Henry VII contrasted with a couple of dogs chasing a bone, St Michael the Archangel slaying the dragon, a pelican in her piety, and the most famous boss of them all – a mermaid with comb and mirror, surrounded by a wreath of oak leaves.

One of the recurring bosses depicted a ram inside the loop of the letter P under the letters SAM, an armorial pun on the abbot who commissioned the work: Peter Ramsam. Legend has it that the master mason employed to build the fan vault was one Teddy Rowe, who completed his great architectural achievement in 1490, the same year that Hinton St George was finished. Rowe was a master of a different order from Hinton's jobbing tower builder. The story is that when the work was completed the masons packed up their tools and paraded through the streets, so the fair has continued ever since as 'Pack' Monday.

The aroma of onions frying lured us outside. Traders spun candyfloss onto sticks, unlocked mobile phones and sold objects of dubious virtue to locals, tourists and travelling folk. At midnight a 'band' named after Teddy Rowe wanders the streets making a deafening racket, letting off air horns, blowing bugles, beating saucepans and the lids of wheelie bins.

A week later, the dog days of summer were ending and we had filled, secured and decorated the vault. Now the work moved outside and I was sat astride one of the flying buttresses that support the choir. Its arm connected with the clerestory of the choir at the usual midpoint of support between the big Perpendicular windows. I was at a loss to understand why the medieval master felt the need to prop this end with flying buttresses when there were none on the nave.

Hamstone tends to delaminate, and the top sections of several buttresses were tired beyond repair and required replacement. The forces of thrust and counterthrust that held up the walls could not afford to be compromised, so after inspection and sounding with a chisel for dullness, replacement of those stones was the only option.

With the end joints of the original stone cut out with a normal wood saw, I didn't wish to challenge the forces of compression upon which the whole building depended for too long, so I quickly levered out the whole section and replaced it with a new one, pre-manufactured in the workshop. Scraping away on the surface with a drag, the equivalent of a carpenter's plane, to dress in the new work, my forearms glittered gold in the autumn sunshine with the dust. Below, the last of the autumn's house martins skimmed over the grass before their great migration to central Africa. I pictured them crossing the downs to the south coast and over the Isle of Portland that projects into the sea like a finger to provide the shortest route to the continent.

I packed up the last of my own tools held in a small chapel off the north transept, admiring the strange Renaissance-era monument that took up much of its space. Upon a canopied four-poster bed rested a pair of knights in medieval armour that was about a hundred years out of date. I counted twenty-two horses' heads, a heraldic pun on the family name adorning the surfaces on coats of arms, protruding from the top of the canopy and on each corner. Over the years working on and off at the abbey I had got to know all about Sir John Horsey who lay interred there under his likeness with his son. In the Reformation when Henry VIII sought to crush the power of the monasteries and refill the exchequer's depleted coffers, they were the principal local beneficiaries. Sir John, it is believed, cleverly bribed the king's chief minister, the vicar-general Thomas Cromwell, to appoint a new abbot who was unlikely to lend opposition to the new order of things. This allowed Horsey to purchase the monastic buildings and land of Sherborne Abbey at a bargain price in 1539.

★

The English Reformation was bound up with King Henry's desperation for an annulment of his marriage to Catherine of Aragon, his first wife, who in the language of the time had not yet produced a male heir and so threatened the future of the Tudor dynasty. An annulment could only be granted by the pope who was more afraid of the wrath of Catherine's cousin, the Holy Roman Emperor Charles V, than that of the English king. So Henry passed legislation through Parliament to curb the power of the papacy in England and moved quickly not only to take control over much of the Church's property but also to remove any reminders that the pope was ruler of the Church in England before 1534, when Henry became its 'supreme head on earth'.

You can see the evidence of the radical steps that were taken in every church, abbey and cathedral. The effects were catastrophic. Apart from the ban on processions and fairs that would have affected cathedral cities like Wells, the changes came in two different ways. Henry's son, Edward VI, introduced the translation of the liturgy into English as the *Book of Common Prayer* in 1549, and this required a rethink of how church interiors were laid out. As the mystery of the Sacrament was now removed and the 'sacred' areas of the church opened up, the vicar was forced to leave the chancel in order that his sermons and readings should be understood by the congregants; if they couldn't hear him, the value of having the service in English was lost. Reading desks started to be used at the east end of the nave and were often combined with a pulpit for sermons and another desk for the parish clerk. This is seen best at St Mary's in Old Dilton with its triple-decker pulpit. There you can also see the typical wooden table that replaced the stone altar, so that during the act of Communion it could be moved into the middle of the nave or chancel for the parishioners to kneel around. Dilton's interior is a precursor to the new parish churches built after the Civil War for the growing number of non-conformist protestants who had abandoned churches altogether in favour of meeting houses such as Avebury's Five Mile or Dissenters chapel of 1670.

However, the biggest change was the systematic demolition of monasteries and the stripping of images, stained glass, miracle-working statues, relics, ornaments and liturgy from every church. The life-sized images of the Crucifixion that were placed in front of the chancel arch – known as roods, from the Saxon word *rode* meaning cross – seem to have been a particular focus for the venom of the fundamentalists as they were thought to represent popish idolatry. The reformers worked hard to remove them all. The Saxon Crucifixion image, several feet tall, cut into the stonework above the narrow chancel arch and now entirely mutilated at St Laurence's in Bradford-on-Avon, could only have been chiselled off with great effort; here defacement wasn't enough. Today, apart from some remnants, not a single medieval rood survives in Britain, although many must have been hidden in anticipation of a future redemption. We had once conserved a remarkable, and terribly defaced, fifteenth-century rood, a foot square, that lay for many years under the pews of St Margaret of Antioch, Leigh Delamere, Wiltshire.

After we had recorded the condition of the rood and given it a gentle clean, one of our number conserved the decorative colour scheme. Vivid crimsons, blues, gold leaf and skin tones came back to life from distant centuries. A corner may have been knocked away and the faces of Mary and John the

Evangelist smashed, but in spite of this it shows a quality that was once common. In its new position by the chancel, it retains a certain power unusual to encounter in English churches today.

The destruction of roods was as much a political as religious act. Always found on the people's side of the church, they were replaced with large royal coats of arms, painted or carved, affixed either on top of the rood screen or over the Chancel arch. Some people were unhappy with this. The bishop of Salisbury was asked by a rare vocal defender of the old faith, Dr Harding, 'Is it the word of God that setteth up a dog and dragon in place of the Blessed Virgin Mary, mother of God and St John the Evangelist?' The greyhound and dragon support the coat of arms of Henry VIII. The power of the royal family over the Church was now such that they determined how people worshipped and the images they were allowed to see. Interiors which were once richly decorated were white-limed over and within a few years all was plain and unadorned. In places, even church bells were melted down and plate, candlesticks and other valuables found their way into the royal treasury. Many successful merchants and the gentry, such as Sir John Horsey, made the most of the windfall. The glum expressions that the Horseys wear on their tombs were, I think, a mask to conceal their pleasure at the price they got when the town corporation bought the abbey from them in 1554.

The corporation would have been delighted to gain control of the abbey from the monks after many years of conflict that had almost led to it burning to the ground in an earlier dispute. Sherborne Abbey was, up until the Reformation, two churches: the Abbey Church of St Mary and, where the car park is now, All Hallows, the church used by the townspeople. A few clustered piers of All Hallows' north aisle wall, built into a boundary wall it shares with the now-famous Sherborne School, are all that remains of the latter church that was demolished after the Reformation. Resentment at their exclusion from St Mary's, which had always been their church, boiled over in 1437 when the townspeople erected a font of their own in All Hallows. The abbot was so enraged that he sent 'a stout butcher' to destroy the font with a hammer. The east end of the abbey was being rebuilt at that time in the new Perpendicular style, and its stripped roof had been given a temporary covering of thatch. In the ensuing riot, a flaming arrow was shot into the thatch, causing a conflagration which destroyed the wooden scaffolding, and the floor of the nave was filled with a deep layer of charcoal and burning debris. The result of this fire can still be seen in the piers and crossing of the nave where the walls were charred a deep red. This dispute was settled by the pope, who directed the local people to rebuild the church – but better than it had been before.

The Horseys' monument led me to think of their effect on secular architecture too. Fresh out of college, I worked on Montacute House, the Somerset masterpiece of late Elizabethan Renaissance architecture. On the entrance porch, a carved coat of arms with the initials 'J H' (John Horsey) to one side indicated that this stonework had been brought the ten miles from the Horseys' family seat at Clifton Maybank and used to extend the west front of Montacute at the end of the eighteenth century. The Horsey extension carries some of the house's finest carvings, with what looked like a chess set of gargoyles lining the low parapet on twisted columns between the original tower and its entrance porch. The corner of the porch was shrouded in scaffold, and it was from there that I studied these fantastic beasts. More common in design than their earlier church-residing cousins, the sitting dogs, slinking foxes and playful monkeys that looked out from the mansion shared the same purpose as their hunky-punk forebears – to ward off evil intent and the Devil in the most Gothic of ways. At the bottom of the scaffolding was an affecting scene, reminiscent of the destruction of the Reformation, where sculptural adornment filled a skip to the brim. Repairable obelisks, apes, dogs and dismantled ornate chimneys comprised a maelstrom of now lifeless stone.

I pulled out one of the bodies – a whippet perhaps and the same size as my own. It seems he had reached the end of his guardianship of the house, split in two because of being carved in the wrong bedding plane. After four hundred years of service, he had been rejected by the architect as beyond saving. Replacing a missing ear and pinning the sections back together proved a nice hobby piece for me. Looking back, I only wish I had had the nerve to repair more.

I remembered Montacute House as the richest haven for wild things during a seemingly endless summer – the low wall, pierced with tracery, that enclosed the courtyard garden and main facade abuzz with masonry bees that busied themselves in their solitary pencil-sized nests, tunnelled out of the mortar that bonded the walls together. The pavilions, situated at the corner of the large square-walled garden to the front of the house, carried the first of many architectural messages. Intertwined above their famous curved roofs, double rings presented a favourite symbol of Good Queen Bess and indicated the fealty of its owner, Sir Edward Phelips, to his queen should she arrive with her retinue on a royal progress. This side of the estate was now open country, but was originally the main entrance; the rings were the first of many statements that a visitor would have encountered before arriving at the wide cliff face of the house's east front. They would have been dazzled by the most expensive of building materials – glass – which filled the facade. Its diamond-shaped panes were held in a lattice by lead strips, or cames, in the same way as a church window. The glass reflected wing walls, which, with the central projecting porch, created an E-shaped plan in another message of homage to the queen.

Sir Edward was equally keen to convey his intellect and fashionable sophistication and so, working with master mason William Arnold, who was later to take his band of twenty-seven men on the five-day walk to Oxford to build Wadham College, he commissioned a building that would project his learning. Under a Flemish roofline populated with squatting beasts, layers of Greek, Roman and Egyptian motifs worked their way down the walls to rest around bay windows of French design. Arnold was clearly well travelled and familiar with the latest pattern books from the continent. The windows of the second-floor long gallery were divided by niches containing statues of nine Roman-inspired worthies: three Pagans, three Christians and three Jews looked down over a courtyard and garden, each with an arm raised and a gripped hand ready to receive the flags of welcome for the guests.

Below the windows were four intriguing, perfectly cut hollows, like the negative of an ice-cream scoop. I enjoyed the shadow that moved quietly, hypnotically across their arc. I was reminded of Galileo's sketches of the phases of the moon, its chiaroscuro motion preceding his observations of the moons of Venus. Unlike the European contemporaries it is clearly imitating, such as Florence's famous Uffizi, the front of Montacute House is much less formal, and borrows equally from the classical and Gothic worlds.

The quarries at Ham Hill started to fade in importance. Their workings fell out of use and soon filled with fern and eglantine. Some stone continued to be used, as it had been since Saxon times, for local, small-scale jobs, but medieval ways of working were drawing to an end and industrialisation was in the air. Only eighteen years after the completion of Montacute in 1601, some of the first shipments of stone arrived in London from the Dorset coast to build one of the most important buildings in the story of Britain's architecture.

The grand Banqueting House is the only part of the Palace of Whitehall that still stands today. It was the first structure to be completed in the neoclassical style that was destined to take over in both town and country, with the palace's designer, Inigo Jones, becoming the first significant English architect of early modern times. He was heavily influenced by the Italian architect Andrea Palladio and had visited his villas, palaces and churches around Venice and the Veneto.

Palladio had been influenced in turn by the first-century BCE architect Vitruvius' *De Architectura*. The pages of Palladio's *The Four Books of Architecture*, published in 1570, are filled with drawings of those buildings of ancient Rome that still survived, as well as Palladio's own designs, which combined clarity in design and execution with symmetry, order and proportion.

The exterior of the Banqueting House was originally made

with alternating courses of stone from Oxfordshire and Northampton, with decorative features in Portland stone from Dorset. It provided the backdrop to the dramatic execution of Charles I on 30 January 1649: the king reached his scaffold by stepping through one of the Banqueting House's large first-floor windows.

The Civil War era was another bad time for the old buildings of the British Isles. Castles were slighted, religious buildings damaged or destroyed and subjected to a second wave of iconoclastic behaviour, where even the remaining stained glass – which had survived the Reformation – was smashed. Most of the damage was directed against royal arms and the tombs and effigies of Royalist families by unruly troops or by military action. As with the church towers of Flanders that were destroyed in the First World War and, more recently, the minarets of Aleppo, high places provide excellent vantage points for observation and directing fire on enemy positions in the surrounding area, which in turn makes them targets. I had seen the scars of the Civil War on the churches of Devizes and Malmesbury, but the worst was at St Michael's Church at Highworth in north Wiltshire, which had been garrisoned and fortified by Royalists in 1644, its walls still dented by cannonballs and pockmarked by grapeshot and musket balls after the bombardment of June 1645 commanded by Oliver Cromwell.

The Italianate court style of the beheaded king, which had fallen out of favour during Cromwell's puritanical Commonwealth, caught on rapidly when Charles II restored the monarchy in 1660. When six years later London was struck down by the Great Fire, Christopher Wren was commissioned to design new churches for the city. Wren's choice of building material, Portland limestone, was brought to the capital from Dorset by sailing barge. Apart perhaps from Purbeck marble, it was one of the first stones to be extracted in industrial quantity and thus to have an influence well beyond its normal geographical limits.

I had decided, while watching the last house martins head south toward Portland from the heights of Sherborne Abbey, to take *Laughing Water* along the Jurassic coastline to the place Thomas Hardy called the 'Isle of Slingers'. To some, the super-stitious, barren, treeless, prison island may seem a strange place to be drawn to, but I wanted to understand the sea roads that had been taken to transport the island's greatest resource to the centre of London. I also had an appointment at a quarry on the island to inspect the stone I had ordered that was destined for the restoration of two eighteenth-century churchyard monu-ments.

The following day I set out from Wareham's stone quay and enjoyed the easy flow into the harbour through choppy waters. The ebb tide soon sped me through the harbour's narrow mouth past the bottleneck of chain ferry, yacht, and fishing craft. Ahead, the distant edge of a tricorn hat that formed the Isle of Wight, acted as a marker for the sea lanes that led to the Thames estuary.

These stone-carrying voyages that involved dodging French and Dutch enemy shipping would have been perilous. The wreck of a nineteenth-century carvel-built boat rests preserved on the seabed in the Solent off Selsey Bill. Its cargo – immense blocks of stone – still stand proud of the seabed to a height of four metres from its submerged hull. The squalls that suddenly blow out of nowhere across these waters would have done for the craft, its high centre of gravity influencing its demise.

I paddled southwards past the pure white stacks of Old Harry Rocks to where Durlston Head's chalk cliffs greyed to Purbeck burr stone. The Tilly Whim Caves sparked a remembrance of the roughly cut inscription by its entrance, prompting visitors to 'Look round and read great nature's open book'. Blue skies and the mildest of easterlies at my back helped ease the canoe along. I was far enough out in the no-man's-land between sea and shore to run parallel to the cliffs that helter-skeltered on westwards to distant Weymouth at the head of the bay, where Portland's great wedge-shaped rock plateau looked like a lost world. The smell of ozone and the dramatic landscape that defines the Jurassic coastline combine to create an atmosphere so eerie that it was not difficult to imagine a pterosaur launching from the cliffs in search of the ammonites that today lie exposed on its surfaces.

The next challenge that waited was negotiating the imposing St Aldhelm's Head around which aggressive currents compress into the worst of tidal races. It was a far more difficult paddle than anticipated. The plan had been to cut from the other side of the headland across Weymouth Bay to Portland but that was a trip for fresh arms and the sun was already lowering out of sight in a blaze of glory. So, on the far side of the head, I sought refuge in the secret bay of Chapman's Pool, and in the shelter of a ruined cottage I laid out the bivvy bag on a flat grass shelf.

At five thirty the following morning the canoe was back in the water, and by breakfast time I spied Lulworth Cove, but it was too choppy to enter through its Pillars of Hercules. Cliffs, stacks, arches and landslides continued along the heights as far as the village of Osmington where the White Horse cut in the hill indicates the last of the chalk. Weymouth Bay was becalmed and I calculated it would take about four hours to reach the protective wall of Portland Harbour at the end of Chesil Beach, the shingle bank that connected the great, four-mile-long Gibraltar-like crag of my destination to the mainland.

Chesil Beach's great arc sweeps away to end at West Bay eighteen miles distant, where the coast eventually gives rise to rocks and cliffs around Lyme Bay, past the flat peak of Golden Cap – the south coast's distant highpoint. In high summer with the heat radiating from the pale boulders of its herb-laden slopes and the sea glittering in the background I could be on a Greek shore, the edge of Mount Athos perhaps, but when the easterlies blow across the Channel it is a different place. The Isle is often regarded as down at heel, industrial and weird. Here the Jurassic coastline plays tricks; where the beach meets the island the cobbles are as big as flattened turnips and have graded down evenly to pea gravel by the time West Bay is reached. A lobster fisherman, who hunts his quarry from one of the last boats to still work the bay, once told me that if he landed his boat in the fog, he would know exactly where he was by the size of the shingle.

The cliff's cross-section at West Weares, which lowers behind the old fisherman's hut that is our toehold on the island, presents a four-hundred-foot high geology lesson with beds of stone that are much easier to work than their equivalent on Purbeck. The rubble overburden near the top of the formation yielded to the solidity of its white Upper Jurassic oolite, the youngest 'freestone' bed on the island: the roach. This is rather coarse and full of distinctive fossils, such as the bivalves the old quarry-men called 'osses 'eads, which make it extremely durable and so the perfect choice for more exposed areas such as plinths or drip mouldings. Next is the prized whitbed, the best beds of which are pure oolite and are largely fossil free. This rests on the curf, which was sometimes called the 'little roach'. Finally comes the basebed, favoured by carvers and letter-cut-ters as the absence of shells and its softer nature provide easier workability. These best beds are found between 30 to 60 feet below the surface, which meant the quarrymen had to work hard to 'win the stone'.

I thought back to my time at St Paul's, the greatest building to have been created from Portland stone, and the pair of medicine ball-sized cherubic heads that look innocently over the east end stretching away towards Canary Wharf. The white-ness of the rain-washed areas of the cherubs' hair contrasted with the black sulphation that represented three hundred years of London life. It created a pleasing distinction that made me question the job I had of cleaning it up. But I worked with a dummy and the usual letter-cutting chisel to gently ping off the worst of the crust of black carbon that helped to define the cherub's finely carved side parting on an otherwise unruly shock of hair.

Overhead, the great, ethereal dome strained into grey London clouds from the circle of the outer colonnade to which the scaffolding perch was fixed. Wren agreed with Inigo Jones's use of Portland stone, specifying it for the rebuild of London churches after the fire of 1666, and thus established it as London's construction material of choice. The outer colonnade, or peristyle, surrounded an inner drum, which is what really holds up the dome and cupola. The dome's design had many influences but was an imaginative interpretation of Donato Bramante's Tempietto of 1502; the colonnade was an extension of an idea taken from another of the eternal city's circular buildings, the second-century BCE Temple of Hercules Victor. Under its makeshift circular hat of terracotta tiles a colonnade of Greek Pentelic marble encloses an inner sanctuary.

The church authorities needed the new St Paul's Cathedral to become a London landmark. The addition of a Gothic spire was out of the question as Wren wished to embrace the latest ideas from the continent. Apart from the Banqueting House, London had no neoclassical precedents. In St Paul's, Wren masterfully developed a restrained version of the baroque architecture of Paris and Rome that also suited the Italianate taste of Charles II. He achieved this by taking aspects of Palladianism and mixing them with Renaissance Italian cathedral and campanile design, all of which had been influenced by the dome architecture of Byzantium and Islam.

Below, pollution-stained statues of saints and Apostles glared down upon unsuspecting pedestrians from the top of a neoclassical screen-wall. This hid a series of stepped flying buttresses that filled the space behind to support the nave clerestory and vault. Although the facade projected an idea of the neoclassical baroque, I could see that Wren had borrowed heavily from the Middle Ages. This was apparent not only because of its methods of construction but also its cruciform plan. Its focus on length over width and powerful projecting transepts reminded me a little of Wells Cathedral. The nave clerestory continued the medieval tradition of towering over the side aisles and the Wells influence continued in the facade's twin bell-towers that jutted just beyond the aisles. I was struck by how much they also resembled minarets, their square bases rising to cupolas like the tower at the Great Mosque at Córdoba in Spain, and how, when viewed from the front where they were designed to be seen, they contrasted harmoniously with the dome in a purely Islamic fashion.

Wren was a great admirer of Islamic architecture and I could see what he meant when he wrote, 'What we now vulgarly call the Gothick, ought properly and truly be named Saracenick Architecture refined by the Christians.'

All domes possess a tendency to spread at their base. At St Paul's I ventured into the base of the dome to see how this was managed. It was hot and claustrophobic inside, and the outer dome of lead-covered boards supported by a timber framework creaked like the planks of a boat in the sun. I savoured the usual church roof smell of hot resinous timber and visualised, buried deep within its base, the solution to the lack of dome-spread – a pair of chains, encased in lead and cleverly concealed in the brick masonry. The chains, I realised, looped around what was a completely separate structure that stretched up as a cone into the darkness. I was squeezed between not one but three domes, a construction method taken, so Wren says in the second of his tracts on architecture, from the Hagia Sophia in Istanbul. The great internal cone did the heavy lifting and was perhaps Wren's greatest invention, as it was upon the cone's 18-inch thick walls that the interior ceiling dome, which can be seen from the nave crossing, and the outer dome depended.

Wren's friend Robert Hooke, the polymath astronomer and

architect, helped to combine mathematics with masonry as part of the dome's design process. Hooke had experimented to find the shape of the perfect arch and the notion had crystallised with him that the way tension passed through the slackness of a chain hung at two ends matched the arc of compression in an arch and dome, a catenary that also followed its line of thrust. This discovery created the dominating outer form that we are all so familiar with. The cone was likewise designed originally as a form of catenary; however, in the end it was constructed with straight sides as it needed to support the additional weight of the large lantern that weighed a formidable 850 tons.

I made my way down by what seemed an endless spiral stairway to the nave and looked up to where I had begun my descent. High in the crossing, the internal dome rested on deep pendentives, a cousin of the squinch. London's, and perhaps the nation's, most beloved church was an impressive monument to the influences of Muslim engineering and architecture. I wondered what my Nan, with her old-fashioned views of 'foreigners', would have thought of that. I remembered her telling me that, when struggling to get through the smashed city to work at the Woolwich Arsenal, as long as she could see the dome of St Paul's rising through the smoke and ruination of the Blitz, then everything was going to be all right.

Tony, the cathedral's master carver, who was taught his craft rebuilding Wren's city churches after the Blitz, took me in hand as he attempted to bring on my skills. He was a natural philosopher and his maxims pop into my head daily: 'Use a punch for roughing out like Michelangelo did'; 'Cut the form right before tackling the detail'; 'Carve as if you were drawing, with your chisel at an angle, never cut down as it stuns the stone to create a sheer plane'; 'Wear different overalls and hat for different materials as stone dust blunts wood chisels'.

In his 1970s cycling hat, Tony showed me the now neglected process of how to use a quirking chisel to create undercuts in situ. All the deep statuary carving around us had been quirked and left rough so the accumulating soot could accentuate light and shade. About two feet long, the quirking chisel had a fire-hardened sharpened tip. This was an unusual tool to me, as most modern chisels have a tungsten tip. But tungsten would chip and fail in the action of quirking where, after each blow on the chisel, it would be turned so that the blade would land with a few degrees of difference.

Suddenly, all hell broke loose around us when Tony noticed that one of the masons was cutting in a newly carved Ionic volute beneath the cherub's head, a job that should have been done by the carving department. This, he thought, was the thin end of the wedge and unprecedented bad behaviour by a management more concerned with cutting costs by blurring the distinction between trades. For a refreshing moment I realised that this was a place where social mores and ways of doing and thinking had, in many ways, remained unchanged since the cathedral's construction had commenced in 1675.

I brought my thoughts firmly back to the present, the Isle of Portland and the business at hand. I climbed up the cliff face to Bowers Quarry to see if the sawn whitbed I had ordered could be collected. The coastal path runs along the edge of the eternally subsiding cliffs; I stopped to study one of the 'bridges' that cross it, from where the quarry waste was tipped to form the enormous scree slope that spread out to the turquoise sea. It looked as if a race of giants had piled up the fridge-sized blocks to create a portal to their world. This one bore a lintel the size of a telephone box laid on its side. The adjacent open-cast quarry was a vast silent moonscape, now unused, but by the entrance to a modern underground mine shaft, blocks of roach stone were piled high ready for the saw. I went over and admired the combinations of fossils it held. My favourite was the outline of the Portland screw, *Aptyxiella portlandica* – carrot-shaped with a thick spiral thread into it, a long-vanished curiosity.

The idea that species could become extinct was first deduced from Portland fossils, mainly in the observation of the giant ammonite *Titanites giganteus*, noticed by Robert Hooke as he visited the quarries to inspect the quality of the stone destined for St Paul's. In 1665 Hooke published *Micrographia*, where he described the observations he had made with the microscopes he had built himself. Among these observations he studied the structure of living wood, coming up with the word 'cell' for its resemblance to the cells of a honeycomb. He concluded that fossilised objects like wood and shells, such as ammonites, were the remains of once living things, thinking them 'so unlike any living species, that they must be the remains of species "totally destroyed and annihilated".' Two hundred and fifty years before Darwin, Hooke identified the true nature of fossils: 'There have been many other Species of Creatures in former Ages, of which we can find none at present; and that 'tis not unlikely also but that there may be diverse new kinds now, which have not been from the beginning.'

It feels entirely apposite that the stairway up the Portland-stone Monument to the Great Fire in London, designed by Wren and Hooke to house a two-hundred-foot zenith telescope, spirals in its Fibonacci way in the same manner as *Titanites giganteus*, its column drawing together the purest and most harmonious parts of the Enlightenment.

When Andy arrived at the quarry, we loaded the slabs of whitbed into the back of the pickup in readiness for our trip to repair the tombs of two Enlightenment gentlemen, two hundred years after their deaths. Thomas Gainsborough resides within the churchyard of St Anne's in Kew, while Granville Sharp was interred on the other side of the river in Fulham. Sharp, who died in 1813, was a man so controversial at the time of his funeral that he was refused a eulogy. William Wilberforce has always overshadowed him, but it was in fact Sharp (along with his friend Thomas Clarkson) who founded the Society for the Abolition of the Slave Trade. Sharp was also a talented musician who could play two flutes at once and signed himself 'G#'. With his siblings, he held lunchtime concerts on their Thames-side houseboat.

Sharp's Portland chest tomb was in a sorry state. We peeled off the smothering ivy to reveal its restrained neoclassical form – a gently pitched plain capstone, fluted corner pilasters and a moulded cornice, all set on landing stones. A lengthy tribute to Sharp was almost unintelligible on the long north face. The effects of acid rain and subsidence were evident as well as the usual rusting cramps, which were applying huge pressures in the tops and bottoms of the ledger panel and on the carved fluted corner pieces, one of which was completely beyond repair. Apart from Portland stone, the two tombs had another thing in common – a creature, inch-long and black as a newly polished shoe, churchyard beetle. They burrowed about like clockwork in their dozens in the soil and debris of both tombs, to emit an evil-smelling liquid from their rear end as a means of defence when disturbed.

We could do all the repairs and cut the new stone ourselves, but the job of letter cutting was best left to a specialist, and so Robyn Golden-Hann came up from Salisbury to recut the inscription in a fine Baskerville typeface, recording that Sharp left:

behind him a name That will be Cherished with Affection and Gratitude as long as any homage shall be paid to those principles Of JUSTICE HUMANITY and RELIGION he promoted by his Exertion and adorned by his Example

When the works were complete, a service of remembrance was held at which the historian Simon Schama delivered the eulogy. He noted that Sharp 'lowered the threshold of shame' in society. A wreath was placed on the tomb. Descendants of Sharp's family were there and an imbalance was adjusted.

Thomas Gainsborough, one of the most famous English portrait and landscape painters of the eighteenth century, lies buried on the south side of St Anne's, Kew. His tomb was covered by London ivy and surrounded by high, brown, end-of-season weeds. Lying under the flight path to Heathrow, its cracks and rusty railings were also covered in a film of black, smutty pollutants. Gainsborough's instruction in his will that 'a stone without arms or ornament might be placed over him, inscribed with his bare name' had over the years come to be ignored, with a plinth and railings added in the late-eighteenth century. We were, in turn, to challenge his last wishes, as we had been commissioned to further improve the design, add a plinth and clad the exposed Victorian brickwork upon which his black capstone rested.

With our gantry and our block and tackle we lifted the horizontal gravestone from its crumbling sidewalls. Peering inside, three centuries' worth of grey cobwebs lay over the contents like a badly woven textile. Three lead coffins in what was a rather shallow grave had been placed one on top of the other. The bottommost one had split under the weight of Gainsborough's successors, and the bones of his right hand were plain to see. I thought back to his paintings in Bath's Victoria Gallery where he made his name as a portraitist and 'pickpocketed the rich'. The sudden memory of the tender, arresting drawings of his two young daughters at the Victoria and Albert Museum compelled me to reach down and gently place my finger on his, in an act of homage and apology at our unwished-for intervention. With the slab fixed back into position Robyn came back and recut the hard, formal inscription in Baskerville capitals that, like my enthusiasm for working in our capital, had nearly faded away.

Finishing up late and without digs for the evening, I gently closed and locked the door to St Anne's behind me and made my way to curl up in the velvety, tasselled plushness of the church's royal gallery in readiness for the long journey home. Looking down the nave I could see that by the mid-eighteenth century, stone vaults had become a thing of the past. The industrialisation that had sparked the development of the stone industries on Portland could now be seen in all aspects of the country – in manufacturing, agricultural life and the transport system, which was one of the great achievements of the early seventeenth century. In the bone-still darkness of the royal church, I studied the route home I was to take the next day, paddling the River Thames upstream in *Laughing Water*, its final journey on what had un-intentionally become a circular route around southern England.

The next morning I awoke much revived in the still darkness. I reflected on the bottoms of kings, queens and princesses that once rested where I now lay in my sleeping bag. Queen Caroline, King George II, Frederick, Prince of Wales, mad King George III and Queen Charlotte would all have made their way here on a Sunday morning across the park from Kew Palace. From my banquette I could see the terracotta blur of the palace's Dutch gables, their ogeed line lifted in limewashed terracotta incongruity across the evergreens of the parakeet-infested Royal Botanical Gardens.

The church's great door clunked shut behind me and I made my way across the pre-dawn green to an unusually quiet Kew Bridge beneath which, waiting to carry me home to Somerset, *Laughing Water* was tethered to a slipway, immersed only in the early mist and the great river's tang. The Thames was what Churchill called the 'golden thread' that drew together not only the fabric of Britain's history but also the network of waterways that made it possible to travel inland along the arteries that were to prime a revolution, and allow trade with the heart of the country.

PART FOUR
CONCRETE

10

SAMHAIN EVE

I was ready to start the longest section of my ad-hoc tour of the waterways of southern Britain. It was a hundred or so miles from Kew to the city of Bath by river and canal, and I was eager to take in some of the places with royal patronage, from an Anglo-Saxon prince's burial mound to the finest royal palace of all at Hampton Court. But I was most keen to learn about what became an arterial route of the Industrial Revolution, and how the profits of that revolution were spent in the city of Bath. This was a route that would bring together the North Sea and the Atlantic, Europe and the Americas, and in following it I hoped to understand how the world became a little smaller.

I pushed the canoe, with the whippet sat regally at its bow, graunching across the shallows that covered a shingle beach; it was a blend of geology and history that gave a snapshot of the shoreline's long story of human use. Mud and seashells mixed in with the white clay stems of old tobacco pipes and potsherds. Further up the embankment a mass of weed-fringed old bricks, boat-shaped in plan, was the final load from a working wherry, traditionally used for carrying cargo and passengers along the river. Today the Thames is less well used as a method of conveyance for goods and people and I imagined joining in with the flow of rivermen rowing along what for several hundred years was the busiest highway in Britain. I was soon to learn that taking the secret route along the Thames through the towns and villages is a good way to understand how these places evolved.

The dog and I went quickly past the limit of the tideway at Teddington Lock and Kingston, where the sarsen coronation stone upon which seven Saxon kings had been crowned waits patiently by the Guildhall to be used again. Royals, the well-to-do and churchmen all kept their estates upstream from the capital, and it was the red-brick Tudor sprawl of the most magnificent estate of its time that I saw in snapshots as I passed the gaps between the long stands of bankside willows. Closing in, the famous chimneyed roofline lifted to project the power and magnificence of its builder, Cardinal Thomas Wolsey, who laid the first brick in 1515.

Hampton Court Palace was a building suitable to host not only the king and his courtiers, but also monarchs and other heads of the Church from across Europe. Unsurprisingly, Wolsey's king took a fancy to the building that surpassed many of his own palaces, and so it inevitably came into the possession of Henry VIII after the cardinal fell from favour in 1529 and rapidly evolved into a true royal palace.

With the canoe tethered to a willow's hawser-like root, I met my bricklayer friend, Emma Simpson, who whisked me up to the remotest part of the palace. Leading the way through the myriad gatehouses and courtyards, she took me up to the roof where a ladder climb onto her scaffolding allowed a breathtaking view of perhaps the best example of the 'great rebuilding' that took place throughout Britain during the sixteenth and seventeenth centuries, when medieval houses were updated or replaced. I realised that what we were looking out on was more important to the social history of Britain than the great hall below, with its wall-hung tapestries woven with a gold thread designed to glimmer in the candlelight during the extravagant banquets that were once held there.

In those early post-Gothic times, buildings moved away from a simple open fire on a hearth in the middle of the floor, the smoke drifting up into the roof space, to the fireplace, flue and chimney. Compartmentalisation became the norm and so changed how people, regardless of class or influence, used buildings. Most readers can see this in their own homes, which owe little to the buildings of the Middle Ages.

The groups of chimneys built from humble red brick that take away the smoke at the palace created a dramatic display. The pinnacle had been replaced as a device to display wealth and power; but the 241 chimneys that twist upward almost in imitation of the fires were much more practical. However, it was not just their quantity that is so impressive but also the ornateness of the detailing contrasting with the straightforward construction of the palace's walls. This was intended to draw the eye and accentuate the message of power and wealth.

Having just finished the job of rebuilding a clump of stacks, Emma was giving me a master class in how the chimneys were built. It was a process every bit as complicated as if they were made from ashlar stone. The patterns of the three spiralling, fluted and diapered shafts – designs that served to dissipate heat – lifted to an even more elaborate crown sat on a base of horizontal cusped horns that taper to a point: unnecessary work that added to their status as a clear display of wealth. None of the original stacks remain, soft Tudor brick proving unable to deal with the caustic properties of soot, weather and later inappropriate repairs in hard cement. The design for chimneys had evolved as a response to the increasing use of coal, which, being smokier than wood, ultimately led to the chimneys' undoing: the damaging sulphates introduced to the bricks left each one as rotten as a pear.

Emma worked in a methodical way with a mindset that would be familiar to most other craftspeople. To ensure a sensitive rebuild she traced a plan of each course onto a plastic template as the stacks were dismantled. Sound bricks were carefully cleaned up for reuse and numbered so that they could be replaced in their original locations. Once templates of every brick had been made, Emma and her team could reproduce the shapes from clay blocks that were fired at a lower temperature than usual to create a brick with a softer skin, known as a 'red rubber'. Placed in a snug box, a newly fired brick would be ready to take a new profile. The wood at either end of the box had a template cut into it to allow easier guidance so shapes could then be cut by hand with a wire-bladed bow saw and finished with a variety of tools: rifflers, rasps, files, or hammer and chisel. Emma could produce any shape in this way. The crown's replacement bricks alone used twenty-one different boxes that were one-offs. To check it all fitted comfortably together and that the bonding in each course worked well, the arrangement had already been dry-laid at the workshop.

In addition to the exacting rubbing and cutting, justice to the Tudor craftspeople was done with the laying of the bricks on the finest joints possible. Emma had reused the waste brick-dust sweepings from the cutting process as a pozzolana in the

Roman way, which helped to toughen the lime, lending the joint a pleasing pink hue.

She mentioned that, elsewhere in protected areas around the palace, the original mortar was red, coloured by 'ruddle', which I supposed was just a variation on 'reddle', the natural earth colour used to mark sheep. It was fascinating to learn how the changing relationship between buildings and people could be understood by simply looking at a palace's chimneys – structures that were a convenient marker for the beginning of the change to our world.

Relieved that the whippet was still happily napping when I returned, I pushed off. The change from ancient to modern was something I would become more aware of as I continued to follow the river upstream.

It was a slog against the flow, even though the Thames had become sluggish, filled with winter flood water and slowed by the several weirs and their locks that effectively turn each section into a slowly moving lake. I had so far paddled about twenty miles from Kew, when the massive silhouette of Windsor Castle grew in size until its sheer cliff-like faces seemed to lift out of the meadows. Dusk had drawn in but, breaking all the rules of the river, I continued to paddle away into the night until I found shelter and privacy at my destination of the village of Taplow near Maidenhead, in the lee of the great mound that gives the village its name.

Tæppas Hláw, Taplow Barrow, rests atmospherically in an abandoned churchyard, enclosed by a brick wall and surrounded by broken down Georgian box tombs. I carefully paced out the 240 feet circumference of the unnamed Anglo-Saxon princeling's seventh-century resting place, before finding a spot to sleep. The tumulus gave off the feeling that it could easily look after itself. Inside, the treasure that had once laid around the nobleman, and which included a Coptic bowl from Egypt, was the largest Saxon hoard to be discovered until Sutton Hoo was unearthed in Suffolk in 1939.

I had strange dreams and only slept fitfully, so I was away at first light, ready for a long day of travel. I was greeted almost immediately by the grotesque Victorian edifice of Cliveden House that piled up in huge tiers out of its landscaped gardens. Further on, Marlow and Henley presented their best sides to the river and it was a relief to reach Kennet Mouth at Reading.

The flow increased at the confluence with the Kennet. Home was somewhere over the horizon from where a cadent sun sent its brightest parts to illuminate the railway viaducts, gasworks and brick terraces of Reading. It was only a couple of days before All Hallows' Eve and a huge influx of starlings, freshly returned from Siberia, added to the surprisingly eerie atmosphere. They populated every horizontal and edged surface, and engaged in a chorus of avian Tourette's. As they settled in tune with the darkness, constellations of polystyrene flecks flowed about upended shopping trolleys, semi-submerged in oily waters, sourced paradoxically from the virginal Swallowhead Spring back in Wiltshire.

The following morning, after a full English, I wandered the bankside ruins of Reading's Norman abbey. William of Malmesbury recorded that it was built 'between the rivers Kennet and Thames, in a place calculated for the reception of almost all who might have occasion to travel to the more populous cities of England'. The adjacent red-brick gaol wall and the surrounding office blocks required a major leap of imagination for my mind's eye to see what would have surpassed Old Sarum and Malmesbury as the dominant Romanesque church of Wessex.

Stone tablets on a wall of the chapter house hint at its status; one records the final resting place of Henry I, the Conqueror's heir, the other, intriguingly, a large rectangular facsimile of a medieval manuscript cut in stone. Musical notation was set to lyrics, the first line reading: *Sumer is icumen in, Loude sing cuckou! Groweth seed and bloweth meed and springth the wode now. Sing cuckou!* This song is the earliest recorded in the English language, and was written down in the abbey's scriptorium in the 1240s in the Wessex dialect of Middle English that people spoke hereabouts. When was the last time a cuckoo had last been heard in these parts, I wondered, as I slipped the canoe back in the canal on the site of the abbey's wharf and paddled through the Brewery Gut lined with red-brick offices, shopping centres and restaurants.

After a day's journey, the river divided from its natural flow at Newbury and became a proper canal, the Kennet and Avon, which climbed away in a series of locks. I simply pulled the canoe out of the brown water and walked around these. A night in a straw-filled open-sided Dutch barn, an early brew and then onwards, the canal shadowing the river as far as Hungerford, where they went their separate ways – the river to Silbury Hill and the Swallowhead, the canal running westward as an artificial man-made cut for a further fifty-seven miles. My aim was to get to the canal pumping station at Crofton before it was dark, where I hoped its pair of ancient engines would be steaming and snorting for the last time before their long period of winter maintenance.

The steady number of locks and bridges along my route were watched over by a chain of Second World War pillboxes. This seemingly slender obstacle, the 'GHQ Stop Line Blue', was one of many designed to draw the river and canal network into compartments throughout the countryside and delay any Nazi invasion force long enough for more mobile forces to counter-attack.

Another bridge, number '99' on its small metal plaque, was burdened still with giant 'dragon's teeth' – tank traps that punctuated its back. This bridge, arched with its protrusions, cut an almost antediluvian presence, like a brick stegosaurus. The biggest surprise was passing beneath its arch, which crossed the canal not at the normal right angle, but at an acute skew. This was perhaps the first skew bridge to be put up in Britain. Its vault, quite different from all the others I had passed, was formed by four separate parallel courses of brick, which theoretically gave it extra strength by throwing the stress into the inward slope that forms the batter of the arch.

Judging by the irregularity of the courses, the engineer of the canal, John Rennie, who died aged sixty in 1821, had expected more from his bricklayers. Doing this for the first time would have been a real headache. To keep weight down, Rennie's bridges are broader at the springing point of the arch than at the apex. Setting this out scientifically would have required a difficult piece of geometry probably beyond the skill of country bricklayers and so perhaps was an exercise in trial and error, but one that had at least remained standing for three hundred years.

Leaving the bridge in my wake, I saw the distant polluting pall of the pumping station's chimney smeared across the chilly blue sky before I heard, carried along the waterway, the engine's wheezing beats.

The brick stabling seemed only just able to contain the two beasts inside, as the engines gurgled and grunted their way through the day. The elder, built by Boulton and Watt at the Soho Works in Smethwick near Birmingham, is the world's oldest steam engine still capable of carrying out its original job in the place it was designed for. It has been running on and off since the year of Napoleon's retreat from Moscow. The other engine was built by Harvey & Co. of Hayle, Cornwall, in 1846.

I thought the great brick chimney a piece of architecture far more worthy than the showy domesticity of its cousins at Hampton Court, which do nothing better than aid the provision of heat and hot food. By contrast, this plain exhaust vent was one that, in the century from 1760, helped change everything to create the world we inhabit today.

Inside, the pumping station, which was once at the leading edge of technology, continued its job of keeping the canal at a constant height, drawing a ton of water per stroke up forty feet from the adjacent lake-like reservoir into the canal feeder. This remarkable survivor is the last of the line to have made the Industrial Revolution possible, creating opportunities to access coal and raw materials that, without engine-powered pumps like these to ventilate and drain floodwaters away from the mines, would otherwise have remained in the ground. These 'miners' friends' developed out of the Cornish tin industry, where they soon became as profitable to make as the industry of mining itself.

Until the Industrial Revolution, iron production had been a small-scale operation, based around local extraction of ore that was smelted in small kilns to create a sponge-like, porous mass of iron and slag called a bloom. A blacksmith would then have forged this into shape by hand. Andy Thearle, a master blacksmith friend, once told me this tale: Alfred the Great called together representatives of all the seven main trades of the time. He informed them that he intended to present the one who could undertake their craft without the help of the others with the title 'king'. Each was instructed to bring an example of their work and the tools they used. Alfred, dazzled by the tailor's cloth, presented him with the title, thus angering the blacksmith, who stormed off. One by one, the tools of the mason, the baker, the shoemaker, the butcher and the carpenter needed mending and, with the blacksmith gone, the tradespeople broke into his forge thinking they could undertake the work themselves. Their ineptitude made the king appreciate that only the blacksmith could make and repair their tools and so was the one that none of them could do without; he therefore proclaimed the smith 'king of all trades'. This is an accolade that as a stonemason I am happy to acknowledge, as I remember the tedium of pounding away on that sarsen with a stone maul.

Blacksmiths also worked iron produced by the charcoal-powered blast furnaces, the heat of which had been increased by a watermill-powered pair of bellows, a technology that had been around since medieval times. It was used extensively in the Weald of Kent and Sussex to create pig iron, which could then be cast in a mould, mainly for cannons and shot. This ultimately took the supply of charcoal to the brink of exhaustion, as the once-dense woodlands of the Weald disappeared. But once Abraham Darby substituted coke for charcoal in 1709 in Coalbrookdale everything changed, and the world of small-scale manufacturing and hand-production methods was finished. Furnaces became huge and the use of coke overcame the crippling shortage of wood. Large castings became possible and the component parts of steam boilers, engines and pumps once made of brass were instead cast as multiples in iron. Without these engines and the new world they powered, the further development of trade along quiet backwater routes such as the Kennet and Avon to the rest of the nation and burgeoning empire, would have been unthinkable.

Thomas Newcomen put together the first successful piston steam engine in the first decade of the eighteenth century. Scotsman James Watt, with his business partner Matthew Boulton, created the even more efficient engine in 1781, one that reduced the consumption of coal by three quarters. This is what the elder at Crofton evolved from. As it wheezed its way to the end of its cycle, I retired with the help of an amiable boiler man, happy to spend the chill autumnal evening beside the boiler's warm oily glow on my foam mat and bivvy bag reflecting on the changes that this technology wrought to our world.

Dawn revealed that the night-knitters had been busy. The time of daddy-long-legs had given way to the time of spiders and I awoke amid their deceptively dainty creations, aware that my kit was covered in a thin film of smutty oil that made me disinclined to spend many more nights in the protective Gore-Tex embrace of my sleeping gear.

Barges, multicoloured and comfortable in their gypsy-wagon-like decorations, were tied up along one side of the otherwise deserted, weedy canal. A wind shook the dry reeds like a sistrum, as in summons, for today was the festival of All Hallows (also known as Samhain), the end of harvest and the start of winter. A pair of turquoise darts flashed by, at eye level, the kingfishers' delight apparent as they alighted on the distant handrail of a lock gate. They took off with a jump and came back my way, their approach through a farm bridge heralded, it seemed, by their long, straining, high-pitched call, a warning repeated again and again, like a train's French horn as it enters a tunnel. A few yards on a heron lanced a fish, tossing it into an open beak in a casual way. I watched in revulsion as the bird's elasticated U-bend neck thickened and stretched to the form of a hot-water bottle, the fish lashing about before it gave up to the darkness of the bird's stomach. The heron's crest lifted and I paddled quickly on my way as I felt it eyed me a little too keenly.

The portal of the Bruce Tunnel swallowed me for a few hundred yards and I emerged at the start of locks that descended slowly towards Bristol. The leaves of the outlying oaks of Savernake Forest were loosening after last night's frost, and the brick walls of farmsteads and cottages gave way in a few places to timber frames. I looked out for the half-timbered building that I remembered from many years before and a pang of unease ran through me as I spotted its distant windows watching from across an open field.

Its tar-blackened oak beams and whitewashed infill panels of lath and plaster stood out of a clearing under a roof of wheat-straw thatch. I thought back to the job of rectification we had done there, stripping out bad quality patching-up in cement and concrete block from between the oak frame, which we replaced with something more authentic.

But there was more to this house than there seemed and

the shoe of a shire horse nailed above the front door was the only clue as to what lay secreted beneath its floorboards, between its walls and even within the flue of the chimney. We received a taste of what was to come as we investigated the loft space. The torch shone along the thatch's underside, which was smoke-blackened from a medieval open fire, but it was the line of old glass bottles, their bases smashed, hanging by their necks from lengths of hairy twine that proved a more arresting sight. Elsewhere we found yet stranger things.

Fear of witchcraft was rife during the late-sixteenth and seventeenth centuries, with many taking the advice of 'cunning folk' who for centuries had been the people's allies against witches and bad spirits. One of the most effective tools in their armoury was the secreting away of charms created from daily life in strategic places around the dwelling.

Sometimes these were concealed as a cache of objects. We found tiny conch shells brought from the tropics, a few old keys and a glass bottle full of pins under the floorboards. The thighbone of a horse, the jawbone of a cow and an odd-sized pair of shoes had been placed on ledges in the chimney. It is not unusual to make these finds while opening up an old building; elsewhere behind a loose brick I uncovered a poor frog or toad, punctured with a lattice of hawthorns, that looked as if it had been once dipped in treacle, while underneath the hearthstone a cat had been well preserved by desiccation, its skin sagged round its bones like wet brown paper.

Markings were also to be seen around other weak spots – windows and the chimney – where unwanted forces could enter. The protection of the Virgin Mary was invoked with the overlapping VV and the M as apotropaic marks and symbols.

The daisy wheel of compass-marked petals would bring good luck, while the black marks around the doorframes and chimneys were from candle tapers, left to dwell for a while so that fire could be fought with fire.

Only the house, which was a document of its own history, knew what had happened here. Its items had been secreted away at different times and I wondered what sort of unnatural occurrences the successive generations of farmers who lived here were assailed by. Was it simply a response to the eternal battle between good and evil, with the charms warding off bad spirits, like a gargoyle on a church tower? Was there really something in the trees that surrounded the farmhouse? When I had asked the reclusive owner what he wanted doing with the museum cabinet's worth of finds, he told us to put it all back where it came from; directing my gaze to the protective symbols scratched into the old door frame, he said, 'Sometimes I need a little help living out here.'

It was twenty years since I had last crossed the cottage's threshold and highly unlikely that the then elderly owner would still be rattling about the place. Paddling on I wondered if the current residents had any idea of the 'others' that previous owners were so bothered by. No doubt the festival of Samhain made it doubly difficult to escape the lingering eeriness of the place. In summer, the rolling fields that were renowned for their crop circles opened up towards Avebury, only a short distance away over the downs.

This leg was largely free of locks and by now I could almost move through the water without will, passing the familiar churches of Devizes to the most monstrous obstacle on the whole canal: the giant staircase of twenty-nine locks at Caen

Hill. There was no way I was going to negotiate this horror, which transfers the navigation from the relative heights of the Pewsey Vale down into the valley of the Bristol Avon, and so I pulled *Laughing Water* down the grass verge to the final stretch.

This was territory I knew well. The buildings transitioned from the brick of the south country, where it was a material more readily available, to the limestone ashlar of the west. These bridges and abutments had provided some of the most challenging and toughest work Andy and I had done, work that was of a nature very different from that found on any church. Our hardest winter had been spent in the iced-up and effluent-polluted bed of the drained canal as we took down and rebuilt the transitory walls that narrowed under the bridges to carry the footpath.

The canal waters were held back by square sections of lumber dropped down into a vertical channel on either side of the embankment, which acted as a dam, with giant electric pumps sucking out the water that squirted from between the boards in a great arc. We had to adjust our usual conservative approach when working in the canal. The engineering needs of relaying a new canal bed for many miles are paramount.

The English Heritage inspector was in favour of a more traditional method of relining with clay by 'puddling'. I liked the thought of the main contractor – a constructor of motorway intersections and sports stadiums – managing the flocks of sheep as they were shepherded up and down the cut to soften and compress the clay, as had originally been done, but the move-ment and constant small landslips in the valley made this approach unfeasible and so a new bed of concrete was laid in bays abutted by rubber expansion joints.

Further along at Avoncliffe it was a thrill to paddle over the River Avon, the canal bed transferred by an aqueduct built in a restrained neoclassical style. These were not only remarkable feats of engineering, but also an explicit attempt to associate the glories of Rome (and nearby Bath) with the latest development in technology.

This triumph of elegance and purpose that had pushed what was possible in terms of structural design was not without problems, as evidenced by the sag that appeared in the span of the great central arch shortly after its formwork was removed. Its outer faces abound with masons' marks: pentangles, triangles and directional arrows that aided the tallying of those responsible for cutting or dressing the stone. Nevertheless, here, uniquely, they appear on a number of the particularly large blocks in combinations to indicate that three separate individuals were working together. The nearby limestone quarries at Limpley Stoke supplied the raw material for what was to become an arterial route of the Industrial Revolution. Coal wagons loaded with stone once ran down from the quarries to the wharf on iron rails that created an early trolley way. The stone sleepers still survive, and allow the routes to be followed through the woods.

I shadowed Brunel's Great Western Railway for much of the latter part of the journey, as it hugged close to the canal along river valley and across pasture. Both canal and railway enter Bath side by side through Sydney Gardens, the only pleasure gardens to have survived from Georgian times. This approach confirmed my belief that the best way to understand and appreciate the origins of any place is by the watercourse that flows through it. Although it was a commercial route, John Rennie, the chief engineer, took great care to make sure that the canals, bridges, buildings and approaches to the long tunnels reflected the city's Georgian architecture. This was plain to see as I passed under a particularly refined tunnel entrance portal with recessed niches to either side surrounded by blocks decorated with a type of vermiculated rustication under a head of Sabrina, symbolic of the spirit of the Severn. The Cleveland Tunnel runs under Cleveland House, the old headquarters of the Kennet and Avon Canal Company, which was one of the first purpose-built office blocks in Europe. A trap-door in the tunnel roof was where paperwork was exchanged between the barges below and the administrators above.

This legacy of excellence in design was one that only thirty years later Brunel was obliged to continue as he integrated the route through the garden landscape. Brunel had learnt so much from the construction of the canal that it seemed a 'dry run' for his own great project.

It was near journey's end and I tied up the canoe and visited what was still a unique piece of railway theatre where a succession of InterCity 125 trains arced into and out of Bath Spa station around the base of a high revetment wall still smoke-blackened from the age of steam. I imagined Victorian families coming here to a prototype technology-based theme park to marvel at the latest developments that chugged and steamed by on the other side of the low neoclassical balustrade wall.

In common with the times, Brunel used a mix of architectural styles on the Great Western line. From its foundation in 1833 it took only seven years for the first stages to open, with the short section from Bristol to Bath opening in 1840, and the longer section from Bath to London operational from 1841 following the completion of the tunnel dug through Box Hill, between Bath and Chippenham. The final railway ran from Paddington station to Bristol. Austere stock bricks mirror the workers' terraces of west London, whereas on the approaches to Bath a simple classicism is observed. Soon after leaving Bath there is a great viaduct in a castellated Tudor–Gothic style, a theme continued in the tunnels and bridges that terminate at Temple Meads station in Bristol. Everywhere along the route there is evidence that Brunel had more in mind than simply speed and directness.

In Bath, the backdrop of Gothic arches contrasts well with the rest of the ancient city's homogeneous architecture. The city is important to the story of architecture in Britain because funds from the Industrial Revolution poured into Bath as speculative property investment. Money was also frittered away in the city's baths, theatres and card clubs. Income was boosted by the canal's connection with Europe and the North Sea, and to Atlantic approaches and the Americas at Bristol. I know the city well; we have spent many hours carefully restoring its buildings, crumbling from the polluting after-effects of the very industrial revolution that built them.

The Roman streetscape is a result of the genius of two generations of the same family. John Wood the Elder and Younger were romantics, architects and property developers whose great ambition, as a consequence of the Palladian revival, was to build a new Rome among the ruins of that civilisation. Their hallmarks can be seen in the uniformity of the grid-like streets of the first planned city outside London, exceptional with its arrangement of circus, square and crescent as well as the elevations that provide a frame for Bath's rich architectural identity.

It is a place to stroll and the only way the eccentric design of the Woods can be fully appreciated. Their re-creation of a Druidic shrine, the Circus – Bath's historic street of large town-houses that forms a circle – was also an interpretation of the Colosseum, but one turned outside in: the three curved segments display their impressive columns on their concave face. Standing by the group of old plane trees that inhabit its green middle, one can best enjoy the horizontality of the three classical orders visible in the columns – plain Doric at the base, followed by Ionic and Corinthian. Symbolic carvings that could be deciphered only by eighteenth-century freemasons enhance the mystery of the place that was purposefully laid out by Wood to be of the same diameter as the henge embankment of Stonehenge. The identical facades of individual mansion blocks are divided into bays, and when passing number 17, I always give a nod as this was once Thomas Gainsborough's studio.

Many buildings were put up speculatively in the city's heyday from 1714 to 1830, during the reign of the Georges. Lodgings were provided for visitors to the spa. During the 'season' that ran from the beginning of May to mid-September, grander visitors stayed in the Royal, Lansdown and Camden crescents, where a quarter-millennium on, the failure of architectural detailing is a continuing problem. After a hard winter, when saturated and frost-damaged, the swirling volutes that project from either side of the flat Ionic capitals of the best known of Bath's crescents, the Royal Crescent, will in some years drop like autumn fruit. One such we found exploded like a bag of flour on the flagstones after it had pinballed through an ancient magnolia.

However, airborne pollution causes the biggest problems for these facades that were created from a material so soft that it can be sawn. Bath is surrounded by hills that create a bowl around it. The sixteenth-century traveller John Leland thought the city a fine sight situated 'yn a fruteful and pleasant botom' that has always held a soup of air pollution. Now it is diesel fumes that poison the residents, but until recently coal from nearby collieries – high in sulphur – fuelled the hearths and industry that poisoned the buildings.

The city is also perhaps a victim of fashion as its architecture is more suited to the southern Mediterranean, and ultimately ill-equipped to deal with the damp phlegmy humours that are tossed at it from across the Mendip Hills. Facades designed without gutters and downpipes mean that rainwater from the roof has to be channelled along lead-lined wooden gulleys through attic spaces to the rear, with predictable consequences when a dead pigeon does its worst.

I remembered back to the Royal Crescent's Volutes, and how the five-foot deep undecorated entablature that rose from them as a wall was of the same monumental scale as the Avoncliffe aqueduct, which was of the first order of classical architecture, the plain Doric.

Here, however, the second order of classical architecture – the Ionic – was easily recognisable from the scrolls or volutes that projected from either side of a column, a style that came out of the Greek Aegean islands during the archaic period.

On the lead of a rooftop dormer, hidden behind the balustrade, a daisy wheel apotropaic mark indicated that the lead was original and had never been replaced. Other good quality conservation work had been carried out to either side of the high-class hotel that sits at the Crescent's centre, but a shocker awaits on the front of the hotel itself.

Sometime after we had repaired the volutes, a youth was let loose with a bucket of wet mortar. Go and stand and see this work that was signed off by some administrator – it will have its photo taken by every one of the millions of visitors who come here every year. I wonder how many will puzzle over why the finely cut joints, so thin that a cigarette paper would not fit between them, had been smeared to a width of three inches over the interface between every stone. It is as though a chimpanzee had been let loose on Audrey Hepburn's face with a lipstick, in the dark.

The other crescents have their idiosyncrasies: sheep graze in an arbour protected with a ha-ha in the front lawn of Lansdown Crescent. Its plain facade lacks fine carving, but this is more than made up for by the quality of the wrought metalwork that forms lanterned entrance archways to each doorway.

Camden Crescent, put up in 1788, stood as a unified whole for a century before it was truncated when the nine eastern-most houses were taken by a landslide. What survived has some of the finest architectural carving in the town, superior in every way to that on the Royal. Here, the sweep was of the third of the classical orders, where squared, fluted columns lifted to Corinthian capitals. This was the order the Romans preferred, with Sulis-Minerva's temple in the valley below offering proof of this, if in a debased form. The deep capitals hold two layers of finely detailed and stylised acanthus leaves that lean forward like a teapot spout, which crumbled under a smoke-blackened crust thick with spider's webs.

Once the black carbon had been removed with the poultice method, the stone could be brought back to life with the usual mix of lime repairs and newly carved work that complemented the replacement scrolls. But when we opened up the walls, we were surprised by how thin the outer skin of ashlar was. Extracting the stone was expensive, so it had been supplied in smaller pre-sawn blocks: a departure from earlier practice when the Romans and subsequent builders used external blocks that were much larger. The outer stones are generally only four or so inches thick, clad onto a core of compacted rubble walling filled by cheap labour and held in position with staples, hidden in the top course.

As the crescents and terraces were built speculatively, each purchaser of a mansion block employed their own architect to design a house to their own specifications behind the facade. This created a ramshackle mixture of differing roof heights, juxtapositions and window placements, structures with 'Queen Anne fronts and Mary-Anne backs', buildings that if proposed today would probably be laughed out of the office by the city's planning apparatchiks. This financial speculation, created by the effects of trade with the Americas, slavery and industrial advances created the city we see today.

My journey in *Laughing Water* concluded at Widcombe Lock, where the canal meets the River Avon in the middle of the city; and without the popping of champagne corks, I finished my journey by loading the canoe into the waiting pickup for the last time.

Before sliding into the passenger seat, I studied Bath's pseudo-classical SouthGate shopping centre, which glowers discordantly over the old city. Its method of construction is a continuation of the clad approach, but here the facades are made from panels of Bath stone, which are more of a thin veneer, glued onto a concrete backing panel. The craftless hulk is architecture without meaning and everything that the rational and sublime buildings of the Elder and Younger Woods are not. It is architecture that would be more at home as a Trump casino in Las Vegas and the words of Peter Smithson, a more recent architect, sprang to mind, 'Bath's thinning blood is being leeched away by a creeping timidity, but her bones are a marvel.'

Returning the canoe to my workshop, I wondered what that most influential building preservationist, William Morris, would have thought of the despoiling of the city. I remembered my pilgrimage to his Oxfordshire home in Kelmscott, when I was sponsored on my travelling fellowship around the British Isles by the Society for the Protection of Ancient Buildings – or the SPAB, as it was affectionately nicknamed – the charity that Morris founded in 1877 and what he considered to be his greatest work.

There, wisps of river-mist clung to a door in its high enclosing wall that opened magically when the latch was tested, and I was drawn in to explore the garden. Ahead, a flagged path was escorted on each side by a reducing line of fruit trees that converged with other lines of perspective upon a front door under a little porch. The walls lifted to leaded windows that terminated with a pair of Elizabethan gables. In the dawn's half-light, after a strange moment of déjà vu it was a surprise to recognise the view from Morris's socialist proto-sci-fi fantasy, *News from Nowhere*. This was a place I knew, but had never been to, and was unknowingly the point of reference for my philosophy of work.

Enjoying the utopian view of Kelmscott, I recalled the caption within the woodcut print of 1892 that forms the book's frontispiece: 'THIS IS THE PICTURE OF THE OLD HOUSE BY THE THAMES TO WHICH THE PEOPLE OF THIS STORY WENT'. I found the book a struggle at first, but the tale of the time-travelling William Guest soon won me over as he undertook an upstream journey in 2102 from London.

As he passes the familiar cattle-strewn fields and willows, he discovers a deep satisfaction that concludes with his arrival at 'this many-gabled old house built by the simple country-folk of long-past times'. The impressionable hero realises as he is shown around that a humane socialist future in a society governed by the aesthetics and art of the Middle Ages is an ideal worth striving for. I was as young, idealistic and impressionable as the hero when I first read it, but now understand that Morris's ideals were of course too ambitious to effect real change. Morris's move to Kelmscott in 1871 provided him with a much-needed foil to a busy London life. Funded by a private income and thus detached from the realities of ordinary working people, Morris mastered a range of luxury crafts, printing his well-known wallpapers and chintzes as well as designing his stained-glass windows and weaving tapestries.

May Morris, William's younger daughter, thought Kelmscott the 'undertone to all his future activities and where he developed his ideas'. It was in this worn-out Elizabethan house that Morris's genius found its true home. Here he established the Kelmscott Press, which published his poetry and writings about social reform and socialism. He said in a letter that he was moved by the 'melancholy' he felt at Kelmscott that was 'born of beauty', which he found 'stimulating to the imagination'. Morris was so tireless in his endeavours that when he died, his doctor pronounced that the cause was 'simply being William Morris, and having done more work than most ten men'.

Morris's nostalgia for medieval craft skills and old buildings still resonates today. He appreciated that old buildings embodied the past and needed to be cared for if that spirit was to be maintained.

At Kelmscott, he developed a builder's eye as he appreciated that its rubble-stone walls had been 'buttered over, so to say, with thin plaster which has now weathered to the same colour as the stone of the walls'. The gabled walls supported a roof covered in the 'beautiful stone slates of the district'; their diminishing courses gave him 'the same sort of pleasure in their orderly beauty as a fish's scales or a bird's feathers'. Details like this were to strengthen his appreciation of the traditional crafts-manship and know-how that had built Kelmscott, that had in turn been so mellowed by time and nature until it appeared, so he thought, to have 'grown up out of the soil'.

This exposure to the old ways of the vernacular inspired Morris to start what he thought his greatest achievement: the protection of old places, landscapes and buildings. His pioneering activities, in turn, informed the philosophy of conservative repair that was once a new road for me, but one that I have been travelling ever since.

The interconnectedness of place, materials, people and nature can almost be felt to breathe out of the walls of Kelmscott, and Morris became sensitive to the irreversible change wrought by over-enthusiastic restoration and development. It was from his time at Kelmscott that he began to promote the concept of 'anti-scrape', the idea that old buildings can best be respected by leaving them be – preservation, rather than restoration. Six years after moving in, he formed the Society for the Protection of Ancient Buildings – the SPAB.

Morris's ideas about the nobility of handcraft, and that hand-made goods contain the spirit of the people who put them together, chimes with the Japanese philosophy of *wabi sabi* that gives a name to the appreciation of indeterminate beauty manifest in the marks of wear or use, a concept that can be equally assigned to place, building, landscape or thing. We appreciate it in the undulating wall of an ancient house, or in a 'ghost sign' above an old shop. Damage and repairs vividly reflect the life of an object, like duelling scars.

So it is with our day-to-day work where, for example, the 'golden stain of time', as John Ruskin put it, can sometimes be difficult to define to potential clients who do not understand the importance of a building's history and patina. If they want a restoration job, then I walk.

I wondered how deaf to claims such as these was a man whose thoughts were as radical as those of William Morris but his polar opposite – Isambard Kingdom Brunel. Brunel's vision was to harness the products of mechanisation and industrial-isation, which were a consequence of the Industrial Revolution, and to use them to drive forward technological change. His Great Western Railway was conceived to connect London to New York via Bristol and his steamships SS *Great Western* and SS *Great Eastern*.

Perhaps they would have got on, Morris being not averse to train travel and the introduction of labour-saving machinery in his manufactories. He was interested in new building materials and construction methods, and he approved of railway architecture as long as it was authentic and of its time. Morris did, however, consider the undisguised nakedness of the Forth Bridge that opened in 1890 as 'the supremest specimen of ugliness', which is surprising considering his ideas centred on being true to materials, which the rail bridge most definitely is.

In some ways Brunel, who took great care that the route of the GWR through Bath respected the Georgian cityscape without cutting through the city itself, was conservation-minded. In engineering his line from Yeovil to Weymouth, he was persuaded not to drive a deep cutting through Poundbury Hill with its Bronze Age fort and still visible channel of the Roman aqueduct dug into its rampart that supplied Roman Dorchester, and instead found the extra money to tunnel beneath it.

An immediate effect of the triumph of the railway was the loss of the regional building materials that had come from the soil of each area. Homogeneity became the norm as new houses and churches tended to be built of London-stock bricks under a roof frame of Baltic pine covered with Welsh slates. Regional and vernacular style virtually disappeared, but in a few places, where it was still profitable to use local materials, the old ways endured.

The lime-buttered rubble walls that held up the stone slates of the Cotswold Hills in Gloucestershire was one such area, and towards the end of the nineteenth century many crafts-people were drawn that way from London as a response to Morris's call for a return to a golden age of making. Many came together as communities that made good use of the rail network to get their products to the large metropolitan markets, where they supplied the aesthetic requirements of their wealthy patrons. As with Morris's vision, these designs based on past styles were made with traditional skills, which created work that went beyond the mass-produced imitations. These idealistic groups of thinkers, craftspeople and architects were responsible for what came to be known as the Arts and Crafts movement.

One of the hottest spots in the Cotswolds was to be found in the enclave of Sapperton, where a regional building revival took place led by Ernest Gimson, who was considered to be the greatest architect-designer of his time. Working to the theories of his mentor and Morris's disciple at the SPAB, William Lethaby, Gimson created a 'school of rational building' that developed Morris's ideals in a way that, unbeknown to them, was to help shift the world and send it off in the most surprising of directions.

In the summer of 2016, a week after the Brexit vote, with 'Leave' posters still tacked to the approaching avenue of beech trees, I went to Sapperton village to survey the medieval monuments of the church of St Kenelm. This felt a strange time to visit a place that had in a small way influenced the most internationalist form of architecture yet to be seen.

The architect in charge of the now-redundant church took us under the darkening churchyard yews, past hedges clipped seemingly with scissors, to look at the homely village hall. It sits comfortably under a steep pitched roof, which Gimson and his artist craftspeople had designed and built as the storm clouds gathered at the start of the twentieth century.

The hall, in common with the other buildings Gimson and his team had put up in the village, presented an imperceptible fusion where the ache of modernism can be felt to have fused with what had come before. The style reflected the beliefs of Morris and the SPAB that the past was not reproducible, and thus for the first time buildings became aesthetically streamlined.

Would Gimson have baulked had he known the impact that his rationally constructed buildings were to have, as their fame travelled well beyond the homely Cotswolds to catch the attention of the next generation of design and architecture schools and workshops on the continent.

In Germany after the First World War, Walter Gropius, the founder of the Bauhaus movement, fused craft tradition with machine culture in an urban context as a response to poor design and the worst by-products of industrialisation. He believed that his teachings needed to highlight social injustice and poverty and help bring about social change, and the romance and idealism of handmade high-back chairs in the Cotswold Hills was going to change nothing.

Nonetheless many Arts and Crafts design ideals found their way to Germany where they were adopted by the Bauhaus: excellence in craftsmanship, the use of only the highest quality materials, belief that art should meet the needs of society and that there should be no distinction between form and function. The Bauhaus, also known as the internationalist style, was marked by the absence of ornamentation and by harmony between the function of an object or a building and its design.

To these may be added the desire to create; as the architect Le Corbusier put it in 1923, houses should be a 'machine for living in'. In the same year, Gropius announced that 'art and technology should form a new unity', in a revised syllabus oriented away from crafts towards industrial design based on what then was the most modern combination of materials – steel and concrete.

The winds that ushered in the modern world had been increasing in velocity since the mid-eighteenth century when a type of concrete was reinvented that was quite different from the *opus caementicium* of Roman times.

In 1756 the engineer John Smeaton came up with a design, modelled on the shape of an oak tree, for the troubled lighthouse that perched on Eddystone rocks off the coast of Plymouth. This was the third attempt by the Trinity House maritime charity to create a beacon on the site, the previous constructions having collapsed as a consequence of the weak nature of the bonding mortar. In imitation of the Romans, Smeaton added powdered brick to the mix that had been fired from blue lias limestone, which was known to have the ability to cure underwater. This, combined with the clever use of granite sections that interlocked with dovetail joints – an idea he had when he was walking in London and saw stonecutters dove-tailing kerb stones – and pinned with marble dowels helped a lighthouse that still survives, albeit in a different location. (Its top half was dismantled and re-erected on Plymouth Hoe in the 1870s, a relocation that was rendered necessary when cracks appeared in the Eddystone foundation rocks.)

The development of modern concrete gathered pace when in 1824 Joseph Aspdin, a Yorkshire stonemason, patented 'An improvement in the mode of producing artificial stone' which was the first modern artificial cement. Aspdin termed it 'Portland' because it looked like the natural stone product of the island when it dried. It was soon recognised that the hardness of this Portland cement could be increased if it were burnt at a higher temperature and so began the long trail of ever-worsening environmental disaster, aggregate famine and CO_2 release from its manufacture and curing. CO_2 is one of several greenhouse gases that causes climate change, with the concrete industry accounting for about 5 per cent of global emissions, unlike lime mortar that achieves its set by absorbing CO_2 from the atmosphere. The next step was developed by Joseph Monier, a French gardener who made concrete garden pots reinforced with an iron mesh armature to enhance the material's tensile strength. This reinforced concrete was soon adapted for slab or shell constructions and low-rise structures.

British architects were late adopters of the use of steel and concrete in their buildings. Unlike the 'honesty in materials' approach of their European colleagues, trained by the Bauhaus, who liked the finished texture exposed when the wooden shuttering into which the concrete was poured was removed, we preferred to clad them over with Portland stone fixed with iron cramps. The cement plants that fed this completely new way of building grew only where there were pre-existing kilns that burnt limestone with a clay content. These were mainly on or near the coastal chalk or the seam of blue lias that follows the limestone belt and runs diagonally across country from Dorset to Yorkshire. Here, where the seam was exposed, and along harboursides where both raw material and fuel could be easily transported, kilns were a common enough sight.

Inland away from the blue lias they were scarce, but in the secret vale that stretches away below my hilltop workshop, where the whippet gets exercised, the ruined and collapsing cylinders of the pre-existing type occur in great abundance. The Mells river and Egford brook twist and turn through the narrow wooded gorges of Vallis Vale, having cut their way through the rock with an alpine meltwater intensity. Creepers hang down from the dominating stands of ash, suckering wych elm, and small-leafed lime and oak.

We had spent a spring working to rebuild a kiln that had collapsed in on its flue, and it was hard to believe that this place was once tortured and tormented as it was stripped of natural things through the quarrying of valuable carboniferous limestone for road stone or for firing in the kilns. At dusk, the vale filled with bats. The winged creatures flew around the rubble-stone cylinder from which they emerged in their hundreds. They were watched by the whippet, head tilted in puzzlement. She sat on a bank thick with the dark glossy tongues of hard, hart and lamb ferns, their tops partially unfurled, an image that I noted would, one day, be good to carve.

An innocent passing this way in the mid-nineteenth century might have thought they were entering Hell. Once the kilns were lit, they would be fed morning, noon and night; the cost of reheating would have been too great to allow the process to halt and the flames to drop. As the ashes and lime were extracted from its mouth, coal and limestone were tipped into its flue. Summer sun would have been obscured by smoke, and at night-time the surrounding crags and cliff faces would have reflected and echoed to the sulphurous noise and red heat of the Industrial Revolution.

At the bottom of the flue, we hit an unexpected mound. Spading off the thick covering of earthy leaf mulch revealed the chalky whiteness of the final lime burn, a century old but still fit for purpose. It had a consistency of Cheddar cheese, but knocked up into the nicest lime I had encountered and it was only right that this should be incorporated into the rebuild to bond the firebricks that lined the flue and the outer rubble together. To me this smothered post-industrial ruin represented the end of the old ways of the small scale, the local and the vernacular at the start of the twentieth century, when the fusion of old and new ceased to operate and centralised industry became the norm.

A little way upstream in the village of Mells is a monument to international events that brought about the final changes that can be seen in the landscape of Vallis Vale to this day. Following the river, the heights above the cliff faces are dotted with hill forts that suggest what a busy place this has been since prehistoric times, where the flux and reflux of humanity and nature has repeated the cycle of use, demise and resurrection. The early tools of flint, fragments of which are a common find in the fields above the vale, indicate where the use of stone first started to become woven into our lives as the material that defines our species, the working of which for the first time allowed hand, head and heart to come together. Stone created Mells, as the ancient inn, its homes, manor house and church are all paved, walled and roofed from the local quarries. Its chemical manipulation in the Vallis Vale kilns keeps the elements out, the walls glued together and interiors plastered.

Stone is a medium that even allows us to express a faith in something eternal. Positioned prominently in Mells, a white Tuscan column hewn from Dorset's Isle of Slingers lifts to a backdrop of silent yews. The inscription beneath records that it was 'RAISED IN THE HOME OF OUR DELIGHT'. Here, on a street corner at the heart of Wessex, the monument quietly invites the passer-by to stop, look and read the surnames, some familiar to me, of the twenty-one young men of the village who were killed in the First World War.

On the face of it, the way this community commemorates

its dead appears to have changed hugely since the West Kennet Long Barrow's sarsens were first hauled into position. But I can feel the connection through time and space between them and the Windmill Hill people who, when they built their monument on what is now lonely open downland, also created an important hub for their community. In the end, both groups followed the same path. Friends, relatives and leaders came together to make permanent in what some see as the most cold and inert of natural materials the memory of those who have gone on to those still to come.

Stone as a material has allowed the meaning of these monuments to the dead to endure beyond their time. As I have attempted to negotiate my own understanding of the past, I am left touched with the notion that every building, sculpture and structure I have seen in my journey was created by people who felt and thought in a way that was familiar to us, a thread of connection and culture that in some way will continue to run on through the generations.

ACKNOWLEDGEMENTS

When I started to make sense of my commonplace books, never in my wildest imagination did I think that their contents would lead to the publication of a book.

That this has happened is due first and foremost to my agent, Antony Topping at Greene and Heaton. Antony managed to get some early chapters to Georgina Laycock at John Murray who, from the off, was the publisher I had in mind. Unbelievably, Georgina bravely picked up this manuscript and ran with it, so a million thanks to Georgina for understanding what I wanted to achieve and giving the time to make this happen. Thanks also to Kate Craigie for your reassurances and great ideas, as well as to Martin Bryant, Howard Davies and Abigail Scruby for undergoing the pain of knocking these words into shape. I am also grateful to Sara Marafini and Natalie Chen who have achieved a wonderful job of putting the cover artwork together.

Helen Corner-Bryant at Cornerstones Literary Consultancy put me in touch with Eleanor Leese who skilfully encouraged my first steps and helped put my proposal together. Cally Worden and Louise Harnby later assisted with additional freelance copy edits.

I am extremely grateful that over the years I have been able to work with many skilled and entertaining individuals on the projects outlined within, particularly Sharra Oram, Peter Yorke, Seth Mallock, Jason Battle, Henry Gray, Sam Peacock, Bryony Johnson Mayhew, Michael Poulson, John Wilson, Andy Jones and all at J&J Masonry in Melksham and the Leach Clan at Limebase Products.

Particular thanks are due to Nell Pickering for wise words and wonderful craftsmanship – I know that I have not done your work justice here; David West on the early projects, the gift of *Laughing Water* and accompaniment in parts of the early journeys; Emma Simpson for lunchtime help and Hampton Court discussions; Michael and Violet Hardy, who were the first to open my eyes to art and architecture – sorry, Michael, that I caused the loss of your index finger on the circular saw; also to the late Christopher Zeuner at the Weald and Downland Museum for taking the time to get me started and Geoffrey Teychenné for an education and the gift of tools; Michael Drury, for responding to questions about Lake House; Tim Daw for letting me use his theory about Stonehenge stone 56; Tony Webb for the gift of time at St Paul's Cathedral; A.M. Juster for permissions to use his translations of 'St Aldhelm's Riddles'; Siân Echard, University of British Columbia, for permission to use her translation of 'The Ruin' from the Exeter Book of Riddles.

I am particularly grateful to John Bucknall for creating the SPAB William Morris Craft Fellowship. Within the SPAB, Rachel Bower, the late Sonia Rolt and Matthew Slocombe have been particularly supportive over the years.

Thanks to Susannah Walker for tips and advice; James

Laurenson and Cari Haysom, for reading the first drafts and coming back with such encouraging words; Martin and Margaret Cariss-Wade for the 'Victory' dinner and encouragements; Paul and Leila, Amelie and Ben for enthusing so enthusiastically.

Family thanks are due to Mum and Dad, Jean and John (Florian) Ziminski, for your love and support in sending me away on this path, what a shame you will never know about this.

Terry and Alison Venables. Lisa Venables and Esther and Reuben for sound boarding and London stays, and to Daren for introducing me to subjects that I would have never have guessed were so interesting, and your friendly advice.

Andrew Sharland and I have been business partners for the past quarter century. His is an unseen, benevolent presence throughout most of the tales in this book. Thanks, mate, for your patience, encouragement and allowance of time so I could just get on with this – here's to the next one.

Almost everything within this book has come into my mind as a consequence of the journeys and places visited, lectures attended, or books read over the past four decades. As a consequence it is inevitable that I have unintentionally omitted the many churchwardens and custodians of ancient places who unknowingly assisted in the creation of this work. I cannot hope to acknowledge them all except in a general way.

I mostly want to show my gratitude to Clare, my wife, for putting up with my being incapable of cooking, cleaning or doing little else over the past few years. How you managed to do so much and still find the time and care to create the wonderful linocut artworks within as well as the cut letters without, I just don't know. Violet our daughter also cut the 'piecrust' chapter headings. I could not have done this without you both.

NOTE ON THE ILLUSTRATIONS

Maps by Clare Venables.

Part titles: 'Piecrust' patera by Violet Venables Ziminski.

Interlude: Surviving angel from now destroyed crucifixion scene. The Anglo-Saxon chapel of St Laurence, Bradford-on-Avon, Wiltshire (c.1000), by Clare Venables.

Chapter illustrations: linocuts themed around doors, openings, portals and porches, by Clare Venables.

Samhain: West Kennet Long Barrow entrance passageway viewed from the blocking stones (c.3650 BCE).

Winter Solstice: Stonehenge. View of midsummer solstitial sunrise axis from inside the stone circle (c.2500 BCE).

Quinquatria: Temple of Sulis Minerva, reconstruction, Bath (c.90 CE).

Maundy Thursday: The Anglo-Saxon chapel of St Laurence, Bradford-on-Avon, Wiltshire. Chancel arch and view of the altar (c.1000).

Armageddon: Church of All Saints, Lullington, Somerset. Romanesque north door (*c*.1150).

Whitsuntide: Wells Cathedral, Somerset. North porch and upper setting-out room (*c*.1190).

The Feast of the Transfiguration: St Mary Redcliffe, Bristol. North porch (*c*.1325).

Autumnal Equinox: The church of St Michael. Glastonbury Tor, Somerset. Remains of the western bell-tower (*c*.1350).

Michaelmas: Isle of Portland, Dorset. Waste stone tipping bridge (*c*.1850).

Samhain Eve: Cleveland House. Former offices of the Kennet and Avon Canal Company, situated above the Cleveland tunnel, Bath (*c*.1800).

GLOSSARY

Acrow prop: a vertical metal screw-jack support system used to prop overhead loads such as lintels.

Aggregate: a broad group of particulate material used in construction, including sands and the dust of crushed stones.

Architrave: a main beam resting across the tops of columns.

Ashlar: a type of finely dressed stone blocks of similar size, shape and texture laid together in mortar.

Banker: a waist-height mason's workbench.

Bath stone: Jurassic-age limestone extracted from around the city of Bath.

Beaker folk: an archaeological culture of the late Neolithic–early Bronze Age – from about 2,500 BCE – defined by a beaker style of pottery that has often been found in burials.

Billet: an architectural moulding composed of a repeated series of small cylinders, cubes or prisms.

Blind arcading: a series of interlinked arches without openings, cut into the surface of a wall as a decorative element.

Boss (in vaulting): the keystone at the intersection of a rib vault often extravagantly decorated, e.g. with foliage, green men or mermaids.

Capital: the topmost part of a column.

Chert: a hard quartz that forms as nodules in limestone; flint is a type of chert formed in chalk.

Chevron: a zigzag pattern carved into Norman-era mouldings around church windows and doorways, similar to beakheads.

Claw chisel: a metal chisel consisting of a shaft with a toothed cutting edge at one end.

Corbel: a weight-carrying masonry element built deep into a wall so that the pressure on its buried portion counteracts its potential to overturn or fall outward.

Corinthian capital: the topmost part of a column, carved with layers of acanthus leaves and surmounted in a pair of volutes to each face.

Cornbrash: a Jurassic-age limestone found in south-west Britain, composed of layers of fossilised shells and molluscs.

Cornice: a horizontal decorative moulding which projects to divert water away from the top of a building.

Crocket: an ornament usually found on the edge of a gable or spire in the form of curved or flowing foliage.

Cusp: a pointed projection or lobe formed from the intersection of two arcs within a church window tracer, e.g. the cloverleaf forms of the trefoil's three lobes are divided by three cusps.

Dolmen: a megalithic type of monument, composed of two stones fixed in the ground supporting a horizontal slab; from the Breton for 'stone table'.

Drovers' road: a trackway created by livestock over many generations as they were driven to market.

Entablature: the horizontal upper part of a classical facade supported by columns or a colonnade, comprising the architrave, frieze and cornice.

Fosse: a long defensive trench used in fortifications which gave its name to the Fosse Way, the Roman road that ran from Exeter to Lincoln; it is possible that a defensive ditch ran alongside the road for some of its length.

Freestone: an ashlar stone that can be freely worked or sawn in any direction.

Frieze: the part of the entablature between the architrave and cornice.

Garth: the central open space of a cloister.

Gorgoneion: a protective amulet similar to that worn by the goddess Athena (or Minerva) that sometimes bears a border of snakes and the head of a gorgon.

Green Man: a sculptured representation of a face enclosed by, or made from, leaves; foliage or vines may sprout from the mouth or nostrils.

Groove-ware: a flat-bottomed and decorated pottery type of the late-Neolithic period from about 3100–2500 BCE.

Hereweg: an Anglo-Saxon military road.

Jack-in-the-Green: a term synonymous with representations of the green man.

Lewis: a device for lifting large blocks of masonry.

Lierne: a short rib that connects the bosses and principal ribs of a church ceiling vault.

Lintel: a horizontal support across the top of a threshold or opening.

Long and short work: ashlar corner stones or quoins found in Anglo-Saxon buildings and arranged alternately horizontally and vertically.

Long barrow: a long, earthen burial mound sometimes found with a chamber or chambers, used from 3500–2700 BCE.

Mandorla: a frame for images of Christ and the Virgin Mary, usually in the shape of a *vesica piscis*.

Marl: a lime-rich mud with an amount of clay that was widely used as a soil conditioner and sometimes as a walling mortar.

Menhir: a single megalithic standing stone.

Oolitic limestone: Jurassic-age limestone found widely throughout southern Britain, made up of small spheres called ooliths, stuck together by lime mud.

Opus signinum: waterproof Roman building mortar or plaster made with crushed tiles.

Parcae: the trio of goddesses who were Roman personifications of destiny and presided over the lives (and deaths) of humans.

Pilaster: a shallow, rectangular column found initially in Graeco-Roman architecture that projects slightly beyond the face of the wall.

Porticus: small rooms found in the Anglo-Saxon church as extensions to the north and south sides of the chancel which formed a cruciform plan.

Portland stone: Jurassic-age limestone, widely used in London, sourced from the Isle of Portland in Dorset.

Pozzolana: volcanic ash added to mortar by Roman masons to strengthen and waterproof it.

Punch: a long, pointed metal masonry tool.

Purbeck marble: Jurassic-age limestone from the Isle of Purbeck in Dorset; although not a true marble it assumes the appearance of marble when polished.

Quirk: the use of a long metal chisel as a drill to deliver alternating blows to form an 'X' shape.

Quoin: a corner stone of a building.

Render: an outer protective wall covering rubble or lower-quality brickwork in lime or cement.

Reredos: a decorative screen behind the altar, usually highly carved.

Round barrow: a burial mound, generally containing Bronze Age Beaker remains from 2500 BCE.

Sheerlegs: an 'A' frame of long timbers used to lift a heavy weight from a guy rope suspended from the point at which the frame is lashed together.

Silcrete: a particularly hard layer of surface soil formed when gravels or sands are cemented by dissolved silica; sarsen is the best-known example.

Slight: to demolish a castle intentionally, to prevent its further use.

Spandrel: the near-triangular space above one side of an arch.

Springing point: the point at which an arch lifts from the horizontal.

Squinch: an arch that bridges the corner of a right-angle wall to allow support for a dome or spire.

Stiff-leaf carving: a form of stylised foliage motif found in Early English Gothic architecture in capitals and ceiling bosses.

Strapwork: stylised ornamental representations that imitate inter-laced straps or bands in a geometric pattern.

Tas-de-charge: the point above a column or pier from which the ribs of a roof vault spring through several masonry blocks.

Tracery: stonework elements that support the glass in a Gothic window.

Transepts: the north–south crossing arms of the church.

Triforium: a galleried arcade at second-floor level, often in the aisle roof.

Volutes: ornamental spiral scrolls found on capitals.

Voussoirs: the wedge-shaped stones of an arch.

Windmill Hill people: a general term, now considered obsolete, for a culture of early agriculturalists named after the type site near Avebury, Wiltshire.

FURTHER READING

Stone, Geology, Materials and Craft

Ashurst, John, and Dimes, Francis G., *Conservation of Building and Decorative Stone*, Routledge, 1998

Clarke, Marie, Gregory, Neville, and Gray, Alan, *Earth Colours: Mendip and Bristol Ochre Mining*, Moore Books, 2012

Crossley, J. H., *English Church Craftsmanship*, Batsford, 1941

Daniels, Chris, *The Craft of Stonemasonry*, Crowood Press, 2012

Geddes, Isobel, *Hidden Depth: Wiltshire's Geology and Landscape*, Ex Libris Press, 2000

Hackman, Gill, *Stone to Build London: Portland's Legacy*, Folly Books, 2014

Warland, Edmund George, *Modern Practical Masonry*, Batsford, 1929

Art, Architectural Guides and Individual Buildings

Betjeman, John, *Collins Guide to English Parish Churches*, Collins, 1958

Campbell, James W. P., *Building St Paul's*, Thames & Hudson, 2008

Fitchen, John, *The Construction of Gothic Cathedrals: A Study of Medieval Vault Erection*, University of Chicago Press, 1997

Fletcher, Banister, *A History of Architecture on the Comparative Method* (17th edn), Athlone Press, 1961

Hillenbrand, Robert, *Islamic Architecture: Form, Function and Meaning*, Columbia University Press, 2004

Ison, Walter, *The Georgian Buildings of Bath, 1700–1830*, Kingsmead, 1969

Jenkins, Simon, *England's Thousand Best Churches*, Allen Lane, 2012

Mâle, Emile, *The Gothic Image: Religious Art in France of the Thirteenth Century*, The Fontana Library, 1961

Pevsner, Nikolaus, The *Pevsner Architectural Guides* (Yale University Press) have been invaluable, particularly those for Gloucestershire and the Forest of Dean, North Somerset and Bristol, Somerset (south), Wiltshire and Dorset.

Platt, Colin, *The Architecture of Medieval Britain: A Social History*, Yale University Press, 1991

Rodwell, Warwick, *The Archaeology of Churches*, Amberley Publishing, 2012

Smith, M. Q., and Wood, Rita, *Malmesbury Abbey: A Short Guide*

Strong, Roy, *A Little History of the English Country Church*, Vintage, 2008

Summerson, John, *The Classical Language of Architecture*, MIT Press, 1966

Toynbee, J. M. C., *Art in Britain Under the Romans*, Oxford University Press, 1964

Vitruvius, *The Ten Books on Architecture* (Books I–X), Dover Publications, 1960

Wright, Peter Poyntz, *The Parish Church Towers of Somerset:*

Their Construction, Craftsmanship and Chronology, 1350–1500, Avebury Publishing, 1981

Archaeology, Place and Landscape

Burl, Aubrey, *The Stone Circles of the British Isles*, Yale University Press, 1979

——, *Prehistoric Avebury*, Yale University Press, 2002

Clifton-Taylor, Alec, *The Pattern of English Building*, Faber & Faber, 1973

Cunliffe, Barry, *Roman Bath Discovered*, History Press, 2009

——, *Britain Begins*, Oxford University Press, 2014

Gelling, Margaret, *Signposts to the Past: Place-Names and the History of England*, Phillimore & Co., 2010

Gillings, Mark, and Pollard, Joshua, *Avebury*, Duckworth Archaeological Histories, 2004

Hawkes, Jacquetta, *A Land*, Cresset Press, 1953

Hoskins, W. G., *The Making of the English Landscape*, Little Toller Books, 2013

Massingham, H. J., *English Downland*, Batsford, 1936

Parker Pearson, Mike, *Stonehenge: Exploring the Greatest Stone Age Mystery*, Simon & Schuster, 2012

Piggott, Stuart, *The West Kennet Long Barrow: Excavations 1955–56*, HMSO, 1962

Smith, A. C., *British and Roman Antiquities of N. Wiltshire*, Wiltshire Archaeological and Natural History Society, 1885

Wood, Eric S., *Collins Field Guide to Archaeology in Britain*, Collins, 1975

People

Deller, Jeremy, *Love is Enough: Andy Warhol and William Morris*, Modern Art Oxford, 2015

Drury, Michael, *Wandering Architects: In Pursuit of an Arts and Crafts Ideal*, Shaun Tyas, 2000

Fermor, Patrick Leigh, *A Time to Keep Silence*, John Murray, 1957

Morris, William, *News from Nowhere*, Reeves and Turner, 1891

Parry, Linda (ed.), *William Morris*, Phillip Wilson, 2001

Rolt, L. T. C., *Isambard Kingdom Brunel*, Longmans Green & Co., 1958

Scurr, Ruth, *John Aubrey: My Own Life*, New York Review Books, 2016

Miscellaneous

Golding, William, *The Spire*, Faber & Faber, 1964

Hardy, Thomas, *Wessex Tales*, Macmillan, 1888

——, *Wessex Poems and Other Verses*, Harper & Brothers, 1898

Juster, A. M. (trans.), *Saint Aldhelm's Riddles*, University of Toronto Press, 2015

Lapidge, Michael and Rosier, James L., *Aldhelm: The Poetic Works*, D.S. Brewer, 1985

Macfarlane, Robert, *The Old Ways: A Journey on Foot*, Hamish Hamilton, 2012

Thomas, Edward, *In Pursuit of Spring*, Little Toller Books, 2016

INDEX